ADT 18/12/79.

SOCIAL TOPICS SERIES

Policing Freedom

To
Irené,
Gordon
and
The Good Police

SOCIAL TOPICS SERIES

Policing Freedom

A COMMENTARY ON THE DILEMMAS OF POLICING IN WESTERN DEMOCRACIES

John Alderson

Q.P.M., C.B.I.M. (Hon.), LL.D., EXETER 1979
Barrister of the Middle Temple
British Memorial Fellow (Aus) 1956
Chief Constable, Devon and Cornwall.
Formerly Commandant of the
Police Staff College, Bramshill,
and Assistant Commissioner,
Metropolitan Police

MACDONALD AND EVANS

Macdonald & Evans Ltd.
Estover, Plymouth PL6 7PZ

First published 1979

© Macdonald & Evans Ltd. 1979

ISBN 0 7121 1815 2

Printed in Great Britain by
Latimer Trend & Company Ltd, Plymouth

Foreword

It is 150 years since Peel's police made their first appearance on the streets of London. The profound social changes since then which have taken place have not been fully reflected in the philosophy which underlies the accepted attitudes and activities of the British police. This is the theme of Chief Constable Alderson's book, the result of many years of observation and reflection.

His primary concern is to present both police and public with possible answers to such fundamental questions as these. In what way can a forward-looking and socially sensitive police force match the expectations of a liberal and permissive society? How far is it possible to modify the traditional, legally orientated functions of the police, in protecting the public through the enforcement of sanctions against criminal behaviour, by adoption of a more positive and constructive response? To what extent is it necessary for the police to advance in their thinking and acting, not merely *pari passu* with contemporary attitudes, but also in anticipation of future trends?

The text of *Policing Freedom* gives clear and deeply-felt emphasis to the need for a new ethic of police responsibility, to the nature of what the author calls a "superior" police and to the steps by which this philosophy of policing would be transformed into a reality, for the future strengthening of democratic society.

I believe that John Alderson's book has an important message, not simply for senior police officers but for central and local government, for all the community-help agencies and, indeed, for all those whose awareness of the responsibilities of citizenship makes them constantly vigilant on behalf of justice and liberty.

August 1979   Sir John McKay

Preface

The aims behind what is written in this book are twofold. First, it is intended to provide an extension to our thinking about and appreciation of the police. By development of ideas and concepts it is hoped to aid discussion when police talk with police or when others with an interest in police affairs seek an "inside" view. Secondly it is offered as a celebration of the modern police system founded in London in 1829 and as a tribute to all who have aided the successes and triumphs of its progress.

Important as our history is, however, and it is very important, it is not enough to dwell on it. The police need to make their own contribution to the growing debate on their existing condition and their future.

The narrative has been arranged in four parts, each examining some novel aspects of the subject. The first part attempts to analyse the nature of policing and its many variations. Some abstract as well as some concrete matters must be considered if the subject of policing is to lend itself to philosophical speculation. The concept that the police need to develop their own ethical bases is little more than touched upon, but it is hoped that impetus will be given to further discourse on this vital subject, vital that is to advanced civilised police.

The second part takes a few familiar and some unfamiliar views of the police, both from inside and from detached aspects.

The third part attempts to give the subject of crime a few fresh perspectives in the belief that its perplexing and defiant characteristics can be given rational focus. To tackle crime means to understand it as a phenomenon so that it takes on wholly new dimensions which may set a pattern for police and other action.

The final part is intended as the main contribution to democratic policing ideas. An attempt is made to isolate essential principles, to propound a fresh set of criteria and above all some refined objectives for police to match the brave new world. The need to question some of the police folk images and to design new systems to fit new people is fraught with pitfalls, though it should be attempted. An attempt is made.

August 1979

John Alderson

Objectives of a police system in a free, permissive and participatory society

1. To contribute towards liberty, equality and fraternity in human affairs.

2. To help reconcile freedom with security and to uphold the rule of law.

3. To facilitate human dignity through upholding and protecting human rights and the pursuit of happiness.

4. To provide leadership and participation in dispelling crimogenic social conditions through co-operative social action.

5. To contribute towards the creation or reinforcement of trust in communities.

6. To strengthen the security of persons and property and the feeling of security of persons.

7. To investigate, detect and activate the prosecution of offences, within the rule of law.

8. To facilitate free passage and movement on highways and roads and on streets and avenues open to public passage.

9. To curb public disorder.

10. To deal with major and minor crises and to help and advise those in distress, where necessary activating other agencies.

John Alderson

Acknowledgments

I am pleased to express my gratitude to Geoffrey Gorer and the Cresset Press for agreeing to my using extracts from the book *Exploring English Character*; to the Controller of Her Majesty's Stationery Office for permission to reproduce the Judges' Rules from Home Office Circular No. 89/1978; to Roger Busby for his encouragement; to Brian Morgan and Colin Moore for material in Appendixes 6 and 8; to Shirley Page and Joy Sibley for typing services; to the Police Authority for Devon and Cornwall for their support, though for the errors and omissions, and all the views not attributed, I accept complete responsibility.

Most of all, I am deeply indebted to my wife Irené for her patience and for the sacrifice of precious hours.

Contents

Introduction

Policing of Western democracies is in a crisis. The internal crisis reflects the desire for ever more freedom for the individual and how this conflicts with a need for some social control. The external crisis concerns the growth of international terrorism with its ever-present threat of the propaganda of the deed. At every turn police methods, organisation and operations are questioned. Royal Commissions, President's Commissions, Committees of Enquiry, Investigations and Tribunals abound and testify to the dilemma of society in the West. Meanwhile, the incidence of crime rises, particularly violent crime. Fears and tensions stimulate reactionary sentiments which foreshadow backlash, causing further crime and public disorder. Progress by protest brings ideology and violence onto the streets. Industrial disputes cast their shadows of social conflict, sometimes spilling over into crime. And so the catalogue could go on.

It is not the purpose nor is it within the scope of this book to weigh in the balance the tremendous gains which the free, permissive, participative society brings to those who live in the West, and who, if given the choice, would continue to pay the price for their liberty, if only crime and its attendant circumstances could be seen to be under some form of rational examination leading to rational policies of control.

When in pursuit of rational understanding of phenomena, the enquirer is almost bound to start by looking for relevant reading matter. In searching for literature on the subject of the police dilemma, the enquirer will find that the library shelves are gradually increasing their stock of comments, accounts and reports on this most pressing of contemporary issues. However, he will search in vain for books which mark the contribution of the police service itself (save one or two exceptions). Such literature as he does find will tend to concentrate on history, the law, organisation and autobiographical accounts.

The police have of recent years become used to being examined by all and sundry, and have developed an amused tolerance of most of this. This state of affairs will not do for a large body of people who see themselves, and rightly so, as underpinning society in many ways.

1

It will not do if the police aspire to improvement in the quality of their contribution towards the changes going on around them. It will not do if the police aspire to an understanding of that change. Neither can the police complain if people who are interested in their cause are so misinformed as to worsen the police predicament through ignorance. Therefore, the police have a duty to themselves as a group and to the public (and particularly to the interested public) to begin to question the principles and practices which are historic and traditional and to venture forth with comment of their own, which will help to inform and stimulate the debate which at present rages around them. A modest beginning might therefore be ventured here in the year which marks the 150th anniversary of the founding of the modern police in Great Britain, and which provided a model for other parts of the world where the common law and democracy were joined.

The reader is invited on a journey of exploration, not so much in a Rolls-Royce through the lush pastures of certainty, but rather a bumpy ride through some unchartered ground towards the foothills of police affairs, before trying to ascend to levels where perspectives for the future might reveal themselves.

Although abstract thought comes less easily to those such as the writer, whose lifetime has been spent attending to practical issues, than it does to those versed in the intricacies of philosophical enterprise, it is inevitable that some abstract thought must be attempted if principles are to be teased out for examination, comment and disputation. Thus it is that the first part of this book will attempt to examine the principles of the nature of policing, and although this may sound pretentious let it be said that the task is approached with considerable humility and apprehension. Although in an authoritarian society it does not matter one way or the other whether authority is abused save in the most outrageous manner, in a free society this will not do. If the police are to stand as an example of civic virtue they must be civically virtuous. If they have to pursue this difficult and sometimes elusive status, the pursuit must begin with principles. Of course it will be quite easy to turn to text books on jurisprudence to find the philosophy of the law, but the enquirer will search in vain for much about what might be called the philosophy of the police. For one reason or another, intellectual curiosity has by-passed this most important of social issues. Let the police themselves attempt to search a little in the hope that better minds may be brought to bear on some of those things that exist behind a veil of ignorance.

Beginning with the nature of power, its uses and abuses, is to go to the centre of the police function in society. To set up, appoint, equip and direct a powerful instrument like the police without those who fill its ranks and those who direct its course having a meaningful understanding of the nature of power, its uses and abuses and its potential for harm as well as for good, is not to equip the police as well as it might otherwise be done. It is surprising how successfully the police in Great Britain have managed to maintain a reputation, at least collectively, for the proper use of common sense. This marvellous but elusive police quality, when allied to patience, determination and courage, can carry an institution as far as these great human qualities have done. The point is, however, that, in a complex, free and turbulent society, such human qualities, desirable and valuable as they are, are not by themselves enough. They need to be supported by enlightenment through a knowledge and understanding of the forces which they themselves represent and in some cases control. If they are to counter the sophisticated arguments of the learned in law, politics, education and the whole power game, people who know how to manipulate the communicators and the opinion-formers, then the police have to look to it and buckle on their own better understanding of these things.

Neither can the police and those who direct them ignore the need for an acute awareness and understanding of the ethics of policing a plural multiracial society, or any free society for that matter. Many a police officer, both young and experienced, has found his career and his life in ruins, because he did what he thought was right and proper in the pursuit of the fulfilment of his duties. The belief that the police have to see that justice is done in spite of the rules may be a seductive notion, and for some time it may be got away with. In due time, however, as the practitioners of this belief become emboldened, what starts out as a small and tolerated bending of rules becomes a large and corrupting indifference. Who is to blame when this happens?

Is it the officer himself who in spite of all the guidance, teaching and help defies the moral ethical and legal demarcations? Or is it the organisation (or better still the leaders of the organisation) who have failed to ensure that the ethical principles of policing were inculcated in the training of the officer? Let it be said that there are those, both police and public, who regard it as acceptable to bend rules; but only as long as it does not affect them, or as long as the bending is slight and of small rules. Why should police be encouraged (or at least not discouraged) to risk their own moral integrity in the pursuit of society's murkier side? It is tragic for the police, for the individual police officer, for the member of society affected and for society as a whole when the pursuit of just ends is carried out by the condoning of unjust means. Neither the police nor society can afford to neglect the issues involved in the ethics of policing, and a start has to be made in trying to achieve a better and fairer understanding of this dilemma.

Working as they do in the increasingly disorientating, sometimes neurotic and demented, sometimes violent and anarchical (or seemingly so) milieu of contemporary society, police officers (particularly of the junior ranks) are understandably confused by it all. Bravely trying to cope with problems of mass hooliganism, racial tension, drug addiction, distress and degradation (although very often witness to kindness, bravery and compassion), the police are often perplexed by their inability to understand the apparent irrationality of the behaviour which confronts them. To say that such behaviour is an actual consequence of the brave new world and that it only happens at the edges is not enough consolation to people who work always on the edges.

Clearly, greater understanding of modern society, of the cause and effect of its aberrations, is essential to a proper understanding of the policing function itself. Police do not operate in and from a society of their own, though they do find their own rational world in their institutional confines. They also understand much from their experience, since, if it is anything at all, policing is heavily experience-orientated and a practical person's niche. But again such approaches to model policing are not enough, because change outpaces experience. Bewilderment in police ranks, when the doing of what is considered to be a fair, impartial and difficult job turns out to merit criticism from all angles arises from a lack of understanding of those forces which operate beyond the normal scope of the practical police function.

The impact of police action on the lower orders of a stratified society will not always provoke outrage. People brought up to know their station and to keep it, to be conditioned to taking orders from their betters and to have a good understanding of what is right and proper to do, would seldom quarrel with the authority and significance of the police direction, action or even command. It would, of course, be different if police action were directed at the upper echelons of a stratified society, since the general permissiveness and freedom which reign in those echelons would be easily bruised by the intrusion of police authority. In any case, since the police themselves in such a society would be conditioned to know their own station, it is unlikely that they would attempt such intrusion.

In a society, however, where the mass of the people have tasted the permissiveness formerly enjoyed by a few, they are unlikely to put up with old-fashioned police authoritarianism. This in turn may lead the police in a non-stratified society to retreat behind their legal barricades, only venturing forth to deal with clear, provable criminal

4

acts. This kind of thing, inducing as it does a legalistic reactionary, technological style of policing, only serves to widen the gulf between a bemused police and a truculent public. The situation in turn becomes compounded by misunderstanding, suspicion and even hostility, making the job of the police more difficult to do and to understand. If not corrected, this kind of estrangement gradually leads to the police themselves feeling like a misunderstood minority, only able to police as an occupying force. Of course this is stating the extreme; but it is a possibility and can be seen in some Western democracies where such trends have not gone uncorrected. Nor can such trends be corrected without an adequate understanding of what is happening and what can be done to put it right. The research required on the study of the impact of policing styles is of paramount importance in this connection. It needs to be undertaken by the police and their friends in places where intellectual capacity is at its best, so that it can be explained more clearly for the benefit of both the police and the policed.

It is hoped that in the future understanding and co-operation between the police and other agencies and institutions will improve, but such an improvement will largely depend on intensive research and the will to publish its findings. An attempt to bring about such a desirable state of affairs should begin with the police themselves. The reduction of stereotyping and hostility based on ignorance should start now and the reader is invited to observe the modest though well-intentioned attempt to contribute towards such a dialogue which follows in this book.

Police of course are set up by a society to deal with crime, its prevention, its detection and its proof. But crime, being the law-breaking creature that it is, is often only approached from a legal point of view. An attempt has therefore been made to view it from the point of view of the victim, the offender, the moralist, the economist and the sociologist. In doing so, it is hoped that different views will be obtained to enrich the understanding of this tantalising phenomenon, which in part arises from behaviour, and in part is created by rules. The inevitability of crime is to be pointed out and accepted, which only leaves the levels of crime open to argument. Attention is attracted to considering such things as the tolerance of communities for crime, which may be higher in some than in others.

It is not unknown for crime to be more tolerable than the police activity needed for its pursuit. This is sometimes of course due to the criminal nature of the culture or the reputation of the police or a mixture of both. At all events police should be aware that to pursue the elimination of crime is to lay a false trail, but that to regulate its incidence within tolerable levels is the aim of democratic policing.

5

The drift towards reactive policing is highlighted in the hope that some balance may be encouraged by the strengthening of preventive styles.

The ultimate aim of the book, however, is to draw the attention of the reader towards possibilities of coping in the future. There are of course a number of possible futures. A worsening economic situation, the establishment of a controlled national economy could lead to policing of food rationing, the rationing of goods and supplies of every kind. This scenario, unattractive as it is, has to be considered and allowed for. By considering it one may be taken less by surprise if it ever comes about. If such conditions come about the police would have one of the primary duties to fulfil in combining a fair regulation with proper tolerance of and regard for human freedom.

On the other hand, if trends continue generally in the present direction, it is not inconceivable that police ingenuity and imagination will be just as important as police cars and police radios. The use of imagination and ingenuity in control of crime and public order must rank as high priorities where an economic situation continues to be unable to supply the ever-escalating demands of the present police system. The resources solution to the problems of crime must come to a trickle, or even dry up. In such circumstances a constant belief in the use of reactionary police force against a disturbed and disorientated society would be, if not a betrayal of the democratic police function, at least some kind of dereliction.

It is for these reasons that towards the end of this book attempts are made to come to terms with future uncertainties. If democratic police, like the dinosaur, are unable to adapt to the changing surroundings and to a changing world, they will, like the dinosaur, disappear, and their place will be taken by a much more unattractive method of policing.

The search for new policing emphases and styles, if not for complete systems, must begin in an attempt to define the objectives of a police system in a free, permissive and participatory society. The last time police had their objectives officially set out was in 1829. Police objectives deemed fit for pre-Victorian England might be questioned as to their validity in contemporary society, and an opportunity is taken to question them in the pages which follow. Although the report of the Royal Commission on the Police in 1962 set out the duties of the police as they had evolved from 1829, this is not the same thing as redefining them in keeping with present and future needs.

Pragmatism may be a virtue and evolution adequate and acceptable under certain circumstances, but to indulge in it as a principle is a luxury through which the police leave themselves to be dominated by circumstance. To set out objectives which police themselves see as

6

appropriate and relevant is to avoid being dominated by circumstance, and to have a chance to dominate it instead. To take account of their contribution to liberty, equality and fraternity and to the needs of human dignity and happiness is to express the objectives of the police in a new way. To help reconcile freedom with security is an objective of paramount importance in modern society, whereas in nineteenth-century England the police might have been expected to deny freedom to the mass of the people or at least to assist in its denial. In pursuit of the prevention of crime the police have as an objective co-operation in dispelling crimogenic social conditions. This is a far cry from the legalistic policing and the role of the avenger.

Trapped as they are in the world of criminal statistics as proof of their efficiency, the police need to break out and to seek other measurements of their success. The reduction of fear, through the increase of security and trust in communities and of that tension which can give rise to breaches of the peace is quite in keeping with traditional, though often unexpressed, police aims. Investigation of crime and facilitation of free passage together with maintenance of public order are timeless police objectives, though merely to express the *whole* reason for the police in these terms is to fail to grasp the great opportunity for further and better contributions to the happiness of society. The dedication, skill and determination which enable the police to harass, break up and bring to justice organised criminals and terrorists will of course continue to exert great demands on both public and police. Those demands will be better met by police and public in tune with each other, respecting and understanding each other and finally prepared to trust each other.

The reader is reminded that what is to follow is an exploration of the highways and by-ways of the police function, and of the principles and practices which surround its discharge. The attempt to construct a new model for policing a free, permissive, participative democracy is suggested for discussion, for stimulation of thought and where applicable, for the influencing of policies. What follows is the writer's own personal philosophy of policing, and where policies and models are introduced in the text they exist now or will exist in the writer's police force in the very near future.

It is hoped that the reader will at least have been interested in this base-camp "briefing" sufficiently to want to continue on the suggested pathways of exploration. Whether the view at the end of it all is deemed worth while will obviously be a matter of personal preference.

PART ONE

The Nature of Policing

Chapter 1

The exercise of power and authority

The police are related to power in two ways. By their very existence they deny unconstitutional power to others, while at the same time they have legal power to do their constitutional duty.

Power can be defined as "the production of intended effects".[1] The police are instruments of the legal coercive power of the State to produce effects intended by the legislature. It is, however, the tradition of the common law to grant power to citizens so that they may uphold the coercive power of the State, and in this sense the common law differs from systems which retain the monopoly of legal coercive powers at the centre. Powers to arrest, detain, even to kill in self-defence or in the defence of others and to keep the peace are the rights and duties of citizens. This is power widely distributed but which carries penalties for its abuse. The police are the servants of this citizen power. It is of vital importance that the police should see their power in this light; that is as a vicarious form of authority.

One of the most important concepts for police to remember is that the law is lacking in power if it does not have the general backing of the public; or, to put it another way, the police in using their law-enforcing powers will generally be effective with public support and generally less effective without it. This is a principle which Parliament should bear in mind when passing legislation. The problems of enforcement are sometimes overlooked. Police who are consistently required to enforce unpopular laws will gradually lose public support for their general duties; and where laws are unacceptable, civil violence and even rebellion can result. This leads to the seeming paradox that a weak police with public support, at least in the long run, will be more effective than a powerful police lacking public support. Thus, the concept of policing by consent of the policed, as in the British system, has been carried out by a ratio of approximately one police officer to some five hundred of the population; whereas in Northern Ireland, for example, counting all the security forces, the ratio is approaching one to fifty.

Attitudes towards police power in common-law countries have always been healthily restrictive. The well-known statement of the 1822 Parliamentary Committee on the Police is revealing: "It is

11

difficult to reconcile an effective system of police with that perfect freedom of action and exemption from interference, which are the great privileges and blessings of society in this country." This clearly brings out the feeling that police power is not only a threatened interference with freedom but is even incompatible with it. The Committee further stated that "the forfeiture and curtailment of such advantages [freedom of action, etc.] would be too great a sacrifice for improvements in police, or facilities for the detection of crime, however desirable in themselves if abstractedly considered." In other words, and bearing in mind that crime was out of control at the time, the threat of crime was to be preferred (at least by those who were enfranchised in 1822) to having officials with power to interfere with civil liberties!

Police, of course, became inevitable and provided the minimum interference with civil liberties compatible with controlling crime and disorder. Instead of threatening freedom, superior police became its guarantee. But the tensions concerning the coercive power of the police continue. Bertrand Russell in his book *Power* states the matter forcibly when he asserts that: "In every democracy, individuals and organisations which are intended to have only certain well-defined executive functions are likely, if unchecked, to acquire a very undesirable independent power. This is especially true of police."[2]

Police have to remember that restrictions which the law and public opinion impose are not impediments placed capriciously in their path but safeguards of individual rights and liberties which the police exist to protect. It should also be pondered that there is a correlation between levels of police power and public support for the police. Thus, where police have swingeing powers, public support will be in inverse proportions.

The police represent force as a form of coercive power, and it is regarded as important that it should not be concentrated in the hands of a government or a person. This view has been expressed by a number of Home Secretaries of different political parties and was put by R. A. (now Lord) Butler when he was Home Secretary in 1963: "I am convinced that it would be wrong for one man or one government to be directly in charge of the whole police of this country. Our institutions are based on checks and balances. This has kept our liberty throughout the generations."[3]

Police in superior democratic systems have two sources of authority, one from the law and the other from their reputation. It is an unwise police that begins to feel that its authority lies totally within the law, since this can induce an authoritarian attitude which, if not checked, begins to hinder the success of police operations. By authoritarianism is meant requiring blind obedience to authority which depends on

12

power and force. Since compliance with this kind of authority does not activate the free will, nor always appeal to reason but depends on coercion, it lacks virtue compared with true authority. True authority on the other hand achieves its aim through the excellence of its quality. Whether through respect, love, excellence or other virtue, it attracts compliance through the nature of its appeal to reason and the free will.

Superior police, therefore, always aim to achieve their goals by true authority and persuasion. Force, on the other hand, has to be used if the public peace and safety are to be maintained, but when entering upon a forcible solution police should always use the *minimum* force. Force can be dangerous for both the user and object, since undue force incites retaliation on a bigger scale and is the genesis of escalation. When carried to a peak these competing forces can destroy or irreparably damage the protagonists. In police terms this is catastrophic, as the building up of a new police relationship with the public from which to operate in a superior manner may take generations.

NOTES

1. Bertrand Russell, *Power* (Allen & Unwin 1938), Chap. 3.
2. Ibid., Chap. 18.
3. T. A. Critchley, *A History of Police in England and Wales* (Constable 1978), Chap. 9.

Chapter 2

Ethics in policing

Being concerned, as it is, with power and its application it is very necessary that policing should be bound by ethical as well as legal principles. The morality of policing cannot be expressed in universal terms so readily as, say, the morality of medicine, which is under the Hippocratic oath. This is because police morality will differ with the cultural, moral, legal and political climate under which it serves. Policing systems which serve tyrannies, despotism, totalitarianism and the like are tainted at their source and differ widely from those of liberal democratic states. Even the latter, however, sometimes depart from the ideal and can sprout aspects of unethical behaviour from time to time. The difference lies in the police system on the one hand being unethical by nature, and on the other, whilst being ethical by nature, being adversely affected by individuals or sections within the system employing unethical methods. But it is only within the structure of a liberated democratic state that what I call "superior police" can evolve.

Writing of the totalitarian police state, Brian Chapman expresses the position graphically:

> But within the totalitarian police state it seems that the police apparat, by freezing the ideology into a caricature of itself, and emptying it of its dynamism and creativity does succeed in enforcing a genuine uniformity of thought and political aspiration. This is not surprising. When the policeman turns psychologist, assassin and predator he combines in himself some of the more maleficent arts, and these he uses for the subtler forms of terror.[1]

This form of policing is devoid of ethical content and is morally abhorrent. In such systems the police themselves become an arm of the State, determining their own values in which the end justifies the means. It is in liberal democratic states that the police have the best chance of attaining high ethical standards of conduct; but in every police system abuses can take place and the need for firm safeguards is paramount.

PARLIAMENTARY SUPREMACY AND THE RULE OF LAW

The first and most important check on abuse is in the law itself. The concept of the rule of law, in which all are equal before the law and equally answerable to it, is crucial. This is turn will depend on the supremacy of Parliament, the independence of the judiciary from the executive arm of government and the checks and balances which preserve the police as a force from narrow political direction. If these conditions exist, as they do in Great Britain, then the police are set fair with a chance of developing an acceptable morality based on impartiality within the law. That is the first stage, and constitutionally important, since it removes the police from the corrupting influence of absolute power.

POLICING WITHIN THE RULES

Secondly and equally important are the rules of criminal procedure, because the police, being officers of justice, will be conditioned in their attitudes by the tone and demeanour of the rules under which they operate. It can be argued that, because the police in common-law countries are concerned with more facets of the judicial system than any other profession or group, the importance of a strong ethical code of behaviour is crucial.

The great instrument of coercion in most states is the police, though the nature of its work and the manner of its control will vary from state to state according to the politics, culture and traditions of those states. The manner in which police go about their work is one of the main criteria used in determining the degree of respect for human rights which a given society has developed. But, conversely, a police system which is either pusillanimous, inert or neutralised in any way would illustrate the dangerous complacency of a society concerning the protection of victims and potential victims of crime.

In other words, it is a question of balance. If coercive power is too oppressive then freedom suffers, but if freedom becomes licence it loses its virtue and its meaning. The police stand at the point of balance. It is the "principal question of human affairs" as John Stuart Mill in his famous essay "On Liberty"[2] reminds us.

FEAR AND FREEDOM

There is in most people the desire for both freedom and security; and although these two conditions are not incompatible they can be in conflict if either is taken too far. When people are afraid they will give up some of their freedom to be protected and if the fear is increased (either for good motives or not) then more freedom will be

15

sacrificed. Superior police therefore have an important part to play in seeking only the minimum power in the proper discharge of their task. To exaggerate fear in order to achieve power would be unethical.

A good example of the give and take of freedom and power happens in war, when all manner of freedoms are willingly given up and sacrificed. A more recent example, in England, concerned the impact of terrorist violence by the I.R.A. which, until 1974, had not been legally proscribed in England though, paradoxically, it had been in Eire. Following the horrific bomb attack on a crowded bar in Birmingham resulting in the deaths of over twenty people, Parliament gave the police powers of detention of suspect I.R.A. members and supporters for two days, increased to five days by special consent of the Secretary of State, followed by deportation without trial. The public were quite prepared to agree with this, and indeed it was the least that Parliament could do if it was to retain public confidence. To grant such powers to the police and other authorities, save under conditions of public revulsion and fear, would have been unthinkable. Given such powers police have to use them with proper restraint, though for maximum public protection.

The whole question of balancing police power with individual freedom is presently under scrutiny by the Royal Commission on Criminal Procedure. The need for the police to have sufficient power to perform the tasks set for them by the law and public expectation is axiomatic, though clearly in a superior police system such powers need to have well-defined limitations, and those need to be adhered to in police practice.

The powers and duties of the police therefore will vary from time to time depending on the morality, security and general conditions of society. Furthermore, the police may come under considerable pressure from the public to produce results; for an ineffective police organisation unable to clear up serious crime would soon lose public confidence. Then again, excessive zeal resulting from the understandable desire to see victims vindicated has to be curbed by ethical principles, adherence to the rules and a well understood sense of fairness throughout.

Now there are some traditions peculiar to policing in Britain which have considerable bearing on the conduct of the police. The Royal Commission on the Police in 1962 said "that the police of this country have never been recognised either in law or by tradition as a force distinct from the general body of citizens", and it is this principle which the police generally have in mind when they consider themselves to be servants of the people as opposed to agents of the State. The Royal Commission went on to say:

Indeed a policeman possesses few powers not enjoyed by the ordinary citizen, and public opinion, expressed in Parliament and elsewhere, has shown great jealousy of any attempts to give increased authority to the police. This attitude is due, we believe, not to any distrust of the police as a body but to an instinctive feeling that as a matter of principle, policemen should have as few powers as possible which are not possessed by the ordinary citizen, and that their authority should rest on the broad basis of consent and active co-operation of all law-abiding people.[3]

It is this feeling that public confidence and goodwill is crucial to their continuing effectiveness that encourages the police to avoid overstepping the powers which they do possess. Therefore it is important for the public to register its disapproval when police abuse their authority, since to ignore it is not in the long-term police interests.

PERSONAL LIABILITY

The next point of importance is that which renders the individual officer personally responsible for his own excesses. The fact that he may be charged with crime, not only by his superior officers, but by any aggrieved persons, or sued for damages by the victims of his negligence or overzealousness is a salutary check. This is a sophisticated constitutional device that on the one hand renders a police officer readily liable for his own mistakes and excesses, while at the same time liberating him from any master-servant relationship which might exert undesirable pressures on his impartiality. As Lord Devlin put it in his book *The Criminal Prosecution in England*[4]: "Policemen are not by origin or by training simply creatures of the executive. They are not men in barracks, but citizens living and working among the communities which they serve."

Due to the English preference for the evolution of their systems the police have become a quasi-judicial body operating under remote judicial control. This relationship with the law and their independence from direct political manipulation influence the ethical behaviour of the police in Great Britain. The law, being an abstract concept, is neutral; political intention, on the other hand, is partial. The police in the United States, for example, are much closer to politics than are the police in Great Britain, and this creates a different characteristic and style. The ethics of politics intervene.

ETHICS OF INVESTIGATION

When one begins to consider the rules governing the interrogation of suspects, they have, with few exceptions, moved firmly in favour of suspected persons over the past few decades. This development has

17

meant that the police have been increasingly required to act judicially.

One may take as the starting point the common-law principle that, in order to be admissible, a confession must have been made voluntarily, that is it must not have been induced by fear, promise or oppression; this represented the sole judicial requirement.

In 1906, however, the police (in the person of the then Chief Constable of Birmingham) asked the judiciary to clarify the position, following conflicting advice from different judges. The practice had long been in vogue that in order to prove the voluntary nature of the confession, suspects had been told or cautioned that they need not say anything; but judges had differed about this. The advice given to the police by the Lord Chief Justice was later embodied in what is now a code of ethical and judicial practice designed to protect the accused's rights generally and to ensure the voluntary nature of a confession and its subsequent admissibility. The first four rules concerning questioning and cautioning date from 1912, the other two deal with statements from co-accused persons, and the application of all the rules to other persons in authority dates from 1918.

The police are well aware that proper training in the rules and conduct of criminal investigations are of first importance, though it would be idle to pretend that the present position is satisfactory. Many senior police officers feel that in a sense there is a conflict between the common-law duty of persons to assist in the maintenance of law and order and what amounts to formal requirements to invite suspected citizens not to assist the police with their enquiries.

The most powerful statement in recent times on this issue has of course come from the Criminal Law Revision Committee in its eleventh report.[5] The recommendation that inferences should be drawn from an accused's silence in matters which, had he mentioned them before being charged, would have exculpated him and saved time and expense by allowing the police to investigate his story, is a logical though considerable change. If his story were proved correct he would be cleared at the earliest possible time. If his story were proved to be false, of course, then justice would have been served also, since the proceedings would have been nearer the truth and he would be deprived of a false defence.

This proviso seems so logical and fair to most people that the opposition to it appears to be based largely on emotion, and the ultra-conservatism of the English Criminal Bar. There are adequate safeguards both in the rules of investigation and at the trial to avoid oppression. Equally, if in spite of being invited to help the police enquiry a suspect remained silent, the drawing of inferences would be controlled by the court. The mentally retarded and other disadvantaged people would require special care, but judicial control of police and overt evidence to the court would provide proper safeguards in such cases.

There is often considerable pressure on the police to ensure that justice is effective. Not only are the police more victim-conscious than most other bodies but they are the only officers of the system who can ensure the proper questioning of suspects, for once the proceedings begin the accused may, and in serious criminal cases usually does, play no further part. Not even his demeanour is known to the court. It is often not realised that this situation contains not only the seeds of wrongful acquittal but also of wrongful conviction. It also puts temptation before investigating officers to delay preferring charges to prolong questioning, which is a breach of the Judges' Rules.

For many years now, many jurisdictions in the U.S.A. have used the polygraph or lie detector during the interrogation of suspects and with suitable corroboration there appears to be some confidence in it; but it has never seriously been considered in England and there seems to be no significant desire by the police for its introduction. One issue which has raised its head from time to time, and no doubt will do so again, is the use of tape-recording machines for recording the interrogation of suspects. They are often used to record conversation of suspects during investigation of crime at present. It has been said that the tape-recorded account of an interrogation would, for the jury, surpass all other forms, even of a written statement, since the demeanour of the parties would come across better.

There are of course technical and practical difficulties, many of which were set out in the Criminal Law Revision Committee's report, though a minority of that Committee would not have been in favour of relaxing the rule on the "right of silence" of the accused until tape-recordings of interrogations were introduced. There was a general feeling that a controlled experiment should be conducted; and in 1975 the Home Secretary set up a committee, mainly of lawyers, police officers and civil servants, aided by a technical consultant, to enquire into the feasibility of an experiment in the tape-recording of police interrogations. The committee points out the very considerable difficulties involved and that the concept by no means always favours the accused. In view of the costs involved and the problems inherent in the practice, it was thought that the experiment should be a modest one and only relate to the actual taking of the statement and not to the interrogation leading up to it, though they acknowledge the feasibility of an experiment if limited in this way. The report was submitted in September 1976, and experimental results are anticipated.

There is little doubt that both audio and visual devices will improve technically and be pressed on the police and may well, in the long run, be to the advantage of police officers as individuals. They could well prevent those many accused who go back on their written statements in court at present and fasely accuse the police of malpractices as a form of defence from getting away with it as they so often do. On the other hand, the nature of the interrogator's skill will need to undergo changes too.

Apart altogether from the rights of the suspect guaranteed by the Judge's Rules, there are those which are ensured by the Administrative Directions[6] which from time to time are issued by the Home Secretary. They are very important. (*See* Appendix 1.)

The administrative directions require the police officer investigating crime to record properly statements after caution, the time the statement begins and ends and details of breaks and refreshments, to use the natural language of the suspect and to avoid deterring the innocent from making a statement to clear him of any charge. The directions are all-embracing and demand meticulous care. Times and details of persons present require exact recording. Adequate comfort and refreshment have to be provided.

Children and young persons under seventeen years of age should not be interviewed, save in the presence of a parent or guardian or, in the absence of the former, a person who is not a police officer but is of the same sex as the child or young person. This direction was found to have been breached during the recent enquiry into alleged malpractices by the investigating officers in the investigation of the murder of Maxwell Confait[7], when three youths under seventeen years of age were charged and found guilty but later acquitted of the offence. Administrative directions have been reinforced as a result.

There are further directions to provide for the interrogation of the mentally handicapped, who are generally treated as children for this purpose. Deaf persons and those who do not speak English are safeguarded by provisions for adequate controls.

The rights of all persons who are in police custody are displayed on notices in convenient and conspicuous places, and facilities for writing, telephoning and telegrams are provided. Of particular importance is the question of access to a solicitor and friends. A person in custody is allowed to speak to his lawyer by telephone provided that no hindrance is likely to be caused to the process of investigation or the administration of justice. This proviso acknowledges the facts of life that stolen property, accomplices and witnesses may be disposed of, tipped off or intimidated respectively if contact is permitted before the police have had time to take precautions.

There is no right to have a lawyer present during interrogation though it is the practice to facilitate access and private consultation as soon as possible and practicable after arrest, always having regard to the possible obstruction of justice. This is a pragmatic approach which treats justice as having concern for the accused but for victims and society also. It is frequently pressed that the practice laid down by the Supreme Court of the U.S.A. in *Miranda* v. *Arizona* (1966)[8] should be accepted in England, the latest advocate being Sir Henry Fisher in his report on the *Confait* case.

This would mean that unless a lawyer were present during the making of a confession it would be inadmissible. The *Miranda* case was decided against a background of considerable unease at the malpractices of the police in the U.S.A. and even then the court was almost evenly split, clearly realising that there would be considerable denial of justice in many cases, as the guilty would get away with more and sometimes very serious crime.

Further additions to the human rights of persons in custody continue to be introduced, the latest having been enacted in the Criminal Law Act of 1977. This provides that without delay, or no more delay than is necessary for the procuring of just apprehension of other offenders or the prevention of crime (again this acknowledgment of the facts of life), a person held in police custody is entitled to have one person reasonably named by him informed of his whereabouts. Considerable police effort and time is consequently involved in this new right, which even applies to terrorists! It is another example of more ethical treatment of persons suspected of crime.

Further safeguards concern identification, both in the form of parades and of photographs.[9] There are twenty-two rules altogether as well as fourteen paragraphs of administrative guidance issued by the Home Secretary. The necessary additions to training of police and drafting of internal instructions have now been carried out. It is in the interests of the prosecution that evidence of identification is both reliable and seen to be fair if juries are to accept it.

Of particular importance to the issues of human rights are those connected with bail. The balancing of the interests of the public generally, the sensible administration of justice and the rights of suspected but unconvicted persons is of considerable delicacy.

Although the denial of bail has historically been unlawful, the provisions generally have always required the police to grant bail unless it would lead to obstruction of justice, harm to the person concerned or other persons, and such things as the destruction of evidence and above all the likely failure of a person to come back to answer the charge or charges. If the police denied bail the magistrates usually within twenty-four hours could grant it, though police often opposed it on some of the above grounds. The application to a Judge by the prisoner was the third course open.

Since 1976, however, the emphasis has changed with considerable implications. The Bail Act of 1976 was the result of considerable activity from pressure groups for reform, it being felt that too many innocent people were being remanded in custody. There was also the vested interest of the administration in easing pressure on prison facilities. The two coincided.

The significant change was, of course, to order courts (if the police had not granted bail) to grant bail unless certain conditions were present. Bail is now a right. This change in emphasis the police feel is paid for by society sustaining more and sometimes serious crime involving accused persons. Again the balance between police effectiveness and human rights has to be considered. More liberty for some people can mean more suffering for others.

A CITIZEN'S REMEDIES

In the first place here, of course, are criminal charges against individual police officers brought by members of the public. Where a chief constable receives the report of a crime and he is not sure that a crime has not been committed he must refer the matter for the neutral decision of the Director of Public Prosecutions. Civil action for damages will be against individual police officers as well as the vicarious liability of the chief constable created under the Police Act of 1964. The most common civil actions are likely to be false imprisonment and malicious prosecution.

Further safeguards are contained in the system of complaints against the police officers concerned, which can result in disciplinary action apart from criminal prosecution. Police discipline regulations include such charges as discreditable conduct, neglect of duty, falsehood or prevarication, corrupt or improper practice, abuse of authority and criminal conduct, for which officers can be dismissed, reduced in rank, fined or reduced in pay. Furthermore, since 1977, an independent review body—the Police Complaints Board, whose chairman and members are appointed by the Prime Minister—provides a detached and independent view with power to direct proceedings and establish tribunals. All complaints against police officers must be referred to this board.

There is no other body of people or profession which is as answerable as the police in England for the proper performance of their duties and responsibilities in the investigation of crime. Considering the numbers which are brought to trial for crime other than minor traffic offences (477,900 in magistrates' courts and 68,547 in Crown Courts in 1977) and the numbers of investigations found to be improperly conducted, it seems that the system works as well as any other is likely to do.

Police conduct outside the area of their duties connected with the field of criminal investigation is tempered by an internal code of discipline which demands the highest of standards. The Police Discipline Code (*see* Appendix 2) requires adherence to its tenets which are backed up by a wide enough range of sanctions for the chief officer of police to ensure the maintenance of public confidence in the standards of a force.

In addition the criminal law itself makes special provision for the proper conduct of public officials.

These, then, are some of the safeguards through which the law, regulation and guidance have sought to induce a proper ethical standard of behaviour and conduct from the police.

These provisions should be underpinned by an effective system of training and leadership which builds upon them and induces a collective sentiment towards a standard of behaviour which would be capable of resisting the many pressures put upon the police as individuals. The young officer faced with the temptation posed by the cunning pedlars of petty corruption; pressures upon the detective to produce results; gradual corruption of groups of officers through collective coercion within a department; misguided loyalty that puts errant colleagues before proper principles; these are some of the areas of police behaviour which pose problems if high ethical standards are not inculcated from the start of a police officer's career and reinforced throughout.

NOTES

1. Brian Chapman, *Police State* (Macmillan 1971), Chap. 9.
2. J. S. Mill, "On Liberty" 1859 (Oxford University Press 1975).
3. Report of Royal Commission on Police 1962, Cmnd. 1728.
4. Lord Devlin, *Criminal Prosecution in England* (Oxford University Press 1960), Chap. 2.
5. Eleventh Report, Criminal Law Revision Committee.
6. Home Office Circular 89/78.
7. Report of an Enquiry by the Hon. Sir Henry Fisher 1977.
8. *Miranda* v. *Arizona* 384 U.S. 436 (1966).
9. Home Office Circular 109/78.

Chapter 3

The demeanour for policing

As a society becomes more civilised, more free and educated, it requires of its police greater understanding, perception and skill, that go beyond simple enforcement of the law for its own sake and can use the law as a social tool to achieve civic happiness. The proper constructive use of police discretion should lie at the heart of enforcement policies and styles.

Policing is concerned with social control, often against the will of individuals or groups. Assertion of policing means assertion of law both moral and physical. Since the majority of offences are committed by people who are generally law-abiding, it is necessary for police to acquire knowledge of the condition of the policed in order that a better understanding of their behaviour may be acquired.

This kind of knowledge is available from three sources. It is available in the form of commentaries and descriptions by academics and observers of the social scene, from the experience of others and from personal experience. There is, of course, the opposing view which holds that the law is explicit; if human conduct contravenes the law, then it should be made the subject of legal process. Such a school of thought would argue that it is not for the police to enter into value judgments and sophisticated philosophical notions, but merely to enforce the law without consideration, emotion or other human sentiments. This is a barren, unimaginative approach which can bring both law and police system into disrepute and fails to exploit the potential of the law for soothing rather than irritating social maladies.

The demeanour for policing as an individual differs from that required when policing as a member of a group. Policing as an individual requires that reliance on one's own judgment, discretion and personality should be inculcated by training, precept, example and experience. To stand alone and to fulfil the aims of police is a considerable achievement, which helps to develop one's best qualities. In the first place the temptation to rely on undue coercion is minimised; secondly the potential need for courage of a moral and of a physical nature is heightened. Knowledge and skill have to be developed to a satisfactory standard and an ability to survive becomes

24

second nature. Where officers operate as one-man police forces they are inclined to develop superior policing characteristics.

On the other hand, operations in concert by a body of police require different characteristics. It is essential for the highly-trained self-reliant individual operator to subjugate his individuality and lend himself to the corporate function in action. To do otherwise would result in a rabble, in which individuals pursue their own preferences to the detriment of the whole. It is important for commanders to realise that this adjustment from individual to corporate function does not come easily to those conditioned to the former. Where public order duties in corporate fashion become frequent as in urban conditions, stress has to be laid on the meaning of this conversion.

The ability to operate as a member of a unit is more akin to the military model, but although the unit may have to exert force to achieve its aim, it should exert force proportionate to the objective. There are, therefore, dangers inherent when police change from individual to corporate action. Operations in numbers embolden police who as individuals exhibit exemplary control but in concert might tend towards excessive aggression, thereby inflicting undue damage on persons to the detriment of the goals of police activity, perhaps in both the short- and the long-term. It is for this reason that special groups should from time to time be disbanded and reformed with fresh personnel so that the conditioning created by recourse to power and force is not habituated.

Since police more often than not in a democratic tolerant society operate alone and unarmed they are vulnerable to attack, both on reputation and physically. A finely-tuned alertness and perception of potential aberrant human behaviour is required for protection against such contingencies. The arming of police changes personality by inducing a feeling of dominance and power in the minds of those concerned. In such conditions where this style of policing is habitual, it is likely that the police will become more assertive, even aggressive, as they rely less and less on public respect for their safety and more and more on their own potential for the solution by force. Where such police attitudes are induced more serious casualties may be sustained by the police and every effort should be made to train against this trend.

It is required of police that they become sensitive to social atmosphere and to events out of the ordinary. This is a desirable state of affairs if they are to become more than passive observers of the scene or mere watchmen of pusillanimous persuasion. There are again traps to be aware of, since oversensitivity to disorder of a mild tolerable kind can lead to precipitate and overbearing reaction which can have consequences for police and offender. Here again, lone foot police are likely to have a higher tolerance rate than police parties both foot and mobile. A nice sense of judgment is required in such matters and an easy though not forced sense of humour is valuable, as most practical police will agree.

The demeanour required by the police is not necessarily constant. In a plural multiracial society particular care has to be taken in this regard. The policing of a homogeneous, monocultured classless society, would be sufficiently constant in demeanour not to call for any marked adjustment at any time. On the other hand, where in one single police station area there may be two or more ethnic minorities with disparate cultures and attitudes towards law, religion and custom, difficulties might face the police particularly where minority cultures are not represented in the force. In such situations considerable adaptability is required.

It is often argued that there is only one way to deal with such conditions and that is to adopt a completely neutral attitude and to become involved only in the enforcement role. This might make life easier all round. But such a policy ignores the need to enter the culture of a group in order to understand it and to seek its co-operation in the prevention and detection of crime. It would inevitably lead to the minority feeling that they are being legally policed through criminal procedures, though not socially policed through service to the community. From such beginnings there may shortly open up between police and policed a gap containing the seeds of mistrust, suspicion and animosity. It is argued therefore that a superior democratic police, whilst appreciating the need for objectivity in mixed cultural situations, has to be prepared to be subjective and accommodating with singular cultural settings within the mixed society.[1]

Policing in a hostile environment requires considerable skill and ability if the police are not to reinforce that hostility. Where trust does not exist efforts to create it through non-conflict contact and provision of services should be made. In this way a basis for a *modus vivendi* will be laid down. Relations between police and policed in these situations can be strengthened only if the demeanour of the whole organisation is sympathetic. To have one section working towards the creation of superior relations and another, through insensitivity and even hostility, destroying that effort will, through inconsistency, produce even worse reactions than a consistent though remote attitude. It will also produce dissension within the police.

Thus it is that superior police will develop the ability to be sympathetic towards the policed. Where some police may find difficulty in feeling sympathetic they should nevertheless manifest outward

26

signs of it in their work. This calls for the considerable self-control which lies at the heart of much superior police work. There will of course be times when some police will lack the ability both to work in sympathy with alien cultures and to develop attitudes of understanding; if so, they should not be allowed to police such areas. At least they should be withdrawn if superior policing is regarded as the intention and they should then be redeployed in areas more compatible with their attitudes, though this is only a poor second best since all members of superior police should be capable of the necessary adjustments.

This process will come more easily to police who have accepted that their ultimate source of authority comes from the policed themselves. Seen like this, the situation superficially assessed may appear paradoxical; but the true police demeanour must be based on this notion, in a democracy. It is of the utmost importance that it should be realised that police have no power or authority of their own except that which they can muster through the virtue of their character, both individually and collectively. This is not necessarily a complicated admixture of general characteristics but it certainly includes fairness, resolve, and an over-all caring instinct; although individual characteristics will include integrity, kindness and courage. There are many possible refinements on these and the following is a list in order of priority compiled by members of the public at public meetings in the writer's force.

Camborne: sincerity, helpfulness, understanding, ability, deterrent effect, approachability.

Plymouth: social ability, responsibility, dignity, sincerity, approachability, simplicity, impartiality, co-operation, competence in detection of serious crime and in crime prevention, trustworthiness, understanding, sympathy.

Exmouth: friendliness, helpfulness, co-operation, understanding, prevention, responsibility.

Exeter: trust, public/police partnership, understanding, helpfulness, mutual co-operation, time spent in listening, caring attitude, contact, public relations, problem-solving.

This is a striking list of qualities looked for in police officers as individuals by members of the public. The demeanour required by police is very much a matter for the policed, rather than exclusively for the police themselves. Police should not shrink from seeking out this kind of information.

Heroism of the dashing type is not automatically associated with the police function, as there is a tendency for people to have regard for its unspectacular, stoic and quiet courage. Neither do police see themselves in heroic terms. A poster designed by marketing experts for recruiting purposes depicting police in heroic terms was taken down from notice boards and discontinued at the request of embarrassed and sometimes incensed police. There is an element of the stoic concept of virtue as its own reward among superior police, which is an endearing characteristic. There are, however, countless opportunities for heroism, as the honours lists will testify most eloquently.

The height of heroism and virtue in terms of policing, however, is to be found, for example, where armed police have cornered an armed person who has already used arms to kill or maim, and is believed to be likely to do so again. The approach to and disarming of him by unarmed police who have access to arms and legal and moral justification for killing him, and yet turn away from that solution and achieve it by persuasion, is the ultimate example of achievement of goals through persuasion. The writer has known numerous such instances. Even if superior police are shy of heroic terms, they value appreciation.

In all things superior police must have an instinct or perception for human dignity. Seeing human beings as they sometimes do, in most degrading and degraded situations, bereft of self-control, pride and decency, they are greatly exposed to the influence of cynicism. If police become indifferent they will have lost some of their superior virtue, since such an attitude will debase their judgment of human dignity. Police are very often placed in a position where the dignity of individuals can be reduced by unfeeling action. Police can behave in this way without much self-concern. When they do they fail to meet the standards of superior police. (*See* Appendix 3.)

NOTES

1. Michael Banton, *Police Community Relations* (Collins 1973), Chap. 10.

Chapter 4

Corruption of police

Police can be corrupted in two principal forms. In the first place they can be corrupted like all other bodies with authority, possessed of power and its exercise; for, in Lord Acton's famous aphorism, "Power tends to corrupt and absolute power corrupts absolutely." In the second place, they can be corrupted by bribery and extortion.

CORRUPT SYSTEMS

Police are possessed of two forms of power. The first is the legal power granted by the law itself to enable its proper enforcement. Without clearly defined legal power, police would be compelled to operate capriciously and this in turn would not only lead to confusion but to injustice. Such power should be only sufficient to achieve the purpose of the law and to balance that purpose with democratic concepts of individual rights and basic freedoms. On the other hand, police who are expected to maintain a tolerable level of public freedom from crime and disorder require power to do so unless they are to be demoralised and ineffectual. The gap between necessary legal power and excessive legal power is a difficult one to judge and calls for exceptional legislative skill.

Police are also possessed of informal power in the sense that their existence and organisational strength represents a threat to other over-mighty subjects or would-be malefactors. This kind of power stemming from professionalism and institutional cohesion should, in superior systems, represent a threat only to potential wrongdoers; in inferior systems, it can intimidate law-abiding people too. In the worst systems it can intimidate all but the power cliques and even they can be consumed by its power.

Brian Chapman describes the ultimate corruption of police power in totalitarian systems. "The country is left with the arbitrary implementation of laws which are no more than police regulations, which the police themselves do not undertake to observe, and principles which are no more than tenuous guides to safe conduct." He goes on to say "In containing a position beyond their capacity to comprehend, the police become instruments of their own misconceptions,

29

the victims of their own apprehensions and destroyers of all that the police stand for: law, morality, justice and safety."[1] In this sense, then, police as a whole can be corrupted by power if its power becomes identified with extreme politics.

In a democracy, such corruption can be controlled through the supremacy of Parliament and the independence of the judiciary. The Royal Commission on the Police in 1962 attempted to clarify the point by saying that:

> In the countries to which the term police state is applied opprobriously, police power is controlled by the government; but they are so called not because the police are nationally organised but because the government acknowledges no accountability to a democratically elected parliament and the citizen cannot rely on the courts to protect him.[2]

On that premise, when it holds good, corruption of police systems and their power is prevented.

CORRUPT INDIVIDUALS

At the level of the individual officer or group, corruption of power is less dangerous though quite unacceptable to free people and damaging to police and society. There are from time to time exceptional examples of its kind which by their infrequency testify to the considerable control exercised by the high individual police standards in Britain and to their selection, training and discipline. Such an exceptional case was that of Detective Sergeant Challener of the Metropolitan Police, who, while suffering from paranoid schizophrenia, was found to have seriously abused his police powers and to have embroiled three junior officers in similar misdemeanours. The corrupt practices concerned not only involved widespread abuse of police powers themselves but turned to the more dangerous and illegal practices of planting evidence of guilt on persons in police custody. The story set out in the Report of Inquiry by the then A. E. James, Q.C., later Lord James,[3] gives an insight into the pressures and forces which can build up on even the best police resulting in corrupt practices of this kind. Mr. James continues:

> In any disciplined force there are rules and regulations which must be observed. Nevertheless in order to get on with the job in hand there is always the temptation to disregard a rule, to "take a short cut", or to subscribe to the view that the end justifies the means of getting there. An atmosphere can grow which, if allowed to grow, undermines discipline and produces wrongful acts and omissions. It is the atmosphere in which the lower ranks of a disciplined force know that there are certain things which are contrary to regulations and which are wrong, but they also know they are allowed to do those things provided they are not found

out, and no one is going to try very hard to find out. It was submitted to me, with tact and moderation which enhanced the force of the submission that . . . such an atmosphere had developed whereby police officers . . . could use violence and show disrespect to persons in custody, and could indulge in the fabrication of evidence without exciting attention.

It is therefore possible to see how individual officers can, through a combination of zeal and pressure of work, become involved in corrupt use of power, for in this case there was not a scintilla of evidence that any officer had been motivated by that other form of police corruption, personal gain or bribery.

CORRUPTION THROUGH GAIN

All well-ordered societies make considerable efforts to prevent corruption of public officials by passing appropriate laws and exacting high standards of personal probity. This particularly applies to the police since corruption of the police is a negation of all that they stand for. It is a considerable contradiction. In the main such corruption is aimed at obstructing justice or seeking favours. It may be induced by a bribing of police or by police extortion. It is endemic in some cultures, but in others it is rare or extremely rare. Where it is endemic it follows that a corrupt society will get a corrupt police. Whereas in Great Britain it is comparatively rare in general, it will be comparatively rare in police, particularly if police are of a high standard and properly remunerated and of a high morale. The idea that an ill-equipped, badly-paid, demoralised police can somehow escape corruption is far-fetched to say the least.

The scandal surrounding any vestige of police corruption is an indication of its seriousness since it strikes at the whole edifice of public virtue, as the police are among the guardians of that virtue.

Such corruption can operate at two levels, at the level of the individual dishonest police officer and at the group or departmental level. In the latter sense it can be lateral, that is amongst the peer group only, or it can be vertical, which includes senior officers as well. There are, from time to time, prosecutions of individual officers and internal charges under police discipline regulations. The Reports of Her Majesty's Chief Inspector of Constabulary for England and Wales over the period 1972-7 indicate that the average number of criminal convictions for corruption is probably in single figures. Outside London there is no evidence of the vertical or lateral group corruption on any scale. In London the position, though exceptional historically, over the same period revealed an element of both vertical and lateral group corruption.

The arrest of twelve former or serving officers in February 1976 preceded by a number of earlier arrests had resulted in a decision to institute three separate prosecutions of which the last, involving the former head of the Flying Squad, was not completed until January 1977. Altogether eighteen men of varying ranks from constable to commander were sentenced to over a hundred years' imprisonment, including terms of 12, 10 and 8 years in the worst cases.[4]

The difference between corrupt police individual behaviour and a corrupt police department has to be borne in mind. The former has to be checked and eliminated if the latter is not to develop. The means of achieving the most desirable freedom from police corruptions are numerous.

DEFENCES AGAINST CORRUPTION

In the first place, the general criminal law has to provide a proper range of provisions and sanctions. Secondly society has to exact a high standard of behaviour from public officers generally and to promulgate a suitable code of practice. A police force free of corruption will prevail more easily where social values generally are anti-corruption. The British Civil Service provides an outstanding example of excellence in this connection, as, of course, do the police generally.

The police must take their own precautions and this begins with selection. Considerable care has to be (and in Great Britain is) taken in enquiries into the antecedent history of potential recruits. The necessary judgment of character and its ability to stand up to the hurly-burly of police work and the temptations put in the way of police has to be taken into account at this stage. Only high-quality officers properly trained should be involved in selection procedures.

The basic training of all officers should stress ethical concepts of police behaviour. Being concerned as this is with the exercise of power and its application, moral as well as legal principles should bind the recruit to his task. There are particular problems in relation to the arrest, detention and questioning of people, since as we have seen the police are often under pressure to achieve results; but it cannot be emphasised too strongly that illegal practices should not be condoned to achieve them.

It is important that every effort should be made by senior officers to produce the precise climate in which police come and go to their duties. The concept of high standards of professional ethics has to be constantly instilled in everyday practice and attitudes. This is of vital importance and is easier to achieve in small organisations than in

32

large ones. An outstanding example of the leader setting the tone, and an implacable hostility to corrupt police practice, is that of Sir Robert Mark when he was Commissioner of the Metropolitan Police from 1972 until 1977.

When taking up his duties as Commissioner in 1972, he developed early a strategy for dealing with corruption amongst a minority in the C.I.D., which was based on three principles described in his autobiography.

First, our house was to be put in order firmly, quickly, ruthlessly but without undermining the confidence of the honest and dedicated detective required to run risks in the public interest. Second, to give the public the opportunity to satisfy itself of our willingness to be accountable and of the effectiveness of our corrective measures. Third, from experience of those measures to introduce changes in the system of selection, deployment and promotion so as to make institutional wrongdoing very difficult, almost certain of discovery and conviction and therefore much less likely to occur.[5]

The first two principles concern firmness of intention against corruption and the acquisition of public confidence so vital to the proper functioning of a democratic police. It is the third principle which paves the way for precautions against the resurgence of corruption. It is a matter for regret that earlier indications of unhealthy disciplinary systems and departmental chauvinism in the Metropolitan Police had not been eradicated in 1964. In that year a Report of Inquiry known as the Mars-Jones Report[6] found that the investigation of detective malpractices by detectives was faulty in itself because of its obvious tendency to partiality. C.I.D. malpractices should of course be investigated by officers from other departments or from a special department of selected impartial officers.

The report also revealed the blatant and improper use of senior C.I.D. officers to intimidate officers of the uniformed department who showed any lively concern for improper C.I.D. practices. The so-called "firm within the firm" has its genesis in higher rather than lower echelons at times and the failure at the top is more to blame than that at the bottom. It is important therefore to develop internal policies which require inter-departmental transfers which will constantly break up coalitions of officers, and give those achieving promotion opportunities to see the other and broader aspects of the police function. Nor should officers be assigned to duties for protracted periods which bring them into contact with disreputable practices and activities which concern vice and other corrupting influences.

Frequent changes of officers performing these duties are in the interests of the officers themselves as well as of the police and the public. Even the best of officers can lose their sense of proportion by constant exposure to vice as well as being rendered vulnerable to blackmail and conspiratorial complaints.

Superior police, therefore, have to deploy a whole battery of measures to frustrate corruption, to internalise high ethical values and to create a corporate and individual demeanour of police of the highest possible standards.

NOTES

1. Brian Chapman, *Police State* (Macmillan 1971), Chap. 8.
2. Report of Royal Commission on Police 1962, Cmnd. 1728.
3. Cmnd. 2735.
4. Sir Robert Mark, *In the Office of Constable* (Collins 1978), Chap. 20.
5. Ibid., Chap. 10.
6. Cmnd. 2526.

Chapter 5

Styles of policing

An examination of the nature of policing will reveal considerable variations in styles. Styles will vary according to cultural, religious, legal, social and political systems. Even where a system as a whole manifests one dominant and seemingly universal style, closer examination will reveal many variations and mutations. Even in a single geographical location styles may differ as the population changes. This is noticeable in city centres where the daytime may present a different range of problems from those of the night.

INFORMAL POLICING

Among the most successful checks on crime in a society are those stemming from traditional and informal social controls. Superstition, taboos, religions, customs, shared values and moral standards in one way or another have preceded the laws upon which the more formal policing arrangements of an advanced society are developed. Where a society retains the cohesion and stability of family units it is likely that the behaviour of the members of that unit will be controlled and that each and every other family unit will be likewise adding up to a cohesive and stable society. As societies develop and the restrictions of the family unit are lessened, it is likely that young people will be in increasing conflict with the law. As the institution of marriage becomes less fashionable, for example, more children are likely to feel the effects and imbalance of one-parent family culture. This can be redressed to some extent where the informal social concept of the extended family exists or where the close neighbourhood is a surrogate family. Because the family has been at the heart of Western civilisation it has been the most important informal social control of all.

Superstitions and taboos also play their part in controlling social behaviour. The idea that if an individual breaks a taboo, some evil will befall him is probably one of the earliest and most primitive of social controls.

Religions are of considerable importance in this connection as the ten commandments of the Old Testament manifest. It must surely be acknowledged that in Christian countries not only have the ten commandments prevented more crime than any other single code but that they have formed the basis of a mass of secular legal codes as well. The *Koran* of the Islamic faith, of course, represents another striking example of a code of behaviour which, like those of all other religions, impinges very strongly on the secular world.

Of considerable importance to the catalogue of informal policing mechanisms are the great schools of philosophy such as those of ancient Greece and of Buddhism. The moral philosophers of their time present the world with some of its finest opportunities to reach high standards of social behaviour and civilising forces. As in the case of religion, such movements lay firm foundations upon which following legal codes are built.

PASSIVE POLICING

Passive policing is characterised by police whose main purpose is to provide a presence, a "scarecrow", and to achieve their aim of maintaining order through informal means. Passive police are reluctant to activate the law save in serious crimes or in blatant cases of public disorder where there is little alternative. Where passive police operate it will usually be an indication of high tolerance levels in the subculture of a neighbourhood (for example an amusement area of a holiday resort) or on the other hand it may be an indication that a higher standard of residential neighbourhood is likely to reject police activity or to discourage it.

There are some advantages for a community in the passive style of policing, since it permits a good deal of self-regulation, avoids petty scandal and generally makes for a live-and-let-live atmosphere in which recourse to remedies through the criminal courts are kept to a minimum. On the other hand, one has to look below the surface of passive policing. It may be that the passivity is an indication of incompetence or even of corruption. The lack of will to enforce the law may stem from defective leadership or it may be that hostility of minority groups renders it difficult. At all events the vacuum created by pusillanimity may allow the growth of extortion rackets, bribery, blackmail and organised crime. This in turn could lead to corruption of the police and for that reason alone passivity is to be studiously avoided.

It could arise that police will be uneven in their styles by displaying passivity in one area and industry in another, which might be an indication of social expectations in the areas concerned.

PUNITIVE POLICING

Punitive policing has been described as "policing by suspended terror".[1] It works on the assumption that provided the penalties for crimes are sufficiently horrible people will be deterred from committing them. It presupposes firstly that sufficient people will be caught to render it plausible and that sufficient potential offenders will anticipate that they too might be caught.

Both these presuppositions are considerably undermined in practice. Certainly, without an effective police to back up the draconian code, its effect is likely to be considerably reduced. Radzinowicz, one of the leading authorities on the subject, writes in his book *A History of the English Criminal Law*:

> Rich and poor, thief and lord, gentle and simple attended to see the hanging and cracked jokes at the sufferers' expense. The assemblage of so prodigious a crowd naturally offered excellent opportunities to thieves. Magistrates' offices were later thronged by people who had lost their watches, pocket books and purses.[2]

This occurred at a time when hanging was the punishment for such offences. On the other hand, policing through punitive terror is the more likely to succeed as the prospect of certainty of detection increases. To succeed, therefore, there must be a strong correlation between extreme severity and certainty of detection and neither can be guaranteed sufficiently.

As a society becomes more gentle in its attitudes and manners, a condition that usually coincides with higher levels of knowledge and civilisation, it is less likely to permit inhuman penalties. Even where provided, the penalties will fall into disuse, as did corporal punishment before its repeal in 1948 and because juries will acquit rather than convict offenders (or find them guilty of lesser charges) when they feel repelled by such punishment. Under totalitarian or despotic regimes the law may have better chances of being enforced severely and implacably by virtue of the monopoly of power to convict, sentence and punish. It can also survive in religious form, as in Islamic countries at this present time.

The doctrine of policing by severity of punishment reached its peak in England in the latter part of the eighteenth century when over 300 offences could result in the death sentence. Yet crime continued to increase.

The theory directs its attention to policing the criminals and not the crime or its prevention. If the criminal could not be eliminated by death, or if society revolts against such punishment, as it did towards the end of the eighteenth century in England, other ways have to be found. The answer was to be found in transportation to the colonies, which until the mid-nineteenth century provided a remedy for the increasing number of convicted persons in Great Britain. The method is still used in Soviet Russia today through imprisonment in the Gulags followed by restricted movement thereafter, particularly for political dissidents, as evidenced by contemporary writers such as Solzhenitsyn and Bukovsky.

PREVENTIVE POLICING

Of all the strategies of policing it is the preventive one which is superior. It is superior in the ethical sense, since by preventing crime it saves people from their follies and the moral obloquy which confrontation with the criminal justice system brings. It marks the concern of society in reducing criminality which victimises both the perpetrator and the person who is the object of the crime. In this way a dual purpose is served. Prevention is not only ethically superior as a strategy but its utility is greater since it reduces the cost as well as the suffering of crime. The diminution of crime eases pressure on all facets of the system of criminal justice and should be the primary police aim in all systems. Declared as the strategy for the New Police in 1829, its tactical implementation lay with the omnipresent patrolling police whose beats were arranged along the lines of military sentry duty. Influenced as the early police were by military traditions, their fixed patrols not only mirrored their military counterparts but the retort of the constable to his supervisor, "All correct", which in London is still the main form of address, follows that still in use in military sentry duties.

But it is in the tactical sense that this nineteenth-century preventive style is now inadequate and new preventive concepts have to be created. Therefore, a newer philosophy of policing is required in which policing is not only seen as a matter of controlling the bad but also includes activating the good. This idea represents the point where modern preventive policing tactics part company with the traditional or Peel model. Peel's preventive police were created to control the criminal classes, the mob, and the battalions of London's lower orders. It follows in a modern society where concepts of criminal classes and lower orders are no longer current, where most people are potential criminals or victims, that newer preventive policing methods are desirable. There are three identifiable levels of policing a modern community, each with preventive characteristics to a greater or lesser degree. These levels may be called primary, secondary and tertiary policing levels.

PROACTIVE POLICING

Primary prevention may be called proactive policing since it represents the antithesis to reactive policing. Proactive policing describes any lawful form of human activity which results in a diminution of conduct forbidden by the criminal law. It embraces activities to penetrate the community in a multitude of ways in order to influence its behaviour away from illegality and towards legality. Unlike its counterparts, preventive and reactive policing, its style envisages a more persuasive effect, for it involves carrying anticipatory initiatives into practice to head off criminality.

Proactive policing seeks to strengthen that greatest of all prevention, social discipline and mutual trust in communities. Its methods will therefore vary according to community *mores* and culture. As an abstract concept with idealistic overtones it is not easily put across to police officers, who have a healthy scepticism for such things. But once introduced to the tactics required they have been known to become enthusiastic for its introduction into their communities. It easily converts from abstract to concrete and has numerous applications in practice.

Proactive policing envisages a high degree of co-operation with other agencies of government both local and central. It needs to be passed down from the strategic policy level to the tactical ground working level and into action. It requires an approach to social problems adumbrating crime, disorder or social agitation of one kind or another together with social services, health, welfare, probation, employment, social security, housing, planning and other statutory and voluntary services. Removing or foiling crimogenic social conditions is its purpose.

Having a broad and long-term strategic characteristic it also has a substantial and meaningful commitment in the field of education at all its levels and must therefore commend itself to education authorities, teaching staff, parents and pupils. In the educational setting it offers for the police an important non-conflict contact point in which a meaningful human relationship can be achieved on issues affecting youth and the police. It is a matter which should commend itself to higher education where its philosophy can be tested by rigorous intellectual research.

Proactive policing should lead to the lowering of barriers between various agencies from which increased trust and better combined operation can flow to stem criminality and its trail of suffering for victim and sometimes offender and offenders' families and friends. As the future will demand that resources are to be used to the maximum advantage, the existence of rigid professional demarcations between different agencies is inimical to the public good. This is particularly so when it is seen that a number of agencies are all working towards the same ultimate goal, namely the welfare of society.

Proactive policing begins with a frame of mind, a philosophy, and requires the will to pursue its goals in the face of conventional scepticism. It is forward-looking in the sense that it can readily adapt to social and cultural change unlike legal policing which suffers from its in-built rigidity. The nature and variety of the course of proactive policing is limited only by the imagination, since it is not heavily dependent on resources but mainly on ideas.

The police must seek to strengthen trust in communities or where it is lacking to create it, and from this position they, together with other agencies, stimulate the community itself towards self-policing. The police are particularly well placed to provide social leadership for proactive police purposes though care is needed to avoid excessive contributions to this work to the detriment of greater priorities of a short-term nature.

The news media have a considerable role to play in the propagation of proactive policing throughout the communities since, ultimately, it involves all people both as individuals and as members of organisations.

The education and training of a police force in advanced proactive policing would take much time and effort, but as it is considered to have ethical and utilitarian advantages over other policing strategies it is worth the effort.

Secondary prevention is a term which might be used to cover those activities which are normally associated with the narrower and better-understood police function. Preventive policing, by the presence of foot and mobile patrols, is that part of policing which is heavily dependent on manpower, communications and mobility for its success. Foot patrols have a greater deterrent potential, when skilfully deployed, though the response capability is naturally much less than mobile patrols. The latter, however, have less deterrent effect and do not impress themselves on the public. The ideal is clearly a control through community effort or a mixture of community and

Secondary prevention also includes the use of crime prevention advice to the public, particularly of advice against property crimes. Police auxiliaries such as traffic wardens or school-crossing patrols are additional elements of preventive strategy at the secondary level. The use of citizen volunteers in uniform such as a police reserve is dealt with elsewhere more fully, but it is a valuable part of secondary prevention and helps to canalise citizen power away from vigilante groups.

Tertiary prevention might be used to describe the detective aspects of the police function, coupled with correctional work of many other agencies. The belief that detection and conviction are the best deterrents is true at least in this context; but unless detection has a high degree of certainty its deterrent effect is rendered less, and if the certainty of conviction is not high further erosion of the principle takes place. Tertiary prevention also includes a meaningful penal policy. Imprisonment is an important preventer of crime during the period of incarceration, though it can increase criminality through association of criminals inside. After-care, probation, intermediate treatment and other forms of social and penal experiment are all part of a preventive strategy at tertiary level.

REACTIVE POLICING

Police have to be capable of reacting to emergencies which rate high priority in public estimation. They not only have to possess the necessary mobility and communication to do this but they also have to be deployed in such a way that other matters such as bad geographical distribution will not impede their adequate response. The time taken from receipt of a call to arrival at the scene, known as "response time", is regarded as a key measurement of police efficiency. Any police system which cannot keep pace with public demands for quick response in emergencies is in danger of losing its reputation. But there are a number of dangers inherent in police preoccupation with reactive policing which should be studiously avoided.

The first tendency to be avoided is that which regards reactive policing as the essence of the art. Sometimes known as "fire brigade" policing, it is the creation of technology. The impact of science and technology on the police over the thirteen years from 1966 to 1979 was very considerable. Just as the same issue has raised questions for medical ethics, for broadcasting and above all for war, it has had a profound effect on police methods, public image and reputation, to say nothing of police psychology. The police have been helped considerable, even crucially, by technology; though in some ways they have been seduced by its brilliance. Stemming from the universal introduction of personal pocket radio some twelve years ago, together with the availability of cheap motor vehicles and later on expensive computerised command and control systems, what was basically a preventive foot patrolling force has become a basically reactive mobile patrolling force.

The police have been considerable losers as well as gainers from these changes. The loss of non-conflict contact with the public has severely curtailed police understanding of their public, and most serving police officers in this new age have become technological "cops" who barely meet their public outside conflict or crisis. The recent introduction of the Police National Computer with the entire vehicular and criminal information available to every police unit within seconds of its demand, completes the seeming omnipotence of police technology. Policing under these conditions becomes a matter of mobility (motor vehicles), communications (radio) and information (computers). The world of the reactive technological cop has arrived.

And yet this situation contains the seeds of many problems for the police. Loss of human contact, knowledge and understanding, the very essence of democratic police, is too high a price to pay for technology. The gulf that can arise from these conditions can open up as police drift further into their own reactive style—a gulf which can lead to misunderstanding, suspicions, even to hostility. But however much one may deplore the loss, the gain is considerable. The police could not now deliver the services they do and cope with the work-loads they carry without the many aids which place the police in this country technologically high amongst the police systems of the world. They are enabled by technology to police the world of technology, and that is essential.

This seductive power of technology has resulted in a false assumption that, together with the legal powers, it provides the essence of policing. This is a profound mistake. A superior democratic police knows that the essence of policing lies in human care, understanding and education, resulting in a deep attachment of police to public and vice versa. Getting this wrong can have lasting deleterious effects on policing.

In their necessary authoritarian role as controllers of public order it is likely that the police will have greater confidence and feel less threatened by public hostility, and the people, on their part, will view the police in their total role with greater understanding and sympathy if the police have opportunities on a day-to-day basis to be guide, philosopher and friend. This is of crucial importance where policing of nervous minorities renders purely reactive policing quite dangerous.

Therefore the police have to develop a dual character in being able to respond and react and, at the same time, to take care to invest heavily in activities which provide a non-conflict meeting ground with the various types of public which they serve.

The police therefore require resources and understanding to avoid the trap currently being set by the growth of police technology. A purely reactionary police force, however efficient and well-equipped, would be a disaster.

REPRESSIVE POLICE

Repressive police exist to serve strong or alienated government. Rulers or governments lacking in popular support will rely on repressive police to maintain them in power. Colonial governments, never quite sure how the native population is to react, equally require repressive police or military services if they are to stay in power against popular sentiment. Although much colonial government can be benevolent, it remains true that it is alien and an occupying power. It is possible for the governor of a colony to suspend the constitution and govern from a position of strength. This is an inevitable consequence and no doubt a practical necessity in colonial government. In such circumstances the police, supported by the military, have to be endowed with considerable emergency power of search, arrest and detention.

In such an arrangement the police have to be capable of maintaining a strong image, since if they lose the support and approval of the native population their own power and strength are crucial to their success. To maintain their reputation they will have to act firmly when required to do so. Repressive policing generally, though not exclusively, tends towards alienation of police from the community; and this can be further compounded by living in barracks apart from the community.

It is not in the interest of repressive police to become over-familiar with those whom they police, as to do so would be likely to erode their will to repress and to lessen the community apprehension which is part of the stock-in-trade of repressive police. Such police are almost invariably likely to be armed and of a quasi-military nature, since disciplinary control, fire power and military training are necessary for success.

Repressive police have to take care to balance their power effectively. If they are over-repressive they are likely to spark off anti-police riots, but if they are under-repressive the apprehension of the public essential to success is removed.

A repressive style of policing may also be found where the culture accommodates it and where the law and tradition sustain it. Many of the European systems based on the French, following Napoleon Bonaparte, such as Italy and Spain and many South American countries, have strong centralised systems with a repressive capability well above those grounded in English common law.

COMMUNAL POLICING

Communal policing describes at least four distinct styles of social

43

control through community effort or a mixture of community and government effort as opposed to that solely of government.

PRIMITIVE COMMUNAL POLICING

Communal policing is first seen in its ancient form in what would be called primitive or undeveloped societies. In civilisations where only small and vulnerable settlements existed, social control through the immediate family or group of families in combination, provided early examples of communal policing. Referred to by Sir Henry Maine in his classic work *Ancient Law* as the Patriarchal model in which the eldest male parent is supreme, "his domination extends to life and death and is as unqualified over his children and their houses as over his slaves".[3] In contrast with modern Western societies it was not a society of individuals with individual choices but "it was an aggregate of families" with collective choices. In such static societies the social unit was the family extended to the limit of its blood ties. The despotism of the heads of households provides the key to primitive social models of communal policing. The community was the extended family in which: "The aggregation of the Families form the Gens or House. The aggregation of the Houses makes the Tribe. The aggregation of the Tribes constitutes the Commonwealth."[4] The *Patria Potestas* of ancient Roman society was all-embracing before its gradual surrender to civil government, which through its superior power gradually took over the policing of the Commonwealth.

The concept of the primitive form of communal policing is also found under ancient Anglo-Saxon law where the groups of families owe duties for the keeping of the peace to the tythingman or headman of the tens and hundreds who in turn owes allegiance to the king. "From very early times, certainly from the reign of King Alfred, the primary responsibility for maintaining the King's peace fell upon each locality under a well-understood principle of social obligation, or collective security."[5]

It was, however, a system which was largely orientated towards primitive legal, as opposed to social, concepts of control. Critchley, quoting Professor Sayle, says: "the primary importance of the vills in governmental life lay in the police duties which came to be imposed upon them. The most serious problem of everyday administration was to discover and punish those evildoers whose deeds struck at the roots of an orderly society."[6]

Early concepts of communal policing, it seems, allowed unfettered power to be vested in the hands of the family head, with the concept of family depending on blood ties. The latter variations, at least in Anglo-Saxon society, depended on a communal policing duty and responsibility being imposed on headman and tribe alike. These primitive concepts have of course grown into the sophisticated legal systems of modern states with nations assuming policing responsibilities of the legal kind. It is important to note, however, that the Anglo-Saxon ideas of communal responsibility still lie at the heart of the legal police system of Britain as well as that in the U.S.A. and the older Commonwealth countries.

TOTALITARIAN COMMUNAL POLICING

The difference between totalitarian communal policing and democratic communal policing lies in the presence or absence of political manipulation. Totalitarian communal policing is the creature of the party and is used for spying, oppression of the people and the persecution of political, religious or cultural minorities. In this way people have been manipulated to serve demagogues and regimes throughout the ages. In more recent times we have seen both the Soviet Union and Nazi Germany use local groups to police their localities while all the time keeping a rigid grip from a central hierarchy. The latest example of this kind of social/political control has been seen in China. The communist Red Guards placed a firm, oppressive and at times brutal grip on their communities.

Tom Bowden in his book *Beyond the Limits of the Law*[7] records the growth of the Red Sentinels in the factories as guards and as controllers of discipline and ideology on the factory floor in 1969. There were also "listening posts" among the workers. If originally spontaneous they later became the tool of the party. "Thus in the course of some six months what had begun as an *ad hoc* police agency, operating without any statutory recognition, had become firmly established throughout China's industrial and commercial centre." This kind of totalitarian response is clearly offensive to the British idea of communal responsibility.

UNOFFICIAL COMMUNAL POLICING

Unofficial communal policing is to be found in areas where official policing is weak, allowing various power groups to arise in neighbourhoods and localities to exert an unofficial control. This can be a benign or malign control.

In benign control, residents will freely subscribe to the local leadership which may centre around a charismatic leader. In this sense it is akin to informal policing. Kibbutzim in the Israeli culture offer one example of benign unofficial communal policing where all the residents subscribe to the rules (or have to leave!). This is unofficial in the sense that Kibbutzim are self-supporting and do not use or have government agencies and resources. They are of course policed in the legal sense by the official police system, though the aim is not to have to invoke this service or interference if at all possible. This system although bearing similarities to ancient communal policing differs in so far that it exists in a modern developed state and alongside official controls and legal systems.

Malign unofficial communal police systems can be seen where power groups get their ascendancy through violence or intimidation. This can happen within a democratic state where a criminal sub-culture pervades a neighbourhood. Local social control of this kind flourishes in spite of the existence of official police. The outstanding example of malign unofficial communal police in a democracy is the Mafia, with its origins in Italy and Sicily and its new roots in the inner city neighbourhoods of the U.S.A.

Where minorities or popular movements begin to challenge legitimate government and its laws, there are always dangers that pressure groups will exert sufficient power to allow malign unofficial communal police to grow. This kind of thing is most noticeable in areas dominated by terrorist violence. In Northern Ireland it is particularly noticeable in the Catholic or Republican enclaves of Belfast and Londonderry.

DEMOCRATIC COMMUNAL POLICING

Communal policing in its purest form is difficult to find in a modern developed country since there are many forces working against it. It would exist in its purest form where all the elements in a community, both official and unofficial, would conceive of the common good and combine to produce a social climate and an environment conducive to good order and the happiness of all those living within it. It leaves legal policing to the police and concentrates on social measures for its success. The forces and conditions which work against this state of affairs are many and varied, particularly in the cities. The concept of the common good is elusive in a society where individualism and permissiveness are established, as in Great Britain. The cultural diversity of some neighbourhoods makes the concept of the common good difficult to envisage, let alone achieve. Furthermore, communities are divided by politics, religion and class as well as by economic disparities. Additional divisions are found in the young, the teenage, the young married, the middle-aged and the elderly, all belonging to at least two communities, one within the other.

It is this condition which Halsey notes in *Change in British Society*[8] when he reminds us of an aspect of English society of fifty or so years ago.

Working class districts, including those where incomes were very low, and housing and amenities poorly provided, were also areas of domestic peace and neighbourly trust of a standard which we do not know today.

People never thought of locking their houses if they went out during the day, and theft would have been cause for amazement.

In one sense democratic communal policing aims to produce conditions of "domestic peace and neighbourly trust" since it is conducive to the common good. But such conditions are much easier to bring about in a static society with modest ambitions for self and a stoic acceptance of one's lot. In a dynamic, restless, egalitarian and individualistic, permissive society the task is overwhelming and dispiriting, though perhaps not quite impossible. If democratic communal policing is to be tried it is necessary to spell out the principles upon which it is to be based and to outline the strategy.

The aim of democratic communal policing should be based on a concept and understanding of the common good. The creation of a neighbourhood or community climate free from fear and uncontrolled delinquency and crime would be its primary aim. In respecting the dignity of the individual nobody should be regarded as unworthy of its concern. On the other hand it should have due regard for the privacy, individuality and freedoms of all, including the freedom to be left alone. Community-based, it should be motivated only for the community as a whole and not for political or sectarian causes or concerns.

In setting out to achieve its aims it should involve all the statutory bodies and agencies whose work in any way affects the quality of community life so far as control of crime and delinquency is concerned. The common interest lies in the creation of lower social tensions through a more wholesome environment. The statutory agencies should then come together with the voluntary bodies whose social aims bear relevance, and with individuals whose concern is to represent the residents of the community. This team should be non-sectarian, and non-political (in the party sense). It need have no special powers of its own but should achieve its aims through benign influence and persuasion. The community concerned should be kept fully informed of its existence and of its activities. Indeed the starting point of its work is to inform and educate the public about crime, its incidence, causes and effects within the community. It should be victim-orientated also, for by succouring its victims it manifests condemnation of crime.

In order to operate effectively, democratic communal policing has to have regard for the twin pillars of its existence. In the first place it has to define the term "community" and seek to strengthen or create such a phenomenon through fraternity. Community should be seen as a group of people who live in sympathetic proximity, with (to a greater or lesser degree) some significant factor in common. Residential commonality is one thing, but it may contain elements of

47

animosity, even hatred. Thus where a community exists it should be strengthened; where it does not exist it should be created.

Democratic communal policing relies for its success principally on social action, and apathy is its greatest enemy. It should not be too intrusive into peoples' lives, but should strive to attract them to its virtues by the quality and genuineness of its motivation. Law enforcement in communites should be the province only of the police and other enforcement agencies, though the community should be educated in the role of the law and criminal justice as a necessary support of the social policing being carried out. This policing idea is as yet undeveloped, but offers much to advanced societies. An experimental scheme has been tried in Exeter since 1976 and has shown some ability to sustain itself. Under the guidance of a Community Policing Consultative Group it endeavours to fulfil the criteria described above. It is used as a model for further comment in the final chapters of Part Four. (*See* Appendix 4.)

NOTES

1. Radzinowicz, *A History of the English Criminal Law* (Stevens & Sons 1968), Vol. 1.
2. Ibid., Vol. 1, Chap. 6, Part II.
3. Sir Henry Maine, *Ancient Law* (Dent 1917), Chap. 6.
4. Ibid., Chap. 1.
5. T. A. Critchley, *A History of Police in England and Wales* (Constable 1978), Chap. 1.
6. Ibid., Chap. 1.
7. Tom Bowden, *Beyond the Limits of the Law* (Penguin 1978), Chap. 8.
8. A. H. Halsey, *Change in British Society* (Oxford University Press 1978), Chap. 3.

Chapter 6

The doctrine of minimum force

Force of itself is neutral. Its potential for harm however is great. In modern states the State itself claims monopoly over the ultimate use of force. In organised society the use of force or the threat of its use by authority therefore requires the explicit or implicit sanction of the law. Use of force not sanctioned by the law is therefore, even when used by persons in authority, described as unlawful. Thus although a parent may use physical force against its child as reasonable chastisement it would be unlawful for a police officer to do so. The old idea that a "clip across the ear" by the police was a good thing never was legal.

The doctrine of the use of maximum force by those in authority has no place in police affairs in Britain, though it has considerable meaning during war when turned against an external enemy where the aim is to destroy that enemy. It is important to remember, however, that although individuals and groups within the State may indulge in unlawful behaviour so that they are called "enemies of the State", in popular jargon, the doctrine of maximum force can never apply. Even terrorists who may commit or threaten to commit extreme forms of violence cannot be met by this concept. Nor can acts of treason be met by it, even though they are still capital crimes. The rule of law still applies and official violence must be commensurate with the need.

In moral terms violence of itself is evil, therefore force is only justified where it is used to prevent an evil greater than itself. There are, however, countries in the Western world where it is lawful for the police to shoot at criminals fleeing from them, under certain circumstances. In Australia, for example, police are permitted to shoot at "fleeing felons" in order to apprehend them, and the same applies in some jurisdictions in North America. Notoriously the police of the German Democratic Republic (East Germany) shoot at and kill people who climb or attempt to climb the Berlin Wall or attempt to flee the country unlawfully. In moral terms the shooting in all these cases represents a greater evil than the crime itself. It is therefore an abuse of force in moral if not in legal terms.

An historical example of the legal, though immoral, use of force in

49

England concerned the now repealed Riot Act of 1714, which provided that after the reading of a proclamation the crowd must disperse, and if after one hour twelve or more persons still remained assembled this would constitute a breach of the law which permitted the use of maximum force; and any deaths resulting from the use of force by the authorities though otherwise unlawful would be excused. This was a fairly tough provision obviously meant to maintain law and order though it could lead to regrettable disasters. The by now infamous "massacre" of Peterloo Fields in 1819 where some 60,000 people assembled to demonstrate for constitutional reform is an example. The precipitate charge of mounted yeomanry resulted in four hundred casualties and eleven deaths.

The British police idea has always contained, at least implicitly, the concept of the doctrine of minimum force. From the outset in 1829 and until the present this idea has been best exemplified by the unarmed nature of the police. Unique amongst the major countries of the world the police in Britain operate through public co-operation as alternatives to the use of major force. This represents a crucial point of balance, for the correlation between police power on the one hand is likely to be in inverse ratio to public support on the other. The more powerful the police the less the public support and vice versa.

The seeds of the doctrine of minimum force are contained in the common-law provisions which control the use of force generally. These provisions place the police in no more or less favourable position than any other member of the public. They require that the degree of force used should be commensurate with the degree of force it is (or is likely to be) used against. Thus to shoot a fleeing murderer in England would, unless he were about to murder another, on the face of it be illegal. The use of the police truncheon is likewise controlled by the need to weigh its use against anticipated illegal force against oneself or others. Again a passive or fleeing person cannot lawfully be struck save, in the latter case, if he flees whilst using further force.

The doctrine generally has resulted in the police in Britain being one of the lightest equipped in the world in the matter of offensive weapons. The truncheon remains as the symbolic evidence of this.

Thus the doctrine of minimum force is a key behavioural element in superior democratic policing.

PART TWO

Police and Related Topics

Chapter 7

A superior heritage

The British and their police have inherited a peculiar advantage in the form of a relationship which renders them indivisible. Of course there are strains now and then and there are particular stresses in one or two cultural minorities, but it still holds true that in Britain police and public have a better working relationship than most other systems seem to possess. It is all the more important, therefore, that the situation inherited should not be dissipated through apathy or complacency.

In one sense it exists as it does because the public generally do not feel threatened by the police; and, conversely, the police feel safe with their public. There are many reasons for this state of affairs but undoubtedly the police tradition has been a cultural phenomenon. (*See* Appendix 5.)

The police as a British type institution *par excellence* have gradually modified themselves and have simultaneously caused modifications in public behaviour. This social modification resulted in a remarkably precise juxtaposition of police and public which has been shaken, though not completely destroyed, by the manner and pace of social change over the past twenty years or so.

A Frenchman, Bertrand De Jouvenel, in his book *Sovereignty*[1], published in 1957, was able to express felicitously the behavioural implications of police style in England. "If the man who is 'dressed in a little brief authority' treats private citizens rudely, contemptuously, and even brutally, his conduct will be imitated by private citizens; they will see it as a way of showing themselves superior." But on the other hand if "the least important private citizen is treated by the authorities with politeness, and if the ruler behaves with the greatest consideration, this attitude will be imitated in the relations with private citizens." Thus he was able to say, "For instance, the courtesy of the police in England is a formative element of the general behaviour."

A little earlier than the Frenchman's comment was that published by Geoffrey Gorer, the psychologist and researcher, in *Exploring English Character*[2] (1955) using as his vehicle a Sunday newspaper, the *People*, which claimed to have an appeal to the widest variety of the population at the time and to be read by 12 million people. His sample numbered 5,000. The main part of his thesis in this connection will be found in Appendix 8. The main thrust of his argument at the time was that during the previous century "the policeman has been for his peers not only an object of respect, but also a model of the ideal male character". He wrote the following:

I have already stated that there are relatively few attitudes and beliefs or practices which are subscribed to by two-thirds or more of a population so diversified as the English. Besides the attitudes to child training and childish character, already described, another subject on which three-quarters of the population, who have any views at all, are in agreement is enthusiastic appreciation of the English Police.

This result, I admit, came as a big suprise to me, perhaps the greatest reversal of expectations which occurred in the whole research. I had asked the question "What do you think of the police?" with the expectation that a very considerable number of the respondents would take advantage of the anonymous questionnaire to express feelings of hostility to the representatives of the state, of law and order, of the repressive aspects of society. I had also thought that a considerable number of people would give their replies a political tinge, referring to one law for the rich and another for the poor, or describing the police as the servants of the capitalist class. Such replies did occur, but only from a very small proportion of the population, chiefly those describing themselves as upper working class; some 18 per cent of the population had criticisms to make of the police (5 per cent did not answer and 2 per cent gave irrelevant replies) but, as will be shown in more detail later, these criticisms were mostly on points of character or behaviour, that the police as individuals are "no better than anybody else", on the human failing of persons in the police. There is extremely little hostility to the police as an institution.

As far as I know, no parallel survey of attitudes to the police has been undertaken in any other country; but all the evidence available to me from my own research or observations or those of others strongly suggest that the amount and extent of enthusiastic appreciation of the police is peculiarly English and a most important component of the contemporary English character. To a great extent, the police represent an ideal model of behaviour and character, an aspect about which many respondents are articulate.

An attempt was made to divide the favourable judgments into "enthusiastic" and "appreciative"; but the division is so subjective that little value can be put upon it. For what the figures are worth, men, particularly the married, are more enthusiastic than women; there is most enthusiasm in the lower middle class, in the two Southern regions and in those with incomes of under £12 a week. When all the positive judgments are put together nearly all these differences disappear; there is, for example, only 1 per cent difference between men and women (73 and 74 per cent respectively). By nearly every criterion, the positive attitudes are most evenly distributed; the only areas in which there are a variation of 3 per cent or more from the national average is the regions with very high appreciation in the North-West (78 per cent) and low appreciation in the North-East and North (69 per cent); and in the extremes of the social classes, the upper middle having 79 per cent, and the lower working class 65 per cent; the class differences are not very surprising. Young people under 18 are also particularly enthusiastic, with 82 per cent positive; after the age of 18 there is very little variation.

The more recent work of Doctor William Belson[3] of the London School of Economics, in his 1975 study of London's police and their public image, tends to show that the views of people in Geoffrey Gorer's time generally persist, in spite of all the change in attitudes towards authority and the almost universality of motoring in which police and public relations are often at an acute point of strain. He notes that:

> In terms of being broadly satisfied with the police, liking, trusting and respecting them, the judgments of adult Londoners tend to be markedly favourable. Similarly, there was a marked tendency for adults to rate the police highly in terms of personal characteristics and abilities such as well trained, calm, efficient, courteous, fair, kind, intelligent, friendly.

Young people were also generally quite favourable, though less so than adults. Sadly the police themselves appreciably underestimate the degree of this regard.

It is interesting to speculate on the institutionalised element of the police as a system, which most people in Britain respect, as being separate from the attitude towards the human fallibility of the police as individuals. If the police are so well regarded it may be asked, for example, why more of our highly-educated university graduates do not join the Force? The reason so far has been a mixture of poor starting pay, antipathy towards the authoritarian role, and the dislike of having to start at the bottom as a constable. The position is undergoing a slow change perhaps only resulting from improvements in starting pay and the shortage of jobs, or is it that authoritarianism is becoming fashionable again? Only time will tell.

Among the exceptions to this otherwise reasonable picture of police/public relations are one or two cultural groups whose traditional relations with the police in countries where such cultures originate are hostile. Thus some West Indian and some Indo/Pakistan cultures do not rest so easily on this assumption. The heritage differs. It may be as cultural differences in Britain merge that this relationship will improve. If the cultural antipathy is based on police as an institution then it follows that even an infusion of such cultures into British police forces will not necessarily solve the problem overnight. It is essential that leaders of both police and cultural groups work towards a better understanding of the problem. The creation of a new relationship between police and minority publics may well be built around the concept of the village in the city dealt with in Chapter Twenty-eight.

At all events police and public should cherish the folk image of the police as a kind of social cement which even in times of stress will bear the strain of conflict. It is a legacy worthy of maintenance.

NOTES

1. Bertrand De Jouvenel, *Sovereignty* (Cambridge University Press 1957), Chap. 5.
2. Geoffrey Gorer, *Exploring English Character* (The Cresset Press 1955).
3. William Belson, *Public and the Police* (Harper and Row 1975), "Main Findings".

Chapter 8

Police and politics

Police are part of the politics of social control. Without a political device to enact laws, and a framework (not a strait-jacket) for their enforcement designed by political architects, policing as we understand the term would lose a great deal of its meaning. But even within democracies it is possible to speak of inferior and superior police systems, and the political framework in which they operate is crucial. Neither communism nor fascism could ever generate a superior police system, since such systems would be tainted with naked power and the tyranny of the one-party state. Superior police are the creation of liberal democratic states. They stand in the way of revolution and on the side of orderly evolution in allowing a tolerable degree of constructive violence and protest. As in Parliamentary democracy such a system has flowered best in Great Britain and its overseas legatees.

Although there is a whole field of policing which has nothing to do with the law at all, the police themselves are very much the servants of the law and instruments of its authority.

In spite of constant disagreement about the nature and content of laws, there is no disputing the need for laws of some kind if society is to be safe and to prosper. Of course the anarchists may disagree, but even they would want at least one law and that it should declare there shall be no laws.

But "where there is no law there is no freedom. For liberty is to be free from restraint and violence from others".[1] When Locke wrote his *Treatises of Government* in 1689 and 1690, it should be remembered that he had lived through the Revolution of 1688 and suffered from the anarchy and violence of those lawless times. But 200 years later in the more stable condition of mid-Victorian England, John Stuart Mill in his classical essay "On Liberty"[2] was also echoing the same eternal truth: "All that makes existence valuable to anyone depends on the enforcement of restraint upon the actions of other people. Some rules of conduct therefore have to be imposed."

He then wrote just one sentence which encapsulates so much in such a few words: "What those rules should be is the principle question in human affairs." In other words, as in so many aspects of human affairs, it is easy to state the abstract principle, but translating it into action is another matter altogether. Police as agents of action are well acquainted with this dilemma.

But both Locke and Mill died before the advent of the modern totalitarian and bureaucratic states. The legal and constitutional issues of their times tended to be concerned more with the freedom of individuals in relation to other and more powerful individuals and groups, the "over-mighty" subjects of their time.

In our own world, as Orwell so brilliantly and devastatingly reminded us in his novel *Nineteen Eighty-Four*, it is the State itself which now poses the main threat to individual liberty as we can see all around us. In this world of Big Brother, both Locke and Mill might have agreed that, although some law is necessary, where there is too much law there is no freedom, for liberty is to be free from restraints and violence by the State. In fact in one of the most famous passages from his celebrated essay "On Liberty" Mill put it thus: "The only purpose for which power can be rightly exercised over the member of a civilized community against his will, is to prevent harm to others."

That is a principle most honoured in the breach in modern society, and no doubt Mill and his contemporaries would have been greatly surprised to find how the *laissez-faire* society of those heady days had now become the province of modern bureaucracy with its reams of controlling laws and regulations. Even so, in Western democracies, the rule of law still holds, though at times by the skin of its teeth, and still represents our shield against capricious use of power which in current society floats around dangerously. If our society is to continue to hold together, it must be accepted that the law remains supreme.

It is therefore important to grasp the meaning and purpose of law in a democratic society and to acknowledge that some laws are needed in an ordered society and that this means incursion into our freedom, though no more than is necessary. Furthermore, it is their purpose to protect individuals and groups not only against each other but also against the power of the State. Such laws should stem from a democratic process and be enforced in such a manner, that is with such proper discretion, as to be acceptable to society generally and to minorities within that society in particular. It is also important that access to the criminal law should remain open to the individual as a matter of right. This common-law tradition is a very important constitutional safeguard not only against over-mighty subjects but also against overbearing officials. The unfettered right of a citizen to prosecute the police for illegality is of considerable importance though it is conspicuous by its absence in practically every system in the world outside that of English common law.

Police in relation to politics pose the greatest potential threat to individual liberty where they are considered to be an extension of political power. This is witnessed in its most potent form in totalitarian systems. It has been said that war is not merely a political act but also a real political instrument[3] and in totalitarian police systems is seen in the same light. The enemy in this case is not the external but the internal critics of the State.[4]

A superior democratic police system must recognise the danger of too direct a link between a political machine and day-to-day police operations; for even in democracies police can be abused by being made to serve the narrower political purposes of those occupying political office for the time being. The latter function would give rise to inferior democratic police systems in the context of this argument. For example, both the French and U.S.A. systems are much more the arm of politics than are the police in England and Wales. In France the powerful centralised police are directly controlled in the operational sense by the Minister of Interior. They are armed and equipped in quasi-military fashion and regarded as a powerful arm of the State. To a Frenchman this is self-evident, and a strong police organisation is very much in the tradition of ancient Rome and the French Revolution.

In the U.S.A., on the other hand, the tradition is very much that inherited from the English common law, but whereas in England checks and balances have continually been devised, the very strong democratic traditions in the U.S.A. have made political manipulation of the police much easier. A good example of the potential flaws inherent in the system is to be found in what were called the Chicago police riots of 1968 when, under the pressure of the then Mayor Richard Daley, the police turned with considerable brutality on the hippie fraternity protesting during the Republican convention in Chicago at that time. The direction of the French police in Paris in the same year against the Sorbonne protesters was regarded as having escalated the violence to such a pitch that it caused General de Gaulle to consider bringing in the Army to control the ensuing anarchy. Allowances of course have to be made for the French tradition of violent protest but it is significant that this is usually turned on the police as representing the State.

The direction of the French secret police against the Algerian rebels in neutral counties outside France was of questionable legality to say the least. Equally unconstitutional were the political activities of the U.S.A. F.B.I. and C.I.A. under numerous administrations.

In England the question of creating a centrally-controlled, and therefore politically-directed, police has been considered on a number of occasions. As early as 1830 proposals were being seriously put forward for a national constabulary.

And again as recently as 1962 a Royal Commission on the Police contained a powerful dissenting memorandum in praise of such an idea. But the then Home Secretary said what many of his predecessors and successors have said, that it would be wrong for one man or one government to be in charge directly of the whole police of this country. Our institutions are based on checks and balances. This has kept our liberties throughout the generations.

It is not so much the uniformed police under national systems which have potential for undemocratic conduct (though that may happen from time to time), for they can be seen in action and criticised by press and public alike. It is the secret police that go with them that have tendencies towards undemocratic growth. The recent concern in the U.S.A. over the growth of the power of the Federal Bureau of Investigation graphically illustrates this point. Nervous governments in democratic countries have a tendency to overplay this card.

Contrary to many popularly-held views and almost as many instances of politically-inspired journalism, there is no national secret police arm in England and Wales. Popularly regarded as providing such a service is the Special Branch, but it should be understood that there is no such thing as a national special branch but that each police force has, as part of its C.I.D. structure, a branch (special) dealing with unlawful criminal actions associated with illegal entry into the country of wanted criminals and the actions of subversive groups who, contrary to the democratically-enacted laws, have potential for damaging the stability of institutions and of the country. Primarily concerned in the beginning with the violence of Irish terror groups before partition of Ireland in 1922, this has remained their primary function, though new groups both national and international tend to spring up.

International terrorism, the interests of hostile foreign powers in undermining our national stability, together with the cranky and sometimes demented groups practising free floating political violence, all demand police vigilance if the separate police forces in Britain are to discharge their duties. The Security Services' role in addition to the localised role of the special branches of local C.I.D.s is well set out in the Denning Report[5] on the Profumo Case. Paragraph 230 of that report says:

No one can understand the role of the Security Service in the Profumo affair unless he realises the cardinal principle of their operations are to be used for one purpose, and one purpose only, the Defence of the Realm. They are not to be used to pry into any man's private conduct or business affairs: or even into his political opinions, except in so far as they are subversive, that is, they would contemplate the overthrow of Government by unlawful means.

Going on to deplore totalitarian secret police methods, Lord Denning thought that most people would support the above principles It is important to remember that they are not part of the civil police nor, unlike their totalitarian counterparts do they police the police. If the political neutrality of the police is all-important in the maintenance of a superior democratic system, there is no doubt that this principle of neutrality confounds and irritates the extremists of the political spectrum. The National Front, for example, make considerable play on their punctiliousness in their observance of the strict letter of the law, and they are very concerned to create the appearance of a relationship with the police which assists their propaganda for law and order. During the miners' strike of 1974, which brought the unhappy period of the Industrial Relations Act of Mr. Edward Heath's Government to an end, many to the right of centre of politics felt let down by the seeming inability or unwillingness of the police to escalate the confrontation between pickets and themselves at places such as the Saltley coke depot in Birmingham. A retired General, Walter Walker, amongst others, was very active in rallying right-wing elements into a strike-breaking force of an unofficial kind, with the declared intention of securing industrial key points and even helping to police the anticipated impending and incipient revolutionary elements of the left. Efforts were made by General Walker's lieutenants to enlist police support for their movement and to woo their sympathies towards a reaction.

Attempts by extreme left-wing elements to brand the police as lackeys of the right were not infrequent at the time, but the high watermark of these tactics was reached in the case of the so-called *Shrewsbury Pickets* case who were, for political propaganda, even linked in their moral rectitude and courage with the Tolpuddle Martyrs. Unlike the Tolpuddle Martyrs they were not accused of combining for more pay, but for conspiring to inflict violence on their fellow working-class mates who worked during the strike of building workers.

Sporadic attempts continue to claim the police as natural allies for diverse political causes. Nicholas Hyman writing in *Tribune*[6] welcomed the prospect of the police as brothers in membership of the T.U.C. in splendid Orwellian newspeak: "Against tendencies to fascism visible in vigilantism [General Walker?] and private security unscreenable, the police as part of the Labour movement may yet prove a bulwark of democracy."

One may imagine a similar tactic from the other extreme in the following fashion: "Against tendencies to extremism visible in industrial affairs and subversive activities, the police as part of the National Movement may yet prove a bulwark of democracy." The police, the majority of politicians and of the body politic will no doubt wisely continue to think and occasionally to say: "A plague on both your houses".

Speculation on bringing policing within some political ideology should be watched for constantly and carefully and rationally rebutted. Robert Reiner, an active commentator on the police scene from Bristol University, writing recently in *Marxism Today*,[7] thought the police were to be seen "as central to political strategy" and, so far as socialist strategy was concerned, "bringing the police force firmly under the control of popular democratic institutions" was an essential objective.

It is illuminating that at the time of writing the police are being criticised by some for not being sufficiently active in controlling and prosecuting pickets, particularly by those on the political right; whilst, speaking for the left, Reiner feels that "the police would be able to associate more freely with the labour movement and might even seek affiliation. The result of such association could be a reduction in the present virulently anti-union views of many police officers and a lessening of their enthusiasm for controlling pickets."

The neutrality of the police in the face of this kind of political tug-of-war assumes much greater importance as all aspects of modern British society become politicised. But what can not be done one way might well succeed by another.

That other way is to strip the police of their discretion to prosecute, by severing the common-law heritage in favour of alien traditions of central prosecuting officers. This proposal comes in its strongest advocate not from a minor spectator and commentator of the police scene, but from one of the most respected jurist socialist politicians in the land. Lord Gardiner, former Lord Chancellor in a socialist administration, writing as Chairman of Justice in the annual report for 1974,[8] expressed his views that: "In some ways our police are the least controlled and the most powerful in Europe. They are the least controlled in the sense that elsewhere they are national police forces under the orders of a Minister who in democracies is responsible to Parliament. . . ."

It can hardly be a coincidence that the National Executive of the Labour Party adopted a resolution shortly afterwards to follow the Gardner line, but in any case the wilder left was still smarting under the prosecution of their comrades, the Shrewsbury pickets. How nice if some control of the police and their "power" could be devised, but only in partial terms.

Further analysis of Lord Gardiner's statement that "police forces under the orders of a Minister who is responsible to Parliament" may well mean responsibility to a minority Government whose Ministers are vulnerable to parliamentary guerrilla tactics and who have difficulty in guaranteeing the passage of their Bills through Parliament as they would like. Secondly, and very importantly, all our great legal officers of State, the Lord Chancellor, the Attorney-General and the Solicitor-General, are political appointees and only hold office so long as the government by the party in power prevails. There is an element of political caprice in their situation. Speaking recently in the High Court in the *Gouriet* case,[9] the Attorney-General quite properly referred to himself as "a political animal". The police in a superior form are not political animals and never should be so; whatever their motives may be for prosecuting, they should never be political. The same cannot be said with confidence of future political animals.

There are many examples of police being so close to the political majority that ultimately the minority became restive to the point where the possibility of an explosion of public disorder is enhanced. The long reign of the Christian Democratic Party in Italy and the heavy hand of the national control of police forces is a factor to be borne in mind in the analysis of the succeeding bouts of disorder. As outlined in the Hunt Report[10] on Northern Ireland's police problems, the tight control of the police machine by the permanent majority did not serve to raise the confidence of the minority in its impartiality.

It cannot be stressed too strongly that a superior democratic police force should be enabled to and should strive to serve all, since its purpose should be to contribute to the notion of the common good and not to be the servant or tool of the majority. Its aim is to contribute to attainment of general happiness, not just to the utilitarian concept of the greatest happiness for the greatest number, but to go beyond that. Superior policing, however, is not an end in itself in pursuing its contribution to the happiness of all so much as representing a paradox, being on the one hand an extension of the political will in its members' role of officers of the law, whilst on the other hand being a user of discretion to temper the bluntness of the law. There should be about it an apolitical objectivity so that, in the moments of its greatest stress, it can turn to a philosophy fashioned and honed through research, debate and a firm knowledge of enabling legal provisions and constitutional principles.

NOTES

1. John Locke, *Two Treatises of Government* (Dent 1975).
2. J. S. Mill, "On Liberty" 1859 (O.U.P. 1975).

3. Von Clausewitz, *On War* (Routledge & Kegan Paul 1962) Vol. 1, Chap. 1.
4. Alexander Solzhenitsyn, *Gulag Archipelago* (Fontana 1976).
5. Lord Denning's Report, Cmnd. 2152, para. 230.
6. Nicholas Hyman, *Tribune* 1977.
7. Robert Reiner, *Marxism Today*, March 1978.
8. *Justice*, Annual Report 1974.
9. *Attorney General* v. *Gouriet*, Times Law Report July 26, 1977.
10. The Report of the Advisory Committee on Police in Northern Ireland.

Chapter 9

Police culture

Police cultures are most discernible where police feel most threatened. The greater the feeling of threat from a hostile environment the greater the cultural cohesion and group solidarity. This understandable behavioural reaction can be healthy or morbid, depending on varying circumstances. Where the entire environment is permanently and unlawfully hostile it is easier for police to develop a healthy and productive cohesion. It is healthy and productive in the sense that it enables police to survive and to discharge their lawful function against unlawful behaviour. Where only part of the environment in a community is hostile, much will depend on the quality of the friendly part. If the friendly part is for example corrupt, xenophobic or illegal over-identification with such social elements leads to police corruption. If on the other hand the non-hostile element is tolerant, proper and socially constructive, the police gain quality from such support. From this more healthy standpoint, police could work to reduce the hostility of the remainder and to bring about a more socially stable and correct environment for themselves and for the common good.

ENVIRONMENTAL PROBLEMS

It is likely that where police are faced with culture shock by policing environments to which they are strange, there is likely to be a greater tendency to retreat into the cultural familiarity of their own organisation. This is considerably reinforced where police live apart from other communities, for example in barracks or enclaves. As familiarity increases, police can develop a more relaxed set of relationships with the policed which can lead to a diminishing reliance on the solidarity of internal police cultures. Thus it is that where officers are not resident within their policing locations, like many others, they have to accommodate two cultures, their residential and their occupational.

Since ideally police should be capable of sympathetic identification with the policed this has led in some places to demands for police to have residential qualifications. Thus in the United States where police relations with the various ethnic minorities have been tense, for example Berkeley, California in 1971, demands for police to be organised on this basis have been raised. "To police us you should live with us" might be the way this feeling is given expression. Such restrictions rarely stand up to practical implementation. The same sentiment underlies some of the objections to a national police force when police with regional antipathy may be transferred into those areas precisely because they may lack local sympathies and identification. They would be less hesitant in using coercion, for example, because police culture under such arrangements would tend to be reinforced and become dominant in its behavioural influence. Ideally, and certainly in superior democratic police systems, police and public cultures are in sympathetic relationship so long as they are within the law. There are, however, considerable problems where the police represent or are seen to represent a dominant culture which is or appears to be hostile to minority cultures.

In such cases considerable effort is required of police to manifest their legal neutrality on the one hand and their social sympathy on the other. This represents the challenge to police in a plural multi-racial environment. It is a question of balance. Too great a concentration on legal policing would be just as likely to fail as too great a social sympathy. The police after all have to face up to their enforcement role, but they have to see that part of their role in the reality of its social context. It requires what might be called "a nice sense" of understanding.

POLICE PERSPECTIVES

The police generally appear to have tendencies to regard their esteem in the public mind as less good than it in fact is. This has been revealed in the social research programme of the Royal Commission on the Police in 1962[1] and more recently by the deeper research of Doctor William Belson on police/public relations in London.[2] This tendency to feel less well appreciated than they in fact are only increases the need for greater adherence to the group norms.

COUNTER-ATTACK

Relationships with the public in the law enforcement role contain obvious and natural seeds of conflict. It is a conflict-based situation, since the offender has "broken the law" and the police task is to bring the person to account. At this stage police are not only vulnerable to indignant public complaint based on genuine misunderstanding, but they are also vulnerable to malicious counter-offensives aimed at embarrassing them and weakening their resolve and effective-

66

ness. It should be understood that police are very vulnerable to counter-attack in their law-enforcement role, and particularly when dealing with organised and serious crime.

Where the worlds of the detective and of the organised professional criminals come together, attack and counter-attack make play. Just as the criminal gang is most vulnerable to penetration through informants, either internal or planted within the group, so the detective is vulnerable to counter-conspiracy. In this rather obscure and shadowy environment where police are exposed to the machinations of their quarry, the cultural need for cohesion, solidarity and mutual support is most pronounced. Every police officer must realise that if he is not vulnerable today he may be so tomorrow. This common understanding, manifested in fraternity, is a necessary ingredient in proper aspects of police work; it has, however, potential for less altruistic motives to come into play.

CULTURAL CORRUPTION

Police in Great Britain have one of the most outstanding and well deserved reputations for a robust and sturdy integrity. All the more reason therefore to regard the existence of a considerable amount of corruption in the C.I.D. of the Metropolitan Police as a major setback—an illustration of how a police subculture can go wrong and betray the very main culture of which it is part. The solidarity for good is perverted into solidarity for evil. (*See* Chapter Four on police corruption.) The required loyalty to the group as a necessary adjunct of superior policing is corrupted into an alien form. It becomes loyalty to the group above the police as a whole and even above the law itself. This kind of group solidarity spells disaster.

It is based on a misplaced loyalty, that one's immediate colleagues set the standards and ethical values which are to be adhered to, even though they are corrupt and inimical to the interests of the whole: it is seen as in keeping with the need to stick together through thick and thin, that what is wrong and corrupt is part of the moral code of the peer group. This kind of thinking turns police morality on its head and is amongst the most base of police subcultures.

It is sometimes known for groups of junior officers to stick together against the threat of internal supervision and investigation, where standards may be at variance. But the culture that is not only horizontal, as in such a case, but vertical also, in that its corruption flows from the upper echelons into the lower, is the ultimate betrayal and deserving of the most condign punishment. One of the tragedies of this kind of thing is that it involves otherwise innocent and uncorrupted junior officers who find themselves trapped in it, are

67

compromised and can only get out of it through their own destruction.

"REAL POLICING"

Within the broad culture of police there are elements which in internal affairs are either in conflict or at least out of sympathy. There is sometimes talk of what is "real policing" and what is not. Where the majority subscribe to a particular idea of policing care has to be taken to maintain the values and self-regard of others who make their vital contribution to the success of the organisation. Much will depend on how the leadership of a police force articulates the objectives of the force and how plausible those objectives are.

By the very nature of their familiarity with human weakness and proximity to disasters, police develop a scepticism which keeps them from being easily persuaded to abandon old, firm and known ground for new. Thus it is that a conflict can appear, for example, between the general ground cover forces on day-to-day policing duties and those who specialise in community relations. Sometimes the community relations specialists are regarded as having the soft option whilst the "real" police have the dirty end of the stick.

This gap is further widened when the feeling gains ground that the community relations branches are seen to be consorting and unduly sympathising with elements which are hostile, and even violent, towards their colleagues on the ground. It is a paradoxical situation. On the one hand the aim is to produce better understanding between police and policed while at the same time avoiding the impression of letting down those whose duties are involved in hard conflict. This is not an inevitable result of a policy concentrating community relations in a specialist department, but it is a probable result, nevertheless, unless some very skilful persuasion and education programmes are produced to offset it. The alternative is not to create a specialist community branch at all but to make every unit and every officer in it responsible for community relations at the ground level with senior specialists only at the policy level. In this way the apparent conflict can be dissipated, but it is a long hard road to achieve encouraging results.

Conflicts can also arise within the organisation between community constables with responsibility for their own territorial beats and task forces or special groups also operating on the same area. The community constable is preoccupied with creating a *modus vivendi* between himself and those who live on his beat. His success or failure will in some ways depend on how he manages this. Not being a team, he will find it easier to adopt an individualistic style where he can deal with many minor infractions informally. As he builds up his reputation he will begin to expect the people on his beat to support him with his difficult tasks. He is always likely to get help against outsiders who come on to his beat causing trouble but he has to deserve the help he will get against insiders. He may expect considerable support when offences are committed on his beat. He therefore has to invest heavily over a period of time in building his relationships in his own way. It is all the more galling for him, therefore, if a task force or specialist group in pursuit of their own objectives should sweep through his territory leaving a trail of animosities against police generally and many damaged bridges between himself and the community which he has to repair.

Relations between the C.I.D. and ground cover forces can also vary considerably, depending not only on personalities but on the nature of the organisation as well.

There is sometimes a misplaced tendency for the C.I.D. to adopt an élitist posture which is reinforced where officers enter the C.I.D. early in their careers and are then regarded as specialists throughout. There is a natural tendency for the ground cover and C.I.D. forces to grow apart unless special care is taken to avoid this. One of the disadvantages is that the ground cover forces will often acquire valuable criminal intelligence which does not reach the investigators. Not only may this happen through inadvertence but it can be deliberately withheld where conflict between the two branches is allowed to grow. One of the better ways of avoidance of much of this difficulty is brought about through interchange between the branches, particularly on promotion. In this way C.I.D. officers are brought back into the preventive branches in supervisory roles and renew their familiarity with a new range of problems. Not only does this kind of interchange minimise the growth of internal subcultures but it helps to engender mutual respect and diminishes unhealthy élitism and cultural gaps.

There is less of a problem between traffic police and others though a particularly legalistic traffic police can create animosity against police generally.

Relations between police and other agencies with whom they are expected to come into contact and to co-operate are beset, on both sides, with dangers of stereotyping. Police at times feel that other services are working against them and obstructing their efforts. There are equally strong cultural antipathies on the part of other agencies, who see the police as authoritarian personalities interfering with delicate human problems which they are trying to solve. This kind of cultural conflict is inimical to the public interest and has led to censure where it has resulted in unsatisfactory service to those entitled to it. The mutual stereotyping which can lead to antipathy is a dangerous thing, which causes waste of time and energy as well as of resources which would be better employed in mutually co-operative activity in the prevention of crime. When police regard social workers, probation officers, educational welfare officers and others as soft do-gooders in league with malefactors, and when such agencies regard police as punitive, arrogant, unable to form relationships and so on, a good deal of effort should be put into changing these attitudes.

Thus it is that a police culture can be benign or malign depending on its motives.

NOTES

1. Royal Commission on the Police 1962, Cmnd. 1728 (H.M.S.O.).
2. W. Belson, *Public and the Police* (Harper & Ro w 1975), "Main Findings"

Chapter 10

Arms and the police

Whether or not police carry arms will in general be determined by the nature of the society being policed, including cultural traditions.

A repressive police force will invariably carry arms and be supported by paramilitary formations since the concept of the police role unites the alternatives of submission or confrontation. If the policed are submissive then the question of confrontation will not arise, but as they gain in confidence and organisation they will offer further challenges to the police who will find it necessary to raise their own levels of violence to remain on top and in control. If the policed are capable of raising their levels of violence and the weight and size of their confrontation sufficiently high, they will eventually overwhelm a repressive armed police, usually in a welter of violence. In this sense the police will become victims of their own violence.

Police in a violent society have either to respond to the violence or to witness the emergence of alternative power groups and gangs. Where a society is in itself armed, as in the U.S.A., where the possession of arms is a constitutional right, it is not feasible to have unarmed police. The result of this kind of situation is the obvious one of a high death and unjury rate from both accidents and the criminal use of firearms. The police are particularly vulnerable and suffer considerable casualties compared with armed police in an unarmed society.

The policing of an unarmed society by an armed police is a questionable practice. This usually appertains in countries where police have traditionally adopted a paramilitary posture and in spite of the transition from uncontrollable to pacific conditions the police have remained armed. Arms also carry a badge of virility or machismo and symbolise power and a threat.

The ideal civic condition is for an unarmed society to be policed by unarmed police. This has been one of the remarkable features of the British system which traditionally has been not only an unarmed one but has not had paramilitary back-up either. This achievement cannot be unconditionally guaranteed in the face of considerable change. The abolition of the death penalty, the availability of arms, the international mobility of armed terrorists and similar trends of recent years have made it necessary for the police to raise their armed response capability. Most police forces have a significant

71

proportion of highly-trained police marksmen and a variety of small arms capable of responding to armed hold-ups, armed besieged criminals, and the general use of firearms in crime. The need to raise their capability in this direction has been forced upon a reluctant police but the change has been brought about by an increased use of firearms in crime of 305 per cent (1,308 to 5,302) between 1969 and 1977. The increase of violence against persons with firearms over the same period has been of 228 per cent (768 to 2,523).[1]

There are, however, considerable disadvantages in an excessive police response with firearms. It is important to accept that the more that police have to confront armed people the more they have to resort to arms themselves. To expect other than this is not to be realistic. On the other hand, police should take great care not to get too far ahead of the game. It must be expected that armed police will generate some armed criminal response and that police might become less scrupulous in their use of firearms, thus increasing the possibility of accidental shootings. Where police shoot and kill innocent people, even by accident, it is likely to start the erosion of public sympathy, and under conditions where sections of society are hostile it can ignite feelings and cause riot, damage, arson and attacks on police. There is a heavy price to pay where police and public cause an imbalance of violence of this kind.

Of considerable impact on police/public relations is the transition of police from civil to military characteristics. This might happen where the police feel threatened or where a military type response is called for. It is tantamount to the crossing of the Rubicon for the police, and they should consider invoking military aid for the civil power in the proper proportion at the proper time followed by an early withdrawal. Police are not soldiers any more than soldiers are police.

Of the greatest utility, and far superor to response alone, is the setting-up of police teams or squads to concentrate upon seeking out illegally-held firearms (and explosives) and waging a constant campaign upon illegal trafficking in firearms. This should be followed by the prosecution and where conviction follows, the award of condign prison sentences in appropriate cases. This course of action and its intent are of the utmost importance, since what is at stake is the maintenance of an unarmed police force and the control of lethal weaponry.

The police and society undoubtedly stand at the crossroads over the issue of firearms and unless great care is taken the Rubicon may soon be crossed. The need to protect public and police from the armed petty crook or from disturbed persons is one dimension of the problem. The need to grapple with fanatical terrorists is the other. Care should be taken not to allow measures commensurate with the latter to become standard action with the former. Unless great care is taken, the police will lose in terms of both violence against them and public sympathy for them. The stakes are high.

How then should the police go about this task? In the first place they should acknowledge that there may be times when only military weapons and skills will be adequate and appropriate for the efficient control of the highly trained, fanatical and desperate terrorist. The police, therefore, should concentrate on being able to deal with a whole range of situations where firearms are being used against members of the public or against themselves. Since the criminal law has always kept a considerable grip on counter-violence, holding that it should only be proportionate to that against which it is being used, police have to take great care lest they themselves may face criminal charges for excessive violence or use of disproportionate force.

In the first place, lethal firearms should only be deployed against lethal firearms as a general rule. There may be the exception where shooting may be necessary to save the life of another person, e.g. a threat to stab to death, but all other avenues should be exhausted first. It is hardly likely that police would, for example, shoot at an armed or dangerous person fleeing from them; they would endeavour to use other tactics such as encirclement followed by patient dialogue to wear down the offender's aggression before non-violent arrest. Training in the tactical use of weapons for those police permitted to use or direct their use is of considerable importance and the legal provisions and limitations are of paramount importance. Clearly the choice of weapons for police purposes has to be carefully exercised and restricted to those with lowest lethal side-effects and consequences for innocent persons. Since the arming of a person is calculated to bring about a personality change, to the extent that self-confidence is increased, it is necessary to choose authorised marksmen carefully for temperament as well as skill. On no account should highly-strung or irresponsible personalities be allowed to use firearms.

In the final analysis only the officer on the spot or the senior officer in charge will make a decision concerning the use of firearms, since he or she will personally carry the responsibility and it may be a heavy one. The police have to ensure that they are capable of protecting members of the public against armed assaults and to do this effectively requires an armed response. That response should be under the tightest control and certainly arms should on no account be issued to untrained or unsuitable persons. There can be no question of the police taking the law into their own hands.

NOTES

1. Criminal statistics for England and Wales 1977.

Chapter 11

Intellectuals and police

It is odd that, considering the great police traditions in Great Britain, it alone amongst all other Western states has failed to commend itself to the intellectual community generally as a subject worthy of its own place in university curricula at undergraduate level. It is true that a growing number of police officers read for degrees of one kind or another and that at postgraduate level second degrees in police-orientated subjects are now being awarded. None of this, however, can compensate for the failure to establish police studies in a major university at departmental level. In spite of the great expansion—explosion almost—of universities, the intellectual input into police studies is very small indeed (though it is growing).

In 1976, the University of Kent at Canterbury indicated its willingness to establish such a degree course which, if not entirely devoted to police studies, would have certainly covered an area of civil administration capable of embracing the field. The indifference of the police service and its administrators to this brave and promising proposal was an indication that the fault does not lie completely on the side of universities themselves. The lack of awareness in the police generally of the value of university interest, support and research is unfortunate to say the least.

In relation to the Kent proposal, it was also interesting to note that student leaders organised a petition against such a civil administration degree course. They were supported by a number of junior academic staff and the Students' Union thought that the proposal was a proposed interference in university autonomy by outside interest. This, it was explained, was due to the possibility of research being influenced by outside bodies such as the police themselves.

A survey carried out by the student newspaper indicated that 44 per cent of the students supported the university proposal, 30 per cent were against and 26 per cent were undecided. The survey further showed that 68 per cent of students at Kent were in favour of establishing an associated research unit and 76 per cent believed research into law enforcement was a major step forward. Additionally, 60 per cent of students interviewed said that they would not support any

Students' Union action aimed at preventing the setting up of the degree course.

It seemed therefore that, in spite of some resistance, the proposals were viable. Considerable work over fifteen months and discussions between the university, Police Staff College and senior police officers came to naught. The reason? Perhaps it was a combination of lack of will, lack of imagination and lack of understanding amongst the leaders of the police service and police administrators. At any event the proposal failed.

It is also noticeable that visitors from police organisations in Europe and North America who come to study and to admire many of the qualities of the British police system are confounded by the apparent lack of intellectual input into the subject of policing, and of the lack of police awareness of its importance. The problem is worsened since not only is there an absence of learning from which those responsible for police decision-making might enrich their judgment, but also the lack of literature means that some of our most educable youth are not attracted to higher forms of study of the subject and hence do not see the police as offering a professional career structure. The all-round loser from this intellectual gap is society as a whole. The science and art of policing a modern developed society is equally complex and important as those other forms of social administration which attract high status and resources in most of our major universities.

Although there are many degree courses covering the several parts of the system of criminal justice and comparative studies, there is a lack of undergraduate facilities for studying the criminal justice system as a whole, from law-making and police action, at one end, to penal and rehabilitative policies at the other. The result of studying a system of criminal justice in piecemeal fashion is that its administration in piecemeal fashion is perpetuated in practice. Progress in this field will continue to be spasmodic and unsatisfactory, until the police are able to convince their own service and the universities that a great need awaits a great opportunity.

Perhaps a progressive university will consider the establishment of a chair leading to a first degree in "The Policing of Society" or some similar title. There are difficulties to be expected in establishing the parameters of such a course and in developing a range of topics which would be amenable to the disciplines of higher learning. The many elements in universities of course exist already, as the Kent proposal indicated.

The general scheme was to offer a full-term three-year degree course leading to the award of B.A. (Hons.) under the Faculty of Social Sciences; and this was to be called a degree in Civil Administration (problems and process of law enforcement). It is not suggested that such a course should be confined to students from the ranks of the police but that it should be a mixed one of serving police officers, intending police officers and students of social sciences generally. It is estimated that, of some thirteen courses which would have to be taken, existing faculty resources could provide ten.

It will be seen from this that additional resources to set up such a degree course would not be necessarily extensive. It is readily acknowledged that any senior appointment should be at professorial level for the post of director of a research unit, with a centre for research in existing social sciences faculties. In considering the aims and objectives of such a course the University of Kent believe that a better educated police would lead to greater benefits for the community at large and that it was remarkable that no university had yet acted on this principle. It was felt that little seemed to have been done to satisfy the more recent suggestions made in Parliament for intensive research to be carried out by universities and others into the problems of law and order and of the police in carrying out their task. An appropriate course would not only be likely to help police officers who reach senior positions in the police and related services, but to help school-leavers who may be contemplating a career in the police service and others who wish to work in the general field of civil administration.

Any degree course of this kind would need to study in depth the discretionary nature of police power and the accountability for its exercise; the phenomenon of crime and its dimensions, the organisation, social functions and values of police work, together with the social attitudes which are themselves a factor responsible for the lack of objective and balanced study of many of these problems. Other areas of police requiring investigation involve the acceptability of police techniques to the public which so far has attracted less objective and scientific an enquiry than the importance of its demands.

It is felt that in the first year of such a course elements of economics, social history, law, politics, anthropology and sociology, statistics and the acquisition of social knowledge or philosophy might provide a starting point or two. In the second year, and using the subjects already mentioned as a basis for further exploration, all students might undertake a research programme selected in consultation with the director of the research unit and including matters of law enforcement, control and accountability of police and problems of social order. There is a large number of options which could be exercised having regard to existing university resources and departmental facilities.

Although the gallant attempt of the University of Kent at

Canterbury failed some three years ago, it is hoped that their efforts will not have been in vain and that soon both the police service and the Home Office together with academic advisers will feel able to press ahead with taking up the challenge of university studies in relation to police work at undergraduate level. There can be little doubt that the fusion of intellectual power with the practical knowledge and understanding of the police would provide a considerable force for enlightenment and enable the police and society to cope with the challenges which inevitably will come upon them in the future.

Chapter 12

Police and military

The distinction between the military and police functions, at least since the formation of the modern police in 1829, has been marked in Great Britain. The distinction is not so clear in France and other countries much influenced by the Napoleonic police systems where the *gendarmerie* are in fact under military command but have a normal policing function as well. Neither is it so clear where a police reserve, such as the National Guard in the U.S.A., provides an early back-up for armed police action. The policing function carried out by Cromwell's New Model Army after the Civil War of 1641 represents an exception in modern English history. The control of regions under Cromwellian Major-Generals and their military police was of course an aberration, though the Army was largely responsible for maintaining public order from time to time as England became turbulent in the early days of the Industrial Revolution and Reform movements. It is not surprising therefore to find that the Stanhope Memorandum on the Army in 1891 put high on the list of its tasks the continued support of the civil power in all parts of the United Kingdom, and so it remains at the present time.

It is hard to deny that, in the final analysis, since the government in a democracy should have a monopoly of armed power, the military should be regarded as the ultimate back-up to maintain the rule of law. To believe otherwise is to go against constitutional sense. On the other hand it is imperative that the military should always remain under strictest control by the government of the day and in all respects be subservient to Parliament.

It follows from this that the military can never come to the aid of the civil power without the permission of the government of the day. Such force is far too dangerous to democracy to be free floating. That is not to deny that, like any other citizen or citizens, a soldier or soldiers have individual rights and responsibilities for the arrest of serious offenders under the common law.

The difference lies between the actions of soldiers in the military context and the actions of soldiers as citizens. The distinction, on the face of it difficult to see, should in practice revolve around the personal responsibility of each soldier, acting on his judgment and on his conscience and not under the orders of his senior officers, at least when discharging his common-law duties. This of course is quite unacceptable to the military purpose in war. At all events, the soldier in the final analysis would be answerable under the common law as an individual where he acts as an individual. Where he acts under the orders of a superior officer he still remains personally responsible for his own unlawful actions though no doubt the fact that he was coerced would mitigate his blameworthiness. It is conundrums such as these which render the use of the military in civil affairs of a law and order nature a most delicate operation.

MILITARY AID

When we speak of military aid to the civil power we mean just that— that assistance be requested and given. It is at this stage that police and soldiers alike should try to get things in perspective if hostages are not to be given to fortune.

According to Major-General Lunt writing in the *Army Quarterly and Defence Journal*[1] under the heading "Soldiers are not policemen", "the principal task of an Army remains the same as it has always been—to deter war until or unless it breaks out, and if it does, to conquer". But if the primary task of an Army is to deter war, or if it fails then to conquer, it has always been recognised in this country that the Army had a role in the maintenance of law and order.

Defence Fellows Baynes and Kitson in their respective works, *The Soldier in Modern Society*[2] and *Low Intensity Operations*[3] both testify to this axiom. Indeed Kitson raises the soldiers' role in internal security to a high, even to the paramount, role, but then he is more often than not writing about a role outside Great Britain and when normal law and order has broken down, a fact overlooked by his critics. The distinction needs to be made clear since there are political objections to premature paramount military involvement. Recently the Right Honourable Enoch Powell, M.P., propounded some very thought provoking comments on the extent to which the Army should become involved in what he called "the affairs of civil authority". Stressing the point that the difference between the police and the Army was not a difference of armament but of function, he went on to comment about the undesirability of the Army involvement becoming too profound.

Meanwhile it should not be overlooked that it was precisely because the Army was too involved in the maintenance of public order in Great Britain in the early nineteenth century that the Duke of Wellington (then Prime Minister) gave Sir Robert Peel (then Home Secretary) every support and encouragement to get his Police Bill through Parliament in the face of much political obstruction. The Duke was very much opposed to the contemporary use of the military against the unruly crowds of the times as well as against the more legitimate Reform movements and the Luddite rebels of the Industrial Revolution.

It was partly to disengage the Army, therefore, that the formation of the modern police system gained further impetus; although social change connected with other factors, including urban growth, was the main driving force.

It may therefore be helpful to try to establish a principle or two concerning military aid to the civil power. Firstly, the procedure for seeking aid, in the event that it becomes necessary, is as follows.

The chief constable, or in London the Commissioner, seeks military aid to assist in maintaining the rule of law by applying to the Home Secretary who in turn seeks agreement from the Minister for Defence and the Cabinet. The procedures are laid down quite clearly and generally should operate speedily. The problem is in the implementation. If a chief constable is denied military aid, he will have to go it alone, in which case he will make his own decisions for which he is accountable to the law, as are each and every one of his police constables.

If, on the other hand, military aid is sanctioned, a number of important and sometimes delicate questions remain to be answered. Since the police are not generally subject to political direction in discharge of their legal functions, does it follow that the army who come to their aid are similarly placed? I do not think that it follows automatically. For example, if military aid is approved to deal with the arrest or destruction of armed foreign terrorists at a particular airport, it does not follow that such aid could be diverted to controlling a local demonstration by sympathisers outside the airport. Or at least it may not be prudent to do this. Military aid has been sought to carry out a particular task and to go beyond that task would require a fresh consent. If this is accepted as good practice, it leaves us with three important questions.

The first is to do with the proper deployment of a military task force in a police operation once political consent has been given. By that I mean who is to ask the military to carry out the task? I think it is generally agreed that this is the responsibility of the senior police officer in over-all charge of the operation.

The second question is who decides on the nature of the military response to the task? Here I believe it is the responsibility of the senior soldier in charge of the task force who carries the responsibility. At least he is going to be answerable thereafter so he should be

80

endowed with the necessary authority though he cannot expect unlawful orders to be implemented.

The third question concerns the proper withdrawal of the military force. By that I mean when should the military task force be called off? The answer would generally suggest itself or be arrived at by consultation; but if there were to be a difference of opinion about it I think the police officer in over-all command should carry that responsibility. The main reason is that we are considering a police type operation, with all that it entails.

But although the above principles might apply to isolated incidents under the normal law, for example the use of troops at Heathrow Airport to deter terrorist activity, or the standby of special units in other cases, there is also the larger question of emergency legislation and the setting-up of regional or *ad hoc* government bodies at times of extreme emergencies. In such cases delegated powers of government through Orders in Council may be granted to Ministers or senior Civil Servants to set up committees on which would be represented the police and military commanders. My own view is that such police action as needs military support would best be carried out under over-all police responsibility, with military commanders being responsible for completion of tasks allotted in support of the police. I think it is in these circumstances that the Army stands the greatest risk of being sucked into a dominant and protracted policing role which is inimical to the wider military interest. In the first place the police have a duty to avoid involving the military in the policing function if at all possible.

Enoch Powell's comments are interesting in this context. In *The Times* of 4th October 1977 he is quoted as saying:

> The role of the Army in aid of the civil power is perfectly clear and definite; it is a role which had been a hundred times proved and demonstrated in experience and the disastrous consequences of departing from it are a military truism. It is not to replace the police. It is not to supplement the police. It is not to deploy armament which the police do not possess. The true role of the army in aid of the civil power was to act as a killing machine at the moment when authority in the state judged that order could no longer be maintained or restored by any other means. The army was then brought in if necessary to perform the act of killing, albeit minimal, controlled and selective. Having performed this role it is instantly withdrawn and the police and the civil powers resume their function. Any departure from that proven rule of aid to the civil power meant that the army became what is was not and ought never to be, an armed police force, whose very inappropriateness to the task signalised and emphasised still further the breakdown of authority.

On the other hand, Colonel Baynes writing in *The Soldier in*

Modern Society, saw involvement likely to go beyond that envisaged by Powell. He would include widespread looting and destruction of property, physical occupation of forbidden premises, e.g. control tower of a military airfield, interference with military installations or illegal entry into closed zones, kidnapping or abduction of military personnel or equipment, the appearance of really effective uniformed bodies, the overstretching of the police either inadvertently or by design by a plethora of small outbreaks at the same moment. This approach, it is felt, goes too far.

Whether it be by police or soldier the enforcement of the law and the maintenance of public order are subject to strict limitations, both strategically and tactically. The first and overriding factor is the rule-of-law. This includes the principle that all actions must be either sanctioned by law or not specifically banned by it. Under its scope the police and (as I see it) soldiers are equally answerable for personal excesses. To have it otherwise would merely pave the way for those so inclined in the heat of the moment or under great strain to give way to extreme courses of action. This would lead of course to criticism and a diminution of the standing of the forces representing law and order. To seek to uphold law and order by breaching it is a contradiction in democracies.

The need to act without bias or prejudice, to be a servant of the law and of society as a whole is the *sine qua non* of police action. This leads to the third principle of answerability, that is to the broad consensus—to operate in a manner acceptable to public opinion.

It is in these areas of the legal, political and public opinion that police and Army are most vulnerable to campaigns of denigration to discredit them, to shake their self-confidence and to render them less effective.

Military involvement in policing operations should be avoided if at all possible, but should it come to pass then the following principles should be borne in mind.

1. We are considering the use of power, and power in Great Britain is generally the subject of constitutional checks and balances.
2. Police principles demand a recognition of the philosophy that police and people are indivisible.
3. Police (and soldiers who aid them) are personally answerable for excesses.
4. Although police principles may remain constant, social change creates novel problems.
5. Aid to the civil power is not a primary military task but it is well enshrined in history and is constitutional.
6. The army should not be too readily or too deeply and protractedly diverted into civil functions.

82

7. There is need to consider where responsibilities lie between police and military when in combined police operations.
8. All action should be within the bounds of the law, it should be non-political in any party political sense and generally acceptable to public opinion.

NOTES

1. Major-General Lunt, *Army Quarterly and Defence Journal*, July 1974.
2. J. C. M. Baynes, *The Soldier in Modern Society* (Eyre & Spottiswoode 1971).
3. Frank Kitson, *Low Intensity Operations* (Faber & Faber 1971).

Chapter 13

Vigilantism and the police

The police in England and Wales are conscious of the need to exert themselves to procure public concern for crime and its control. They are also aware of the duties to maintain lawful behaviour which the common law places on every citizen.[1] The powers of arrest possessed by every citizen and the right of every person to prosecute any person save the monarch, are notable features of the police system in England and Wales. (Scottish traditions differ.)

These are legacies of a kind of "do it yourself" police idea[2] but which even today have symbolic importance and occasional utility. They are symbolic in the sense that, like the jury system and the lay magistrates, they enable citizens to participate in the major function of policing the State. They are also important in denying a bureaucratic monopoly of the administration of justice. The system does not belong only to police, Civil Servants and the judiciary, but to all. This is an important and valuable concept all too often overlooked by ordinary people with other things on their mind.

For the police the citizen power to arrest for and prosecute certain offences places them in something of a dilemma. To encourage the populace to "have a go" is one thing, but when that becomes the province of organised groups it becomes dangerous. The term "vigilante" adumbrates an extension of casual assistance to the police into that of an organised body for the maintenance of order in a society which is disorganised either when opening up new frontiers, as in Western U.S.A. in the nineteenth century, or when normal controls are disrupted, as in Ulster since 1969, or when people are afraid, rightly or wrongly, and do not have confidence in the official police. The difficulty arises when the vigilante purports to operate within the law, since the police cannot deter this through law enforcement but have to use other means. This can be by persuasion or by the provision of adequate and visibly adequate police action.

There have been and are occasions when, for one reason or another, well-intentioned people concerned for society move to set up organisations, sometimes colloquially called "private armies", in order to uphold law and order. In one sense this might be seen as good citizenship; it is often motivated by the best civic intentions and is far from

84

base in its motives. There are, however, considerable dangers in it. It is dangerous because it may excite other groups of people equally well-intentioned but with different ideas to organise for their own purposes. The seeds of public disorder on a wide scale might be contained within the heart of good intentions.

Police, however, should not just put down such manifestations lightly, since they may well contain indications of a genuine public desire to do something to keep the peace in their neighbourhood or to help the country as a whole. It is here that the urge giving rise to vigilantism should be directed into constitutional channels. The Special Constabulary offers a considerable alternative to unofficial bodies and can be controlled by the police in a way acceptable to the public.

It would not be wise, for example, to use the Special Constabulary in industrial disputes, or to use a monocultural Special Constabulary exclusively against persons of another culture. It would not be wise, since they may be seen as a threat to those policed by them and an inducement to further lawless behaviour. As ordinary members of the general public, the Special Constabulary might also be embarrassed by insensitive use of their services. (For a suggested plan of Special Constabulary *see* Appendix 5.)

There will be many who might be attracted to the logistic side of voluntary service and they can be directed towards service with some of the many voluntary organisations which are constitutionally and socially acceptable.

Thus the police cannot afford to and should not ignore the considerable benefits of citizen participation and support in keeping the peace. Nevertheless the growth of unofficial groups, even lawful ones, contains the seeds of sectarian strife, and they should be channelled into constitutional forms.

NOTES

1. Archbold's *Criminal Pleading, Evidence and Practice*, (Sweet & Maxwell 1976).
2. T. A. Critchley, *A History of Police in England and Wales* (Constable 1978), Chap. 1.

Chapter 14

Police and other agencies

The role of police in a democracy impinges on the responsibilities of many other agencies. Since the police are primarily preventers of crime they have a vested interest in the work of all other agencies which prevent crime too. They not only have an interest but a duty to share their experience and knowledge of crime for the mutual benefit, for by doing so they may be instrumental in furthering efficiently the prevention of crime.

PROBATION SERVICE

It is salutary to recall that the supervision of offenders was a police responsibility until the formation of the probation service in 1925. Under the provisions of the Prevention of Crime Act 1871 police were responsible for the supervision of offenders twice convicted on indictment, and such supervision could be for up to seven years! The provisions of S.8 of the Act are worth noting.

Person twice convicted may be subjected to police supervision.
8. Where any person is convicted on indictment of a crime, and a previous conviction of a crime is proved against him, the court having cognisance of such indictment may, in addition to any other punishment which it may award to him, direct that he is to be subject to the supervision of the police for a period of seven years, or such less period as the court may direct, commencing immediately after the expiration of the sentence passed on him for the last of such crimes.

Every person subject to the supervision of the police, who is at large in Great Britain or Ireland, shall notify the place of his residence to the chief officer of police of the district in which his residence is situated, and shall, whenever he changes such residence within the same police district, notify such change to the chief officer of police of that district, and, whenever he changes his residence from one police district to another, shall notify such change of residence to the chief officer of police of the police district he is leaving, and to the chief officer of police of the police district into which he goes to reside; moreover every person subject to the supervision of the police, if a male, shall once in each month report himself, at such time as may be prescribed by the chief officer of police of the district in which such holder may be, either to such chief officer himself, or to such other person as that officer may direct, and such report may, according as such chief officer directs, be required to be made personally or by letter.

If any person subject to the supervision of the police, who is at large in Great Britain or Ireland, remains in any place for forty-eight hours without notifying the place of his residence to the chief officer of police of the district in which such place is situated, or fails to comply with the requisitions of this section on the occasion of any change of residence, or with the requisitions of this section as to reporting himself once in each month, he shall in every such case, unless he proves to the satisfaction of the court before whom he is tried that he did his best to act in conformity with the law, be guilty of an offence against this Act, and upon conviction thereof he shall be subject to be imprisoned, with or without hard labour, for any period not exceeding one year.

At the time of this enactment and during its currency, it was seen to be at least a task not totally incompatible with the role of the police. The probation service, at least in part, is an offshoot from the historical role of the police in relation to the supervision of offenders. The accent on juvenile offenders was not so marked in the nineteenth century as it later became with the early Children and Young Persons Act, by which time the probation service was in being.

Although the roles of police and probation service are sometimes regarded by both as containing the seeds of conflict, it is certainly not in the public interest that any degree of antipathy should be allowed to develop between them. The important comity of interest is in the prevention of crime.

From the police point of view, to express their interest as being primarily the prevention of victimisation might serve to indicate the bias which police give to their role as protectors of people and their property. This is not to say that they lack concern in the prevention of recidivism and the resettlement of offenders, but this is not seen as central to their purpose. On the other hand, it might be said that the probation service has a bias towards the offender, since probation and after-care is by its nature offender-orientated. To the outside, the fact that some conflict should arise out of so narrow a difference of emphasis on prevention of offences might appear silly, but there are a number of subtleties which have to be considered.

The police are enjoined to regard their task as completed when they have put the offender before the court or have cautioned the offender under police procedures. The reason given for instilling this attitude into the police is a proper one. It is to avoid an unhealthy concern with punishment of the offender, unhealthy in the sense that, since the police investigate crime and compile the evidence, they may be tempted at times to feel it morally if not legally proper to enhance artificially the prosecution prospects. Thus the police attitude should be clinically objective so far as the offender is concerned. It is understandable therefore that the victim becomes the concern of police.

The probation service, on the other hand, is required to concentrate on the offender, and unlike police they will seldom, if ever, see the victim. To prevent their client offending again is their main purpose, and a laudable one. In order to do this they have to develop a relationship with their client quite unlike any relationship which police are required to develop with any person except fellow officers. A probation officer therefore has to be guide, philosopher and friend (a stern one at times).

He is torn, therefore, or at least exposed to being torn, between his responsibility to his client and his duty to the police. Police, for example, may seek the whereabouts of the probation officer's client in order to interview him as a suspect or as an informant. The probation officer on the other hand, anxious to give his client a chance to go straight and to respect his client's right to privacy, may refuse when police ask him to reveal his client's whereabouts or to tell police what he is doing, where he is working, with whom he is associating and so on. It will therefore easily be seen that police, particularly if they are inexperienced, may begin to see probation officers as unnecessarily impeding their function, and to regard them as indifferent to the interests of the victims of crime.

Probation, on the other hand, can begin to see police as perpetrating authoritarian acts and tendencies and being seemingly indifferent to the delicacy of their relationships with their clients and of their whole purpose in life. Here lie the seeds of conflict and are contained the beginnings of attitudes which deprive the public of the best service either can give, apart altogether from reducing prospects of feasible collaboration.

Improvement must begin with an attempt to develop respect for each other's task and to anticipate possible conflict. The pressing need is to reduce such a possibility to a minimum. Co-operation should be founded on the axiom that police and probation are dedicated to controlling crime by its prevention in the first place, and by preventing its recurrence in the second. The process of improved understanding can be considerably enhanced by arrangements being made for selected police and probation officers to be attached to the other's departments for short periods. The immediate effect of such arrangements is to dispel almost totally the stereotyping that has grown up through acceptance of images out of line with reality. Having started to demolish the walls of ignorance and suspicion, the way is opened up for a degree of proper collaboration in the prevention of crime. The conflict that has to remain as inevitable from the nature of both tasks will then be at the irreducible minimum.

SOCIAL SERVICES

Of all the relationships of police with other agencies that which is most conducive to faulty stereotyping and misunderstanding is the police/social services relationship. But it is a helpful start to recall that police for long discharged a number of tasks thrust upon them by statute, or self-imposed, which are now part of the social services' ever-widening role.

The Mental Deficiency Acts 1913–1938 and the Children and Young Persons Act 1933 both placed welfare duties upon the police, which have now been passed over to the social services. The role of the police included the duty to take persons of unsound mind before doctors and magistrates for care to be provided. The removal of children from moral and physical danger was a task requiring considerable adaptability from the police, a task so well carried out by the now defunct women police departments. Self-imposed social services included the acknowledged successful intervention of special police in juvenile affairs. The Juvenile Liaison Officer schemes, initiated by police following the Liverpool City Police scheme of the late Chief Constable, Sir Charles Martin, set out to provide supervision and social support for potential delinquents and neglected youth. Police led the movement which drew together numerous statutory and voluntary agencies to provide succour, discipline and supervision to prevent young people drifting into delinquent habits. This work is now carried out largely by social service departments. The importance of remembering this is to illustrate just how close the police role and the social service role came together at times.

The bones of contention between the two are to be found in the potential conflict of roles and the different orientations of police and social worker. Some would say they even represent polarisation in community work. The potential conflict of role is mainly in the area of law enforcement by police and in the familial, supportive functions of the social worker, where both become involved, as they often do, with the same people.

Police, once again victim-orientated, see their role as getting satisfaction for justice on behalf of the injured party and find it difficult to understand the attitude of the social worker who is more interested in his client than in the victim. Further, the social worker, having anxiously and patiently developed sensitive and delicate relationships with fragile families, sees the role of the police as destroying at one fell swoop months of constructive work. In addition, to give police all the information which they seek may seem a negation of the purpose of the social worker. The role conflict is heightened by the very fact that the social worker is labouring amongst the broken homes, faulty parental and social conditions, poverty and bad housing which contain a preponderance of the seed beds of crime which attract the police in their seemingly avenging role. Small wonder that conflict abounds. This situation is aggravated by the backgrounds and self-styling of the antagonists.

Social workers are in the main products of the blossoming sociology departments of the universities and polytechnics, and they are amongst the most idealistic of those receiving higher education. Having digested their many theories and sharpened their social consciences it is natural that their view of our communities should so often differ from that of police.

Police generally are not products of university and polytechnic faculties, but of grammar and comprehensive schools and police cadet corps, though there are growing numbers of graduate police officers. If they are idealistic to begin with, their earlier experiences of crime and its catalogue of pitiful victims, of courts and the sometimes seeming hypocrisy of criminal proceedings and the denial of their own idea of justice make them more realistic than idealistic, more pragamatic than theoretical and sometimes, though more rarely, cynical. They, in turn, sometimes see the social worker as encouraging, or at least not discouraging, antisocial behaviour through excessive tolerance of civic irresponsibility. Therefore, on the face of things, the two agencies are bound to be in conflict. Yet clearly this is far too superficial a view and unfair in its superficiality to those police and social workers who have developed considerable working relationships.

Police have a social role to play as well as a legal one. In fact, some 80 per cent of all police activity and time is spent in providing services other than legal ones to communities which they police. In all forms of crisis, from family crises to community disasters, the police are always prepared to provide succour, resources and expertise. The very training of police, stressing as it does the saving of life through rescue from drowning, first aid to the injured, rescue from fire, climbing and pot-holing accidents, are manifestations of this "real police work". Time and again police intervene in family crises by protecting the child, the wife or the juvenile in need of care or protection. In spite of all the self-styling to the contrary, the police are in the front line of social workers.

Social services themselves are also collaborators with the police in so many different ways, particularly in preventing crime. Although highly motivated by their concern for their clients' welfare (that after all is their job) they are nevertheless active in concern for victims of crime who require help. The co-operation between police and social workers in dealing with juvenile offenders is now required by statute

90

(Children and Young Persons Act 1969) and certainly in practice. The Maria Colwell enquiry emphasises the need for the client's interest to transcend any narrow police or social worker interest. Police, by their duty to protect life, and social workers, by their commitment to their clients' welfare and both by their commitment to the broader general social welfare, must increase their mutual understanding and respect.

In the words of the Maria Colwell Report,[1] resulting from the enquiry into the tragic death of Maria Colwell whilst under agency care:

> it seems to us that certain local authorities and agencies in Maria's case cannot escape censure because they must accept responsibility for the errors and omissions of their workers; because they are responsible for their supervision, and because at all levels within their competence they failed to devise efficient and so far as is humanly possible, fail-safe systems.

There was to a greater or lesser degree "a failure of system compounded by several factors of which the greatest and most obvious must be the lack of, or ineffectiveness of, communication and liaison". This then is the price of antipathy and indifference.

Improvement in relationships between police and social workers can begin with attachments to each other's departments. This will require careful matching of personalities to begin with, until tolerance and understanding increase. Of particular sensitivity is that of confidentiality between social worker and client. Clients often give personal information to social workers which if imparted to the police may betray the trust, but there are many matters which a social worker can pass to the police to help their own work, including threats to their clients from estranged spouses or bad associations which are destroying their own social work and so on. Police, on the other hand, may have knowledge of matters which would be of considerable assistance to the social worker.

Relationship between police and social worker should be based on respect and tolerance, which can only come if more rational assessment is initially carried out. Often, the welfare of the individual will emerge as worthy of support by police and social worker, but there will be times when the wider public interest may become paramount, and when the law must have its say. When this happens there may occasionally be conflict, but it will be diminished after some soul-searching has taken place.

EDUCATION

Next to the home the influence of the school on juvenile behaviour is

91

regarded as paramount, and yet the school alone cannot be expected to deal with that small minority of pupils who become delinquent. Teachers, however, have the ability to detect early signs of the drift towards delinquent behaviour and with the help and interest of other agencies of prevention, particularly the police, they might be able to bring about relevant behavioural changes. Where this contribution of the teacher is allied to that of the educational welfare officer, social worker, probation officer or police, a significant step has been taken taken towards proactive policing, that is prevention of crime in its early stages. The problems of the children or youths will, of course, vary greatly from problems at home to physical or mental disadvantage, but involvement of other agencies in combination will almost invariably provide prospects of some solution or part solution.

It is beyond all doubt that there is a high correlation between truancy and juvenile crime in the school catchment area. Operations to reduce truancy will lead therefore to a reduction in offences such as thefts generally, theft in shops and breaking into premises. Police should concern themselves with truancy reduction in co-operation with head teachers and it behoves head teachers to ponder on the causes of high truancy rates and to devise ways of reducing them.

Police can offer much constructive help to schools in a variety of ways and in doing so they will be making a most valuable investment in their own better relationships with young people. Not only will young people have the opportunity for a more natural relationship with police but police will gain a much healthier understanding of young people and their problems. Due to the motorised age in which we live, and the modern cult of the nuclear family, police, pupils, parents and teachers are not always able to interact and develop relationships in the streets and market places. The school therefore offers an admirable meeting ground.

Modern policing requires that police find the resources to develop a police/schools branch. This is of crucial importance where there is a tendency towards hostility between youth and police. In some locations due to poverty, culture or other impediment to sympathy for police from youth and vice versa, extra effort and stoic patience will undoubtedly be required.

A model schools scheme may well include the following objectives.

1. To create sound relationships between the police and the school community—pupils, teachers and parents.
2. To assist the school community to prepare pupils to cope with life outside the school and to develop good citizenship.

The first objective is essentially one of developing mutual trust and understanding, since most pupils, parents and teachers will have no first-hand experience of the police. Such understanding of the police which they may have is gleaned from second-hand accounts through the media and from other people, who themselves may only be repeating what others have said. The police image is therefore likely to be received in an already distorted fashion which may easily be confirmed in their minds by glimpsing the smallest view of only a part of the police function. The police therefore have a massive self-interest in this kind of investment in schools and colleges. This self-interest concerns the need for superior democratic police to have the support of the policed, since this will add to their authority and facilitate their work. The many enquiries that operational police, particularly detectives, have to carry out, and the supply of information from the public which is indispensable to their success, are both improved through such efforts as schools liaison. Preventing petty delinquencies and even influencing the harder cases through presence in the schools is a further addition to police success in preventive policing, and is another step along the road to communal policing.

For the teacher, there are likely to be considerable benefits from the involvement of a police/schools scheme. It is better if the teacher regards the police in the first place as consultants. The many incidents or reports of delinquent behaviour which may involve the teacher through his pastoral function can be made the subject of informal discussion. This is a far better alternative for the teacher, in the beginning at least, than having to consider the need for a full activation of the police machine.

It would be quite understandable if the teacher hesitated to become involved in all save the most serious delinquencies of his pupils if the only other available course open to him or her is to invoke the full reporting system. The teacher after all is concerned with relationships almost as much as the parent and no one would deny the parents' right not to invoke the full weight of the police or judicial machine for minor juvenile crimes. The danger is that should the teacher lack the availability of informal discussion this may result in no action being taken at all and the delinquent juveniles might begin to believe that delinquencies do not matter.

So far as the caring and competent parent is concerned, the availability of police involvement is generally acceptable and uncomplicated. It is just another safety net for the growing juvenile and an extra reassurance for the parent. When schemes of the kind being considered exist, this group of parents speak highly in praise of the value they place upon them. There are, however, those other parents who, for one reason or another, are failing to provide an adequate home environment, and this in turn is manifesting itself at school or in outside school activity. One-parent families, of course, are often splendid, but sometimes the strain and responsibility is too heavy, the child gets caught up in the crisis and further delinquency looms. This situation is reflected often in school and combined action is called for. Young people from criminal homes are at high risk and are almost certain to be delinquent themselves. This situation raises special problems for teachers, police, probation officers, social workers and educational welfare officers. Police availability and knowledge in these situations are of the greatest importance.

Finally, there are the advantages of police/schools involvement for the juveniles themselves. No longer is the authoritarian social framework available to provide sure, if narrow, paths for them to tread. The premium placed on individual freedom for all, including youth, leaves them particularly vulnerable, and police concern, care and understanding are of the greatest value. Once more the rationale for police involvement is the prevention of offences, and particularly those offences concerning drugs, sexual matters, alcohol and motoring—all likely traps for naïve or daring youth.

This kind of police role is also "real police work", with its accent on meeting community needs in the field of prevention of offences and the maintenance of order.

In a sense it is superior police work since its aim is to *prevent* and thus to spare both potential victim and potential offender. Police who undertake this work, however, require aptitudes for it. High on the list after a good track record as a successful beat officer is the ability to make sympathetic relationships with a wide range of people. Inability to do this would be a disqualification. In practice, senior police should seek volunteers for this kind of duty and their selection should be made through joint police and education interview and appraisal. No pretension to lengthy training of selected officers need be undertaken but some training is valuable.

They need to understand that school or college is a community with its own wide range of characteristics, needs, aspirations, duties and problems. They need to understand the diversity of pupils with whom the teacher has to cope and the backgrounds of those pupils most at risk. The best of them will develop new roles for police/schools involvement in order to create a better climate of understanding and thus make a useful contribution to helping young people with the many social and moral dilemmas which beset them. This provides the police with a springboard for the much more difficult task of prevention of juvenile offences in the less structured society outside school.

It is a far cry from the neighbourhood school to the university or polytechnic, and the latter examples provide a much more difficult area in which to imagine any police involvement at all, save law enforcement when the campus erupts! It is a fact that undergraduates generally find the police to be a useful target upon which to turn their fledgling social idealism. The liberation of the spirit which university provides, before the business of earning a living shackles it again, would generally seem to rule out much of a role for police, save as a campus official, and sometimes guide, philosopher and friend.

But it would be a mistake for police to adopt this attitude. In the first place, most undergraduates need to know much more than they are often likely to admit about the role of the police and much more than they are likely to acquire without police participation. Police must be prepared to take up the challenge offered by invitations to speak or debate the police issues of the day. To neglect this task is only to leave the field to those who would use it for stressing partial and even ill-informed views of the police. The growing number of police who are now graduates themselves should be particularly suited to participation of this kind. Such involvement as can rightly be entered into will also strengthen any movement to establish better degree courses in the arts and sciences of the policing function. The university campus offers a most challenging task.

Finally, in this matter of police and education, there remain the further education opportunities. A growing number of people of all ages are demanding more information from the police concerning crime and criminals, police procedures, methods, skills and functions. This demand will continue to grow as the democratic society develops and as individuals have time on their hands for further education. Police have a golden opportunity to capitalise on this demand.

Night schools combine the desirable effect of minimum input and maximum effect. People will respond to invitations from the police to attend night schools for ten or twelve sessions throughout the winter months. The police input consists solely of ten or twelve officers with various responsibilities and skills giving up two hours of their time. In doing this they can reach up to a hundred or more people. Indeed, the effort is so minimal that the value of the impact on public opinion is out of all proportion. Subjects may range from "What it is like to patrol the beat" (always a winner) to "The investigation of serious crime", with many variations in between. Such schemes not only give the public more information from which they may develop a better understanding, but they often result in a better flow of information into police operations.

For teenagers who are bored during school vacations or out of work, police may consider arranging morning schools along lines similar to those of the adult evening sessions. The same principles and methods will apply, but the audience is more impressionable and sometimes more suspicious. Since the teenagers are more restive, sessions have to be kept more lively and debates and panel sessions are considered essential. Once more for very little effort from police a great deal of impact can be made. Without in any way committing undue resources to this role, the police have a significant contribution to make in the world of education.

FURTHER POSSIBILITIES

Although education, social and probation services are the larger agencies whose work overlaps that of the police, there are many others, both statutory and voluntary. The youth, leisure and welfare services have need of police support and understanding, for they have considerable influence on young people and their problems. The nipping of delinquency in the bud may be furthered by co-operation. Less likely agencies such as housing, planning, transportation and highways have, on further examination, considerable comity of interest with police. Housing allocations may go some way towards inhibiting delinquency if strategically considered. For example the placing of all the lower social economic groups in one estate is the highroad to higher rates of vandalism and petty crime. Police advice in the planning stages might be more of a boon to the planners than police criticism afterwards. The strategic placing of leisure facilities is of paramount importance in a plan to reduce delinquency levels, and police should prepare and offer advice.

The many voluntary bodies who offer their time and resources for the common good will often gain great encouragement from police interest, concern and advice.

The police have much to offer and to gain from developing this wider approach to their duties and responsibilities for the prevention of crime.

ENVIRONMENTAL SECURITY PLANNING

It is becoming increasingly obvious that the prevention of what might be called neighbourhood crime, such as vandalism, petty theft and break-in property offences, is in part amenable to reduction through environmental security planning.

This approach was a tentative feature of the Exeter experiment in 1976, and police liaison with the City Council Planning Department has shown promise. An attempt was made to reduce anonymity in large housing estates, for example through creating smaller communities by clustering small groups of houses with "defensible space" as in Oscar Newman's theory, providing better street lighting, police patrol access and so on. Recently, however, a new study from the United States has come forward to emphasise the viability of environmental security planning. Called "Design for Safe Neighbourhoods"[2] it emphasises the major thrusts as: that the physical environment and how it is planned can play a major role in encouraging or discouraging the opportunity for predatory crime to recur; that crime prevention and control cannot be limited to law enforcement but must be reflected and integrated in town plans; that town planners and all others who make decisions affecting the physical environment must be made aware of and educated to include Environmental Security in their planning processes; and finally that cities cannot achieve economic revitalisation without dealing effectively with crime.

This clearly calls for a new approach to urban renewal, if mistakes are not to be repeated. The police have a very important part to play in offering an advisory service to planners and architects. Nor should the police wait for the planners to make the first move. Through the development of demographic surveys in relation to crime the police will be able to initiate or impel environmental improvements.

THE PRIVATE SECURITY INDUSTRY

The private security industry, like much crime, is the child of affluence. In a modern developed capitalist or mixed economy it is both necessary and desirable. In countries where there is no private enterprise the task of protecting property is discharged by the State. Just as it makes sense for the individual owner of property to protect it from criminal activity, so does it for industrial and commercial firms. In any event, it is not possible for the public police to protect all private property, since they are neither sufficiently numerous nor sufficiently capable of the diversification which would be required by the extended role. The owner of property will decide on the degree of protection required by insurance on the one hand and by physical or technological security on the other. These decisions represent choices which it would not be proper for the public police to make.

It is also to be remembered that the world of commerce is subject to the fluctuations of market forces, and these in turn will have a bearing on the private security industry, because as industrial and business fortunes rise and fall so will the volume of private security business respond. But although the public police may justifiably feel relief from the efficiency of major parts of the private security industry they have nevertheless to keep a wary eye open for unlawful and improper practices.

It is necessary to distinguish between private security of the in-house kind, where the firm concerned manages its own security, and those which offer specialist services provided on a contract basis. Private detective agencies deserve special attention, since unconstitutional or illegal practices are more likely to accompany their activities. It was to control this threat that the Younger Committee on Privacy (Cmnd. 5012) recommended strict control through licensing of private detectives and criminal sanctions for abuse of licensing rules. Private security has also had a considerable boost from the need to guard against terrorist and organised criminal activity, including personal protection.

The public police generally have had a somewhat ambivalent relationship with private security. This is understandable when it is realised that the industry at its best is an indispensable and valued part of the policing arrangements of society, whilst on the other hand the public police have to police the private security industry. This must be so because the answerability of the public police to the law for its enforcement, to police authorities for efficiency and thereby to the people, to the Secretary of State for efficiency (and thereby to Parliament) and finally to public opinion is unique.

The private security industry, on the contrary, is only answerable to its shareholders for making a profit. Though it must operate within the law it has no answerability other than to those who invest in it. It is this fundamental premise that provides the possible flaw for abuse of the private security industry's potential for injudicious operating practice. It is for this reason that access to the public police records system cannot and should not be made available to the industry. But, having said that, it cannot be overlooked that the growth and size of the industry and its potential influence is giving rise to some public anxiety and concern. It is for these reasons that the Home Office discussion paper "The Private Security Industry" was published in 1979.

The police have a major part to play in helping to control and guide the activities of the industry since its contribution to the prevention of crime is both outstanding and indispensable. Its potential for abuse, if it were covertly influenced or directed by organised criminal syndicates, is considerable. So far the record of major abuses has been minimal. Much credit for this state of affairs accrues to the major part of industry represented by the British Security Industry Association with its own code of practice, rules and conditions. The work of the association is complemented by that of International Professional Security Association which, by providing individual membership and particularly by training and examination to standards, enhances the status of the industry generally.

Though these two organisations possibly account for the majority of those engaged in the private security industry and the majority of business turnover, there remains the problem of fringe operators of low standards and sometimes dubious practices. Relations with the police are therefore easier with the former than with the latter. The work of the Home Office in influencing, though not controlling, the proper development of crime prevention through private enterprise has been and is of particular value. The question remains, however; where do we go from here? The argument mainly centres on control.

Existing controls are to be found in the criminal law itself, in the civil law of such things as contract, tort and comparing law, all of which can be activated either by the injured party or in the case of the criminal law by the public police. The growing custom of standards being required by such legislation as the Trade Descriptions Act offers further scope for development. Specific clauses in such legislation could refer to private security organisations and set out standards of service and guarantee. There also exist advocates of licensing, compulsory registration, as well as of self-regulation, and the vetting by the public police of employees in private security.

These are all understandable, but the public police have to exercise considerable caution against being drawn in to the role of supervisors of such a large and diverse industry. The bureaucratic growth required to discharge such a task would be considerable and unwieldy. It would be particularly risky for the police to certify the credentials of private operators since it would be impossible adequately to supervise them. Access to criminal records surely cannot be allowed where answerability to the checks and balances imposed on the public police would not, and could not, be matched in private. The best and most acceptable way ahead lies in self-regulation assisted by official interest and encouragement. The best of private security deserves police help, the worst should be eliminated by the legal imposition of membership of a professional association. The association itself might well attract official guidance and support. A healthy private security industry is undoubtedly a valuable asset to a trading and commercial nation and the public police have a vested interest in its success.

NOTES

1. Report of the Committee of Inquiry into the Care and Supervision Provided in Relation to Maria Colwell (D.H.S.S. 1974, H.M.S.O.), paras. 149–152.
2. "Design for Safe Neighbourhoods" (U.S. Government Printing Office 1979).

Chapter 15

Police and the media

Modern democratic policing is based on good communication. Apart from communication within the police force, which is another matter, there is a paramount need for effective communication with the public. In this sense the meaning of the word "public" includes the many different publics. It is important to get this right, since there will be nuances which vary according to the particular public being communicated with at any one time. The need for effective communication with the many publics is based on the principle that modern democratic policing is a joint operation between the police and those many publics. It is not possible to conduct a joint operation unless both sides of the partnership are well informed about each other's hopes, fears and aspirations.

On the other hand, policing in an authoritarian society depends, not so much on the type of communication between police and the public which will lead to a dialogue about policing, but rather on the communication of orders, directions and coercions. There is no dialogue, only a monologue.

THE MASS MEDIA

The term "the mass media" is generally meant to include television, radio and newspapers. Each element of the mass media will require its own unique approach, input and output. Since the police have a vested interest in communicating with their publics, an understanding of the three parts of the mass media is important. It is important to reach an understanding of the various impacts of each element; its viewing, listening or reading publics; its own culture, purpose and method.

TELEVISION
Being both audio and visual, television leaves less to the effort of the person receiving the message than do radio or newspapers, which require more action on the part of the listener or the reader. Since television is delivering its message to the eye and to the ear, it has a special impact.

The police are often ill served by television because a great deal of its output consists of drama involving the police. The fictional portrayal of the police, if cleverly done, can induce in the mind of the viewer not only an unbalanced view but even a biased one. If fictional television series are sufficiently compelling, they are capable of undermining public confidence in the police and the self-confidence of the police themselves. In such cases the police have to increase their own input of documentary and current affairs programmes in order to achieve a balance, in addition to offsetting the damage of such fictional series by real-life face-to-face meetings with the general public. In the final analysis, the general public will prefer their own experience to the vicarious experience of the television set.

The police, therefore, are vulnerable to damage from television unless corrective measures are taken. In taking steps to counteract these effects, the police should be careful not to appear to be too defensive, or they will create further doubts in the minds of the general public. The police, therefore, have to make a positive reaction to such problems, by adjusting the balance with the quality of their own input into television.

The same principles apply to teleivision news bulletins. Again, if the police fail to produce their own official and correct version of events, they will suffer from the distorted half-truths and even opinions of other people. Consequently it is vital that a police force should have adequate staff and departmental potential for making their contribution in all aspects of the communication media. Managed by professional advisers who understand the medium, police require training, not only in the characteristics of television presentation, but also in how to handle interviews with television reporters. There is a risk attached to this policy, since it is likely that, from time to time, officers confronted with the difficult problem of making a comment may well make mistaken, imbalanced or prejudiced comments. However, it is felt that the risk can be reduced by training and information. Attention to and co-operation with this most potent form of communication is well worth while when the final results are achieved.

RADIO

There are many more radio sets in existence than television sets. Radio is to be found everywhere that people go, from the shoulder-slung portable set to the car radio through transistors, which are to be found in most homes. There is a constant output of news, current affairs and entertainment. Added to this is the growth of local radio which provides a most important forum for local news, attitudes and impressions. This is perhaps the finest medium for everyday use by the police. Unlike television it does not create instant damage, nor does it provide instant justification and impression, but serves as a general influence over a longer period of time. There are of course certain programmes which make an immediate impact on thinking and attitudes, but generally sound radio has a cumulative effect. Again the police have to be geared up to adjust the imbalance and to use the medium to get across their own creative community relations and police attitudes on issues of the day. Since the use of national radio by police has generally to be confined to matters of national concern, it is to local radio that the police have to turn to exploit its potential for such strategies as community policing, crime enquiries and investigations, disasters, crises, road safety and the messages which, from time to time, have to be broadcast. The potential for this medium in strengthening self-policing in communities is vast. Since most people have a vested interest in the prevention of crime and the production of a more secure neighbourhood, they can be expected to respond to police requests for assistance. Not only will people generally respond to appeals in connection with crime and disaster and crises, but they can quickly become used to being asked to assist at a moment's notice. Participation in crime prevention schemes is one thing, but the almost daily requests to the observant to check up on this or that matter troubling a neighbourhood is of the essence of community responsibility and assistance to the police. There is much potential in the relationships between police and radio.

NEWSPAPERS

There are at least two levels at which newspapers have to be considered; the first involves the national newspapers and the second regional and local newspapers. Each has its own value and presents its own problem to the police. It was the editor of the *Daily Telegraph*, The Right Hon. William Deedes, who, when addressing the Association of Chief Police Officers some years ago, said:

> The one thing all professions and institutions in this country have in common, including the police, is an ardent desire to see the Press exercising an influence for their good. Attached to this earnest, instinctual desire is a theory called "Sucker's Law", which holds that the more you bend over backwards to help and please the Press the closer you will get to the fulfilment of that desire; in other words the more they will exert influence for your good. I cannot speak for the police but I can assure you that the political cemeteries are absolutely crammed with the reputations of politicians who subscribed to "Sucker's Law". The task of the Press, however sedulously it may be disguised, is disclosure. The Press is not in business primarily to foster public confidence in public administration, in the Police, in politicians or in any institution, however

102

admirable. Disclosure is its business and, in fairness, that not only sells newspapers but is often conducive to the public good.

This is a salutary comment and should not be forgotten by police officers, particularly senior police officers. The job of the newspaper is to disclose facts. It is also to give editorial opinions. Above all it has to survive as a viable commercial venture. It has therefore to please its readers through the presentation of news, views and current affairs, whether serious, salacious, scandalous or of great concern. The police provide vast quantities of news. It is very important that the police force is geared up, through its own press relations department, to attempt to satisfy the insatiable appetite of the newspaper world.

The police, of course, have to give as much of their information to the newspapers as they can without breach of secrecy or confidence, as the news value of what they possess is often great. They do not, however, possess information in their own name but in the name of society generally; therefore it could be argued that such information is public property which should be disclosed. On the other hand, information comes into the possession of the police given on trust against non-disclosure, and here the police have to be careful that they do not damage with one hand what they hold in the other.

It is not only news and current affairs that the police have to deal with in relation to newspapers, for, particularly in local and regional newspapers, there is a first-class vehicle for the propagation of the police view of the problems and issues of the day. The police, therefore, should take an assertive role in presenting their own viewpoints ahead of the demands of the newspapers. In other words, the police should take the initiative and, instead of being constantly under pressure from the media to make unconsidered statements or to adopt defensive attitudes, they should strive to balance the strength of the media with the *quality* of their own output.

OTHER MEANS

Apart altogether from the mass media of communication as described above, there are the many journals and periodicals in which the police can put out serious articles to stimulate debate and interest and to test public reaction to proposals. Bearing in mind that, in a democratic, non-authoritarian society, policing is very much a contract between the police and the policed, senior police officers, particularly, have to be prepared to make their own contribution to the debate. This can be enhanced through use of journals and periodicals of one kind or another.

103

CONCLUSION

It should not be overlooked that the spoken word in an interface between police officers and members of the public is the most impressive of all communication, since the receiver is able to see the demeanour of the person speaking and to form a balanced impression having regard to the context, the tone of voice, the confidence or lack of it and so on. Generally speaking, people hold a little reserve against what they see on television, hear on the radio and read in the newspapers. That is not to say, however, that these three media should be in any way underestimated in their potential for supporting or damaging the police cause.

If modern democratic policing is basically supported by adequate communication with the public, all forms and manner of communicating should be studied, understood and used. The police have no grounds for complaint in the treatment they receive if they indulge in a negative approach to the difficulties and challenges of operating in a news-conscious participatory democracy.

Chapter 16

Police and technology

Police are required to keep pace with scientific as well as social change if they are to remain effective. An outstanding example of this axiom is to be seen in the social impact of the motor car. To envisage a foot police controlling society in its motorised activities makes no more sense than does an unarmed police attempting to control an armed society. The impact of technology on motor traffic police control and law enforcement having begun with foot police checking speeds with stop-watches has passed through a number of phases and will pass through more. From mobile police through radar, television, and other electronic checks and controls the police have been able to keep abreast of vast change. The development of computer technology has seen the police move far ahead with the promise of more advances to come.

The same story is mirrored in the field of telecommunications. The transition from rattles and whistles to pocket radio (and to electronic notebooks in the near future) highlights the considerable determination of the Home Office and police forces to exploit technological change. The new wave of command and control systems and computerised information systems are but the beginning of a new police technological explosion.

The intrusion of technology into the field of security and guarding of both persons and property has had a pronounced effect. Whilst increasing surveillance it has cut down manpower growth proportionately if not in real terms. Electronic eyes and bugging devices are now readily available. The technological cop is as much a part of the technological world as his perambulating predecessors were part of pedestrian communities. It cannot be otherwise. Ever since Doctor Crippen and Ethel Le Neve became famous more for the manner of their arrest than for Crippen's crime the investigator has been able to call on science and technology as his aids. It took a Marshal of the Royal Air Force (Lord Trenchard), however, to establish the first forensic science laboratory in England when he was Commissioner of the Metropolitan Police in 1934. Just as science has come to the aid of the soldier, sailor or airman, so it has to the police, and so it must. Nevertheless the police like the military with their destructive potential and massive capacity for overkill, have to weigh in the balance their own potential for overkill.

One scenario of the imagination of George Orwell may be regarded as far-fetched (or might it not?):

> The telescreen received and transmitted simultaneously. Any sound that Winston made, above the level of a very low whisper, would be picked up by it; moreover so long as he remained within the field of vision which the metal plaque commanded, he could be seen as well as heard. There was of course no way of knowing whether you were being watched at any given moment. How often, or on what system, the Thought Police plugged in on any individual wire was guesswork.... You had to live ... in the assumption that every sound you made was overheard.[1]

The world of Big Brother used by Orwell as a warning of the dehumanising nature of omnipresent and all-pervading technological and unseen interlopers is offensive and abhorrent to those Western societies where individual freedom ranks high. Where regimes keep close and oppressive control of their people they usually have police who are loyal only to the party or its adherents. Thus where central control and manipulation of the police is combined with central technological data storage and surveillance a social/political condition may be produced where the use of police may be corrupted. The police have to balance the desire and need to increase their efficiency with the genuine fear of the public against overmighty officialdom.

Therefore a locally-based police system has a better chance of interpreting and accommodating public anxiety than a system which is remotely controlled. This is not to say that storage of data and surveillance has no moral justification, for to say this is to fly in the face of reason. But, just as the police in Britain have always had to operate with the minimum legal power, so they will be expected to do with the minimum technological and informational power commensurate with adequate effectiveness. It is for the police to explain this and make out their case, for without adequate information, and secure information at that, the necessary public protection will be eroded. Efficient police, even in liberal democracies, must collect and store information vital to their task.

As technology increases in scope it will be capable of giving great power to dominate to those who command it. Superior police will therefore have to become accustomed to public demands for disclosure, since this is a healthy democratic reaction to the seeming omnipotence of science. Two important committee reports of recent years only serve to highlight this. The Younger Committee's Report on Privacy in 1972[2] and the Lindop Committee's Report on Data Protection on 1978[3] whilst laying bare the intricacies and anxieties surrounding the threat to personal liberty posed by technological intrusion and storage of information place the police in a dilemma. On the one hand superior police are concerned with protecting liberty from trespass, whilst on the other they need to trespass upon liberty to effect their own purposes for the detection of crime and protection of our institutions. It is a problem which will not go away and has therefore to be understood.

The Younger Committee found that new technology radically increased the threat to privacy, and recommended that criminal sanctions should be established for abuses of surveillance equipment.

Police have to exercise great care if they are not to represent a threat to the very right to privacy which people in a democracy have a right to enjoy. On the other hand, proper use of technical facilities can be an important element in the defence of the lives and rights of people. A proper balance and the means to guard against abuse are of great importance.

Continuing concern about the impact of computer data banks further involves the work of the police, and the Lindop Report devoted a chapter under "Areas of Special Concern" to the issues. After acknowledging the need for the police and security services to hold personal information "in order that they can do their work effectively" they were satisfied that police data storage carried "less risk for the privacy of law-abiding citizens than is feared by some people". The main problems concerning public scrutiny or scrutiny by a Data Protection Authority are to be found in the sensitive areas of confidentiality of criminal intelligence and personal data concerning the security of the nation.

In a significant passage of the Lindop Report (23.12) the Committee said, "We think it most important, if the confidence and respect which, by and large, the public in our free society still has for the police is to be preserved, the major policy decisions about computerised police applications handling personal information should not be taken in secret." The arguments are finely balanced. The police should not claim any more secrecy than is essential to their task, though they have to ensure that the effectiveness of their ability to con-control dangerous organised and habitual criminals is not undermined. So long as society remains free, the tensions and conflicts surrounding the legal and technological power of democratic police will be an indication of the health of democracy and a barometer of social concern.

The twin pillars of responsive and reactive policing are mobility and communication. The police have exploited all phases of transport from the mounted horse patrols, originating under the Fielding brothers (when they were Bow Street magistrates in eighteenth-century London), to helicopter patrols against mobile criminals at the present time. The great mobility of modern policing has ensured much of its effectiveness. There are, however, dangers where too much reliance is placed on this method on a day-to-day basis. In the first place, police become more and more remote from the public who, seeing them as faceless officials, recede further and further from police relationships of the non-conflict or non-crisis kind. Natural trust and understanding may diminish and this in turn will reduce public sympathy and support, often because the police appear to be omnipotent and therefore do not require support. Technology does not give with both hands but, whilst offering increased efficiency, will quietly take away the essence of democratic policing if it is not made the subject of eternal vigilance.

It is not only that the speed of technological change affects police and public relations, but also that it creates problems amongst the police of itself. Consumer resistance to change is well-known though perhaps not so great as it was some twenty years ago when the first rumblings of the police technology explosion began. The first and growing need now is to step up technical training both general and specialist. So far as senior officers are concerned they have to manage technology and need to understand and appreciate its importance. Junior officers, as operatives in the field, need every help from their training and guidance as a feature of police management. Paradoxically, however, it is the brighter and younger of the senior officers who often know much more of the detail than their seniors, who have to rely on a knowledge and judgment of the wider issues involved. The partnership of guiding and controlling from senior officers, with middle-ranking experts (police and civilian) to create systems and juniors to operate them, offers the best formula.

There is therefore little doubt that the police, in order to maintain the pace of technological change, will require both increased general and specialist technical training. The stage will undoubtedly be reached very soon when greater acceptance of the direct recruitment into specialist departments of those who have the necessary qualifications and aptitudes will have to be faced up to. Meanwhile, police should guard against the seductive nature of technological efficiency, which, if allowed too great a place in the nature of policing, may well damage or destroy the immutable essence of superior policing, namely the human side.

NOTES

1. George Orwell, *Nineteen Eighty-Four* (Penguin 1970, Martin Secker & Warburg 1949), Chap. 1.
2. Report of the Committee on Privacy, Cmnd. 5012.
3. Report of the Committee on Data Protection, Cmnd. 7341.

PART THREE

Crime

Chapter 17

Crime and its inevitability

The crime-free society is an impossible dream. There always has been crime; there always will be crime. Crime can be induced unwittingly by social change; it can be increased by legal change; crime is one price for freedom and at times the means of securing progress.

To view all crime as a purely malevolent phenomenon and as abnormal behaviour would be quite mistaken. Crime is not a behavioural but a legal phenomenon. By definition all forms of human conduct are natural. Man is as naturally cruel as he is naturally kind, and as naturally dishonest as he is honest. The Marxist–Leninist theory that, given the right kind of society, man will cease to be a criminal goes too far, since all societies require rules and those rules are going to be broken by some from time to time, even if unwittingly.

If a society decrees that cruelty is a bad thing, then it will adapt its culture to indicate that. This will be followed in advanced societies by moral condemnation and, thirdly, by legal sanction against it. At this stage, the degree of cruelty in a society will gradually have diminished, but in order to reduce it even further there will need to be enforcement of the law by a body created for that purpose. By these means cruelty will have been brought under control, though it will still break out from time to time. It might be argued that cruelty could be further reduced by a draconian punishment, say execution, and even thereby eliminated. But the history of man seems to confound this theory because the cruelty either begins to consume those who use it, as in revolutions (whereupon the theory has gone full circle), or else society becomes repelled and seeks fresh controls.

Society, having experienced this pattern, accepts that some crime is inevitable and ineradicable; therefore the aim must be to contain it within tolerable bounds. Consequently, the existence of some crime is an accepted part of a liberal society. That is not to say that crime is to be condoned; that would be an illiberal sentiment which would expose its citizens to uncontrolled crime, which is another thing altogether. The principle is that the price of wholly eradicating crime is too high to pay. It is too high in moral terms, as it would require punishments which a civilised society cannot accept without losing the reputation of being civilised. It is too high a price to pay in resource terms, since the enforcers would outnumber the rest of society and they would need *their* own police, and so on *ad infinitum*. The administration of the system required would be so large as to consume too high a share of available resources. Society therefore has to compromise with crime.

There are, however, danger signals in levels of criminality which should not be ignored. Emile Durkheim's idea which he adapts from the medieval schoolmen and calls *Anomie*, means in effect that social aims and aspirations can in themselves become so pronounced and competitive that those who cannot compete fall out and develop disrespect for society and its values. This in turn can lead to a kind of alienation which is crimogenic. Therefore, although some crime is inevitable, high levels of crime should not be regarded as inevitable and certainly not as acceptable. Such a situation as *Anomie* cannot be cured solely by reliance on the criminal law, but has to be safeguarded against by social change, including a greater understanding of the need for social justice. Thus if large gaps in the scale of wealth and social privilege are not narrowed from time to time, crime will flourish alongside prosperity.

To talk of crime, however, as if it were one single and simple entity does not make sense, since the disparity between types of crime is great and is rooted in different things. The difference between simple theft and murder is so great that the only thing each has in common with the other is that it is proscribed by the criminal law. It is important therefore to look at crime from as many different vantage points as is possible, from the point of view of the victim, the offender, the moralist, the economist and the sociologist, and this will be taken up in the following chapter.

Chapter 18

Considerations of crime

In trying to get the subject of crime from a police standpoint in perspective, it is possible to approach it in at least six (maybe more) ways.

LEGAL CONSIDERATION

Crime may be seen as a legal matter, for after all it is the law that defines it and makes it punishable. The legal approach, however, unless it is tempered by other considerations, can lead to difficulties. In the first place, as Sir Henry Maine pointed out in his classic work *Ancient Law*[1]: "Social necessities and social opinion are always more or less in advance of the law. We may come indefinitely near to closing the gap between them but it has a perpetual tendency to open."

Police of course know this to be true since much law which is still extant is not enforced by them because of its social unacceptability. If the police were to take a different view and were to prosecute extant though outmoded laws, they would not only become a nuisance but would clog up the works. Even by prosecuting on every conceivable occasion laws which are still socially acceptable, police would represent a considerable irritant in public affairs. Judgment, discretion and establishing priorities in enforcement become major police skills. Another significant defect in police adoption of too legalistic an approach to crime is that, by concentrating on *ex post facto*, the main police purpose of preventing crime becomes increasingly overlooked. Thus, although crime in this sense is the child of laws, police should get the legalistic view in perspective, for it is but one aspect of the phenomenon.

VICTIM CONSIDERATION

One view of crime which provides a totally different perspective is to see it from the situation of victims.

Police more than any other agency are aware of the consequences of crime. They are not only aware of the impact of crime on property but of the much more serious question of the impact on people. Yet it is odd that society has failed to concern itself with the victim aspect of crime to anything like the extent that it does with that of the offender. The resources and effort put into studying the causes of crime and the treatment of the offender are necessary, but that is not to say that concern for victims is not important. Of course many of the victims are quite capable of looking after themselves; or they are large companies and concerns of that kind. Insurance companies also take much of the strain from those who can afford their services and others are able to employ the range of private security services which are available. Legal aid provisions are also furnished to enable the less well off to acquire legal assistance in court proceedings and some socially conscious lawyers provide free aid and advice, or aid at minimal cost through neighbourhood law centres and duty solicitor schemes. Nevertheless, all this tends to be concerned with victims' legal rights against known or suspected offenders; most crimes, however, are perpetrated by unknown offenders.

It has been argued that, if the police only get to know of some 10 per cent of all crime and of that they only detect some 50 per cent (43 per cent in 1978), then the vast majority of victims do not have known offenders to pursue.

Traditionally, the police have accepted the task of offering first aid and advice, and often a comforting presence, to injured or frightened and distressed victims of crime, though society does not give much thought to such cases. This is clearly wrong. There is now a growing awareness of this need, and Victim Support Groups, first established in Bristol, are growing in number. Not only can it be said that a society which neglects the victims of crime *condones* crime, but there also exists another compelling reason for society, through the State, to concern itself with this aspect of the matter.

Since all citizens are potential victims of crime, as of disease, it behoves the State to exert its resources to study the question of victimisation, its likelihood, its consequences and its remedies. There is as yet no such science, though there are signs that one could emerge as a branch of criminology.

The police not only record every crime but keep considerable details of the victim-and-offender relationship. It is important not only that more should be known of likely victimisation but also of its varying nature. This kind of knowledge would considerably affect the disposition and deployment of police resources and know how.

114

There are considerable variations in patterns of criminal victim-isation when related, for example to socio-economic groupings. Some of the most obnoxious crimes are likely to affect the lower income groups to a much greater degree than those in higher brackets. Yet it cannot be said with any certainty that police skills and resources will be deployed to a higher degree in poorer neighbourhoods to give the service on the scale required. An American observation on the subject indicates that "the risks of victimisation from forcible rape, robbery and burglary are clearly concentrated in the lowest income group and decrease steadily at higher income levels."

At the higher levels victimisation from theft rises sharply.[2] An English study indicates, however, that, at least from a reporting point of view, social class shares "no consistent or statistically significant differences in the reporting to interviewers of either offences against the person, or burglary, among respondents of different social classes."[3] Victimisation, however, generally would be expected to be higher in inner city areas compared with suburban or smaller towns and rural areas.

It is of considerable importance for police to develop studies of victim/offender relationships since policies for allocation of resources and investigative procedures may be more accurately resolved from a better understanding of such phenomena. It is well known that the majority of murders are committed not by strangers but by members of the same family or circle of friends and acquaintances. But beyond this there is a considerable gap in police information which would make a useful study and is relevant to proper use of resources.

The idea of approaching the policing of crime from the victim perspective contains considerable promise. Commercial undertakings have given considerable attention to the question of losses from employee crime and from "customer" crime and have, no doubt, built in economic margins to avoid paying for their own losses, or they have built up internal and external security to reduce risks, but of course the costs of these measures as well as insurance can be passed onto customers. This is not to say however that the police should ignore this field of victimisation since the very criminality to which it might give rise will often spill over into other areas of interpersonal behaviour, thus adding to the whole of crime and to further victimisation of individuals—individuals who are often too weak to take evasive or compensatory action.

Victimisation studies can be taken further by examination of geographical and cultural relationships between offenders and offences. It is important in geographical or demographical studies that the information on the location and type of crime should be passed on to the public and local government agencies, for example. The general public are entitled to have information on local crime in order that they may demand action or that they may take action themselves to prevent their own victimisation. It is fatuous to argue against the right of every person to take action to frustrate his or her own victimisation. Vigilantism, in the pejorative sense of the term, is of course to be discouraged.

Cultural patterns of crime also require much closer study. It is well known to those who observe the scene that patterns of crime emerge with consistency in different cultural settings. This aspect of the study of crime increases in importance where homogeneity of society gives way to heterogeneity and the multicultural society. Some cultures manifest practices of abuse of person and property which are unlawful in the strict legal sense and against the declared behavioural norms of a country's standards, though they may have origins in deeper religious, traditional or merely regional customs for their justification (for example, the ritual slaughter of animals which might otherwise be against the laws concerning prevention of cruelty to animals, or the wearing of turbans whilst riding motor cycles which might be against provisions for road safety). In both these cases, special legal provisions have had to be made. Police in a multi-cultural society need more information and understanding of the degree of incidence and the cultural affinities of such "crimes".

OFFENDER CONSIDERATION

It is natural to move from the victim perspective to offender perspective. Much more thought has been given to this aspect of crime than possibly any other, save that of the legal one. The offender perspective of crime is bewildering in its kaleidoscopic nature. At one end of the spectrum are forgetful, incompetent offenders against minor regulations, while at the other are those who kill for personal satisfaction or gain. The law itself excuses persons under ten years of age from criminal responsibility and permits qualified excuses for others. But since ignorance of the law is no excuse, the offenders drawn in to the legal net are many and varied. As society has become more and more complex and the great welter of controlling laws has been passed, most persons at one time or another have committed or will commit a crime or crimes. Thus, being an offender is more and more becoming a matter of degree than of class. The view formerly held that there was such a thing as "the criminal classes" is now totally untenable, though still widely held as a smug belief. This is one of the problems of moral condemnation of crime, since the condemnation cannot be universal if all are sometimes guilty; it is only the *degree* of crime that can be expected to invoke general condemnation.

Since it is argued that most offences never come to official notice (*see* p. 135) it follows that most offenders never come to official notice. It is probably fair to say of offenders, as a whole, that they are truly representative of all kinds of people. Offending is not necessarily an abnormality, being generally within the range of normality. The range of offenders stretches from the professional criminal through white-collar criminals, pathologically violent criminals, petty offenders and juvenile delinquents to the "one-off" or occasional offender.

Professional criminals are those who devote their full time to crime and base their way of life upon its opportunities. The successful ones are never caught and represent an unknown quantity; though many spend increasing proportions of their time in prison with outbursts of major crime in between terms of imprisonment. Close to the professional criminal, big-time or small-time, are the shady offenders who handle the disposal of the proceeds of crime, the receivers or "fences". Professional criminals account for a large proportion of serious property crime and require the attention of special police operations. Criminal intelligence and surveillance are the prerequisites of successful police counter-measures.

The "white-collar" criminal is the product of opportunity since working as he does with accounts, computers, stocks, goods of one kind or another, he is in a position to take advantage of his employment just as the shop-floor worker is with the factory product. It is this class of offender who generally follows a professional or semi-professional life-style based partly on bona fide activity and partly on crime. There is no violence or thuggery involved and the expansion of this type of offence is a fairly modern phenomenon. The extent of business crime through sharp practice and dishonesty is unknown, but it is known to be growing (and that connected with credit cards and cheques growing rapidly). Since it is associated with people who appear to be "decent" it often attracts less condemnation than other crimes committed by "unpleasant" people.

MORAL CONSIDERATION

The fourth approach to the consideration of crime may be a moral one. Of all the approaches to concern for crime the moral one has excited most debate and controversy. "From the time of Plato it has been clear to all thinking men that laws are not necessarily just, and from the time of the Romans, that all that is thought to be moral need not necessarily be embodied in law."[4]

It is a subject too vast and intricate to be disposed of in a few paragraphs of passing comment. Yet, for the police, it is of considerable importance that an attempt be made to develop an understanding of the classical debates on the subject. The great nineteenth-century arguments between Sir James Fitzjames Stephen, a distinguished lawyer and judge, and John Stuart Mill, the liberal philosopher, and a similar twentieth-century encounter between another distinguished lawyer and judge, Lord Devlin, and a distinguished scholar, H. L. A. Hart, the reader must personally pursue, and in doing so reach for these heights. The important thing for police to remember is that some moral principles remain permanent, such as freedom, equality before the law and justice, though in practice their attainment may be uneven, and that other moral concepts change with the times and often do so rapidly.

It is a matter at once profound and highly philosophical and at the same time a matter of practical everyday concern for police. The recent changes in the law concerning some aspects of private morality make the point. Over the last twenty years or so, though not without great debate and controversy, Parliament has gradually withdrawn the law (and therefore the police) from areas of private behaviour hitherto considered important subjects for the criminal sanction.

For the police, these shifting social values and changes in the law have a profound importance. The changes in the law concerning private morality reflect changing social behavioural values and stem very much from the liberation of the individual to decide these matters for himself or herself. Change can be noted particularly from the time of the Wolfenden Report of 1957 which said: "It is not, in our view, the function of the criminal law to intervene in the private lives of citizens."

It was of course referring specifically to interfering with the private sexual morality of individuals, and it went on to say in relation to police action in detecting homosexual and similar acts in private: "It is evident that this law does not command the respect of those who are charged with enforcing it." This is an important matter of principle for the police, since where they have a discretion and do not have respect for a particular law, they will be more likely to neglect to enforce it, save haphazardly, than it if were a particular law supported generally by the public and enforced generally by the police. Other relaxations of laws in recent times which often represented the high point of Victorian moral rectitude include abortion, betting and gaming, erotic literature and stage and screen censorship.

These legal changes, resulting from social pressures and shifts in morality, have led to two discernible and differing reactions. On the one hand, many regard them as the road to decadence and social ruin; others see them as the minimum desirable in a free society, and they press on for further dismantling of laws impinging on the individual's moral choices. It may be concluded that these views occupy the extreme points of the spectrum of public opinion with the majority of people some way in between, and with a large section not taking up a particular position at all. In one sense society is still adjusting to the impact of the moral turbulence created by the relaxations of the law and to some extent it is confused. It seems reasonable, however, to expect that excesses of permissiveness will gradually be checked by public opinion and that the law and those who enforce it will by degrees achieve a reasonable balance in enforcement of morally-based laws. Nevertheless it should not be overlooked that the debate is continuing and there will be further changes in the offing. Equally, it would be out of proportion for those who champion a strict personal morality to regard the indifference of other people as a catastrophe. In any case, the nature of modern society renders it difficult to identify consensus on all save the most outrageous moral issues. The morality associated with different religions alone requires tolerance of diversity, apart altogether from the numerous social and political cults. In this situation, the law and the police have to move with great care and understanding and the police should not enforce laws in a roughshod fashion, merely because they exist.

Police have to learn to respect moral diversity and the pressure for moral freedom; nor should it be overlooked that not all sin is crime. The lesson of the American prohibition serves to illustrate this point. The great wave of moral censure of alcohol in the United States which led to a legal provision outlawing its sale sparked off an explosion in organised crime, and in the end the laws had to be repealed. In the preface to *Law and Morality*[5] by Blom-Cooper and Drewry, Bernard Crick says:

> In many of the questions of addiction, sexual morality, anti-social behaviour, it is necessary to distinguish between permissiveness and tolerance and between disapproval and legal proscription. "Permissiveness" describes the attitude of people who do not care what goes on. Some people are permissive about things that concern others deeply. Often people do care, do disapprove as I do concerning drugs and pornography; but there are ways of expressing disapproval which do not involve legal sanctions.

Superior democratic police should therefore strive to reach an understanding of the relationship between law and morality and should understand that the enforcement of the law in a plural society which demands its moral choices is a very difficult activity requiring considerable skill.

ECONOMIC CONSIDERATION

An economic consideration of crime, its commission and attempted control reveals a thriving human activity. Without in any way being cynical one can say that crime provides a livelihood for a wide variety of people, some of whom become rich (legitimately!) because of it. Its control may take on such dimensions, if allowed to, that it will devour public money at such a rate that it could outstrip the entire budget for education and more. Crime is so widespread that to pursue its total eradication would run the risk of bankrupting the nation. But the economics of crime control must be evaluated.

The commercial and business world undoubtedly suffers much from crime against property. It may insure against losses through crime but the higher the losses the higher the insurance premiums until the point is reached where the cost of insurance against crime is too high. Therefore prevention is introduced, crime drops, insurance premiums are reduced and when the cost of prevention is accounted for the balance of crime costs is restored. Finally, of course, costs are passed on to customers.

In the public sector, the entire cost of criminal justice is immense, yet there are many considerations other than economic which have to be attended to. There comes a point, however, when the cost of police, courts, prisons etc. becomes so high that the public have to accept some crime risks which they otherwise would not wish to tolerate.

At present, the cost of keeping juvenile offenders in custody raises certain questions. Some offenders are so dangerous or criminally destructive when free that the cost of incarceration may be worth it. The value of crimes committed, for example arson, costing millions of pounds, would be offset by retention in custody of arsonists, however expensive.

It is often said that private security should become part of the public service though it is so often overlooked that what is now governed by the values of the market place would soon become subsidised out of public funds and become an added burden to tax- and rate-payers. One great argument for private security is economic.

If public law enforcement were approached on a cost-effective basis it might result in some interesting decisions, to say the least. For example, given that a budget for law enforcement was set, a decision would have to be made as to not only how much law enforcement was to be carried out in a year but also what kind of enforcement produced the best result. Thus how many minor motoring offences could be overlooked in order to prosecute more car thieves might be one possibility. Such considerations would clearly exert new pressures on policing policies and the day may come when a socio-economic cost-effective approach to law enforcement will need to be carried out by police. In such cases, the options available would be put to the public for their consideration. They would be faced with a list of options. How much of the limited budget should be spent on prevention of crime and how much on its detection? Should traffic control be reduced in favour of more foot patrol?[6] Questions of this kind and the many possible variables would undoubtedly sharpen the police approach to its role!

At the present time, for example, the cautioning of offenders by the police is considerably cheaper than mounting prosecutions, and it appears to be effective to a satisfactory level. Many motorists of the responsible kind aver that a police caution and advice increase their respect for the law whereas a prosecution followed by a fine reduces it, particularly where they are fined more for an oversight than another is for dishonesty or malice.

Cautioning of juveniles is carried out on a large scale and is undoubtedly saving much public money. There is also evidence that it is cost-effective, since the rates of recidivism following police cautions are low. Policing cautioning applies generally, however, to first offenders, who are presumably more responsive to a brush with the law. But there is room for further studies of cost-effective aspects of police activity.

SOCIAL CONSIDERATION

Finally, crime as a phenomenon may be viewed in the social perspective. Social change affects crime and is always likely to. Some acts are decriminalised as social morals change. The recent retreat of the criminal law from the province of private morality is a very good example of this axiom. As Victorian moral rectitude tightened up the law to control private sexual morality, so, in the latter part of the twentieth century, the new permissive society released the bonds. But it is with the pace and degree of social change that patterns of behaviour are seen to become erratic.

In *A Blueprint for Survival*[7], the ecologists conclude:

> There is every reason to believe that the social ills at present afflicting our society—increasing crime, delinquency, vandalism, alcoholism as well as drug addiction—are closely related and are the symptoms of the breakdown of our cultural pattern, which in turn is an aspect of the disintegration of our society.

This statement is fairly dogmatic and might be narrowly drawn; yet it touches the point. A society without consensus, shared values and group loyalties, is almost bound to suffer from aberrant behavioural patterns. Groups of youths may coalesce for fleeting periods to commit senseless damage whilst others conspire to steal, rob and rape in city streets, described colourfully as the asphalt jungle (often an apposite label). Changes continue to occur and crime patterns change; thus, for example, a steep rise in female crime, including violence, has coincided with women's liberation movements. Between 1972 and 1976 crime committed by females in England and Wales increased by some 45 per cent. The impetus for social change comes from political power. The death of authoritarianism or the breakdown of censensus, whichever way the phenomenon is expressed, can be traced back to the introduction of universal adult suffrage in the first quarter of the twentieth century.

It is necessary for police to grasp the significance of social change if they are able to adjust their own role to meet its impact. The death of authoritarianism is a matter central to the police function. It is therefore necessary to examine rationally why a society, which proffers so many splendid facets, is much more difficult to police than it was in the post-war years and the 1950s, when crime, though by no means negligible, seemed to be reasonably well under control. Why is it that, in spite of the billions of pounds which successive governments have spent on welfare and new social control systems, crime escalates and public order seemingly deteriorates? Much time and energy have been spent on seeking out the causes of crime and on the treatment of offenders; yet as recently as 1977, after a lifetime in criminology, the world-renowned Director of the Cambridge Institute of Criminology, while considering the rise in crime, was unable to conclude on a note other than that "for the time being we shall have to live with it and try to contain it."[8] Police do live with "it" and to try to contain "it", but it also helps to try to understand it. Is the permissive society just an aberration or is there some rational, evolutionary social force which amongst other things produces more crime?

Through a variety of causes since the advent of universal suffrage, the mass of the people have been largely liberated from convention, dogma and ignorance. The full impact of the political liberation of first men, then women and now the older teenagers, has worked or is working its way through the system of democratic government. This force is bound to have resulted in the acceleration of social evolution and the loosening of some of the older social controls on misbehaviour, as pressures of political thought and action result in a host of socially-liberating legislation.

Perhaps no single instance of social emancipation has had a more profound effect than education. As merit overtook means as a right

122

to higher education, the more articulate and better-informed society was in much better shape to assault autocratic citadels, including police authoritarianism.

The first citadel to fall was that of the parent, as youth distanced itself culturally from parents. Reaching a peak during the 1960s, the "generation gap" manifested almost an alienation of youth as its economic and social independence increased. Youth was on the march, commercially exploited it is true, but all the time assaulting convention and occasionally getting hurt in the process; and police had to pick up the pieces. Thus the liberation of youth through education and communication (television particularly) had been brought about, but to their disadvantage; true authority, that is a sense of civic responsibility, had not been properly fashioned to balance it. The resultant excess of liberty, often commercially exploited, produced a somewhat disorientated generation and some delinquency and crime was an inevitable consequence.

The economic rise of the mass of the people resulting in the virtual elimination of abject poverty, that is poverty of the destructive, degrading kind, produced its own form of liberation giving rise to greater social confidence. Compared with earlier generations, modern Western man stands at the pinnacle of an economic liberation; and yet paradoxically his situation gives rise to more crime. It is because of man's appetite for materialism and for the acquisition of goods that the society of his creation has organic characteristics of a crimogenic nature; in other words it causes crime by its very existence. The possession of stealable property, cars, household goods, supermarkets, credit cards and so on, not only brings social status but also makes the thief. Status is increasingly becoming not so much what we are but what we have.

Further examination of the social changes and their relation to the death of authoritarianism and the growth of crime draws attention to the condition of private morality. The decriminalisation of much private moral behaviour such as homosexuality, abortion, use of obscene literature and so on, all in keeping with the growth of individual freedom, has liberated people from legal criminal guilt. This moral relativism which operates in private still does not operate in public, or not to the same extent at least. What may not be obscene or what may be acceptable in private is not necessarily acceptable in public.

Public morality, therefore, is still in a fairly robust condition but it leads to conflict with those who desire freedom of public as well as of private morality. The "do your own thing" society is exciting, and gradually reduces the degree of consensus of right or wrong. For the police this plural society, made more complex by its increasing multi-

123

racial character, has no place in their historical experience, nor has it much in their textbooks (Michael Banton's *Police Community Relations*[9] is one exception). Policing in traditional terms had been a matter of enforcing consensus; the law and custom said so. There was one law and one morality for all and it seems a paradox or contradiction to police different moralities under one system.

A liberated public and a traditional, authoritarian system of control are inevitably in conflict. The police stand in the way of behavioural excess and often represent only the minimum control necessary even for a liberated society, but sometimes for the heady feeling of social liberation any impediment is too much. Some consequences are more assaults on the police, bewilderment within police ranks and even an ominous crack here and there in the edifice of police morality. There arise inevitable additions to criminal statistics. The price of liberty goes up.

The catalogue of triumph and of casualties in the campaign of social change is long and varied and one could go on. Sufficient may have been written to have made the point concerning social change and crime but there is one phenomenon which both liberates and binds society, and that is the "free" media (particularly the visual medium of television). The appetites and emotions which are nourished by the media are dynamic and can cause crime, though the purpose is far from that.

Joy, entertainment, information, education and fantasy are among the good things which help to go towards compounding the nostrums of liberation, though fears, anxieties, envy and greed march alongside like some fifth column. Police often blame television and the media generally for adding to their sea of troubles and occasionally this may be so, but it has to be remembered that in one sense the media are neutral and are available to all. Police therefore have to develop the ability to use the media for their own legitimate means. Others do it for their own illegitimate aims as is so strikingly exemplified by the cases of kidnapped victims of terrorism: for example the cases of Hanns Martin Schleyer in Germany and the Italian Prime Minister Signor Aldo Moro. The terrorist with his philosophy of the propaganda of the deed rides exquisitely on the back of television into the subconscious of us all.

The sum total of all this enables us to appreciate that increased crime does not represent just an aberration, not just a chance pattern in a seemingly aimless movement, but is a direct consequence of evolution and liberation itself. It might be seen as the price of an increasingly free and unfettered society and some would feel that if this is so, the price is too high and some freedom has to be reduced

124

in order to reduce crime. It might also be argued that social change has no part in this at all, but that the culpability lies only with the individual; and since his excesses threaten our freedom he alone must be made accountable. These two opposing views, the collective responsibility on the one hand and the individual responsibility on the other, represent the poles of current moral values.

But the police have to cope with things as they are, not as they would like them to be, and it does not seem possible or desirable to put all the pieces back in society where they used to be and start all over again. A new society has to throw up new means to help this newness prosper, and, in doing so, some effort has to be made towards bringing crime within tolerance levels.

This requires the police to begin a search for a philosophical base for their actions and, since their primary function in Britain is not the suppression of crime and disorder after it has taken place but the prevention of crime by action before it takes place, this is largely a social concept. Police should not overlook the fact that social causes of crime have produced and can produce some of the gravest situations which can threaten public, police and the quality of life. An example of such a social cause would be found in the violence which exploded in cities in the United States where black people living in the ghettos broke out in a rash of violent behaviour in the late 1960s.

But the glories of a free society in which man is likely to have the greatest opportunity to fulfil his destiny are gains which we should and do value beyond words. The excesses on the fringes are the products of that society, which is thus challenged to find civilised answers against the development of delinquency. The police are in the forefront of that challenge.

NOTES

1. Sir Henry Maine, *Ancient Law* (Dent 1917).
2. President's Commission on Law Enforcement etc. *The Challenge of Crime in a Free Society* (U.S. Govt. Printing Office 1967), Chap. 2.
3. Sparks, Genn and Dodd, *Surveying Victims* (Wiley 1977), Chap. 4.
4. Blom-Cooper and Drewry, *Law and Morality* (Duckworth 1976), Chap. 4.
5. Ibid., Preface.

6. R. W. Anderson, *The Economics of Crime* (Macmillan 1976), Chap. 4.
7. The Ecologist, *A Blueprint for Survival* (Penguin 1972), Chap. 1.
8. Sir Leon Radzinowicz and Joan King, *The Growth of Crime* (Hamish Hamilton 1977), Chap. 11.
9. Michael Banton, *Police Community Relations* (Collins 1973), Preface.

Chapter 19

Tolerance of crime

If society has to compromise with crime to avoid destroying its way of life by trying to eliminate it, it becomes important for the police to interest themselves in the consequences. It is likely that if rational (as opposed to purely emotional or expedient) reactions are sought they are likely to be found in some consideration of tolerance levels.

Tolerance levels of crime, save the most heinous, will vary from civilisation to civilisation, nation to nation, and within nations from culture to culture. In a plural, multiracial society tolerance levels will vary from street to street almost, whereas in homogeneous consensual society there will be much less variation. It must be accepted at the outset that, in police terms, there can be no tolerance of serious offences in the sense that they would regard them with informality and even indifference. But, setting those aside, there are large areas where the police may use their discretion and, for the minor offences, police can, as a deliberate policy, operate within local levels of tolerance. This approach can pose problems for the police since it is contrary to the nature of the organisation to feel comfortable in declaring policies based on this attitude. There is therefore a tacit acknowledgment that some discretion is necessary, but it should be left to junior officers to discharge it. The alternative is to require junior officers to report everything unlawful they encounter, in order to allow some senior officer to decide. The former is a permissive approach and is best suited where there is a high standard of junior officer; the latter is more bureaucratic and formal and limits the use of discretion where it is felt that junior officers are not able to make acceptable decisions.

Officers who work their own beats as community constables will undoubtedly understand the tolerance levels of their beat's population and know exactly how to police within it. Officers who are transient on general patrol, without an adequate understanding of communities, will be likely to get it wrong, causing at times some irritation with the public concerned.

There are other aspects of this theory of tolerance levels which require to be explained, including the preference of some cultures for crime rather than police activity, and the reaction of communities when tolerance levels are exceeded and the police response thereto inadequate.

It may be that some communities will tolerate a high level of criminality, since they may regard police activity as a greater threat. A good historical example of this is contained in a frequently quoted passage of the Parliamentary Committee of 1822 on Policing the Metropolis, which said:

> It is difficult to reconcile an effective system of police with that perfect freedom of action and exemption from interference which are the great privileges and blessings of society in this country and your Committee think that the forfeiture or curtailment of such advantages would be too great a sacrifice for improvements in police or facilities in detection of crime, however desirable in themselves, if abstractedly considered.

This represents a classical example of a society, or at least the legislature of a society, in which crime was running high and almost uncontrolled, preferring its own parlous condition to the introduction of police. This would certainly be the case where an occupying or harsh alien police was concerned, but it can also be found as a reaction where cultural or political antipathy exists between the police and the policed.

In parts of Northern Ireland where the population is preponderantly Roman Catholic or republican in sympathy, the communities tolerate considerable crime and extortion rather than invoke police activity. Again, in the Notting Hill Carnival in London, where West Indians turn out in their thousands to celebrate, there have been complaints of excessive police activity and demands for a reduction in police presence. This has happened in spite of the high incidence of crimes such as robbery and assault.

Recently, in their book *Surveying Victims*[1], the authors have suggested reasons for lack of public desire for police involvement in their criminal victimisation. These include: lack of belief in police response or ability to do anything; higher cost, e.g. loss of earnings or legal costs; exposition of their own illegal or immoral behaviour; the fact that the victim may know the offender and not wish to involve him, or consider that telling the police would involve a harsh step or that they may "let him off". There are many other reasons connected with rational and irrational considerations of involving the police, the triviality of it, apathy, insurance cover and so on.

There are, of course, considerable dangers where tolerance levels are being exceeded and the public do not invoke police activity or where police are passive, incompetent or simply lack the resources for adequate response. In such circumstances one of three things may occur. Firstly, criminality would go unchecked and the quality of life would deteriorate and the weakest go to the wall. Secondly, protection rackets would develop and rival gangs and other racketeers would fight each other for control thus adding to the total communal criminality, particularly the more serious crimes of homicide and extortion. Thirdly, vigilante groups of a more responsible nature would develop—and under the English common law might lawfully develop in appropriate circumstances. Appropriate circumstances would include proper recourse to the courts and adherence to the rule of law.

Tolerance levels which vary may cause displacement of crime to adjacent areas where police activity is not induced or expected. Thus, where a neighbourhood crime tolerance level is low it will seek to induce police action and this in turn will lower crime levels in that neighbourhood to tolerable proportions. The price of this improvement in neighbourhood A may well be an escalation of crime in neighbourhood B where tolerance is higher and police activity is less likely to be involved. In this way the law-abiding become more so and the more permissive increase their parochial crime.

In considering the role of the police, the use of resources, training and deployment, the need to understand the issues connected with crime tolerance is of some importance.

NOTES

1. Sparks, Genn and Dodd, *Surveying Victims* (Wiley 1977), Chap. 5.

Chapter 20

Strategy against crime

In a modern developed democratic society it should be possible to articulate a concept for the control of crime. The traditional idea that the key to control lies mainly with the system of criminal justice must now be seriously questioned in the light of our new and growing understanding of the nature of unreported crime, the complicated web or pattern of behaviour defined as criminal, and the probability that most people are or will be guilty of committing at least minor criminal offences.

It is of course vital for the law to stake out those areas of behaviour which are inimical to a happy civilised society. It can also be expected that those acts considered in contemporary views to be serious (most of these are capable of change from time to time and markedly from epoch to epoch) will be prosecuted with vigour. To prosecute the whole range of criminal offences with vigour all the time is not only a futile aim but also socially silly. This is particularly true of the minor regulatory offences where education offers a far superior avenue to pursue, at least in parallel with enforcement.

It is not, therefore, sensible to talk of one single strategy for the prevention and detection of all criminal offences, but rather of a range of strategies depending upon the degree of social damage being inflicted by the offence. The shock and unacceptable nature of violence, destruction and invasion of one's home and property, its erosion of the tranquillity of life, if allowed to go unchecked, marks such behaviour down for special strategic attention.

There is little doubt among those whose work brings them into daily contact with crime and criminals, or who have studied the phenomenon, that a great deal of crime, though by no means all, stems from inferior living conditions which induce despair and an existence shorn of the opportunity to share in the values which the majority of people enjoy.

The beginning of the strategy for the control of crime must therefore begin with the diminution of abject poverty, discrimination, injustice and urban decay. Much has been done in this direction but much remains to be done. The lead here of course depends largely on the policies of central government. Housing, planning, education, social services and the creation of job opportunities and activities are all key areas in the pursuit of crime control.

One area of crime control which requires special attention is the reduction of juvenile delinquency. There is sufficient evidence available now to suggest that the attack on juvenile crime should begin in what might be called the seed beds. Intervention before a child becomes confirmed as a delinquent (often a self-fulfilling prophecy) is likely to prevent the drift. Not only have delinquent tendencies to be spotted before they harden, but delinquent families have to be given more attention to break the cycle of delinquency. Any strategy should concern itself here. The varied means for disposal of convicted offenders have to be reviewed, reformed and renewed from time to time.

At local level every agency and every member of the community should be interested and involved in crime control. The strategy here is one of co-operation against crime. Every person is a potential victim and most are potential offenders. Few members of our society do not have a vested interest in curbing crime.

Resources are of course a major factor in strategic planning and constant reappraisal; examination to maintain realistic levels is important. Public spending, however, has its limitations and additionally some doubt must be cast on the desirability of the total amount spent on the whole spectrum of social agents and officials in the heady days of growth during the 1960s and early 1970s. There needs to be a firm commitment to the pooling of resources and in co-operation towards crime reductions.

It is surely beyond reasonable expectations that we should look towards one ministry or government to provide the necessary stimulus for the reduction of crime. The efforts of government towards the reduction of crime now require considerable interministerial co-operation. It seems odd now that we should expect the Home Secretary to be held to be almost solely responsible when some of the most important decisions affecting crime are beyond his control. The Department of Health and Social Security plays a considerable role in the care and control of that element of our juvenile population most likely to commit crime and grow up into the hard core of criminals. They also control resources which go towards ameliorating crimogenic family circumstances. Another ministry with considerable power and responsibility in these matters is the Department of the Environment, whose attitude to housing and planning policies can have a highly significant impact on the quality of life and the creation or destruction of circumstances favourable to community care and control.

It might be argued that if the strategy against crime begins in that

Department and in the Department of Health and Social Security, it is next concerned with the impact of the Department of Education and Science. Not only is the content of the education of our youth of paramount importance in this connection but the very environment of their places of learning and the spirit in which communities themselves are involved are other key factors.

It may seem odd to mention the Ministry of Defence in this connection but the Army/Youth teams have shown considerable potential for a very constructive role in the reduction of juvenile crime. By removing delinquency-prone youth from their permissive and sometimes demoralising circumstances and taking them on adventure activities and into the disciplined service organisation, a meaningful contribution is made possible. It is to be regretted that due to cuts in services expenditure this practice was discontinued in 1978. It can only be hoped that ways will be found not only to resurrect but to expand this splendid contribution.

Thus it would seem that at central government level the strategy against crime would begin in joint ministerial plans and initiatives. Having already suggested that too much reliance should not be placed on the system of criminal justice for the control of crime, the new accent should be on social policing, by which is meant a whole battery of co-ordinated and interlocking measures.

A national plan called "Society Against Crime" might begin at the centre and work outwards to involve both local government and voluntary bodies. The police would have of course to play a dynamic and central part of leadership and dissemination of know-how. They would be joined in strategic planning by the various relevant branches of local government, education, youth, welfare, social services, housing, planning and so on.

The probation service and the magistrates should be brought into this scheme of things, for their considerable knowledge of delinquent behaviour and control is highly significant. At the volunteer level the community has, in a developed scheme, the most important and central role, and its involvement in all social measures for the prevention of crime is important symbolically. The manifestation of communal care and concern is a highly potent counterpoise to the incessant demands for solutions only through penal action. There is a need (and there will be a greater one) for community involvement in social action to head off delinquency; and this should become a keystone of local strategy.

Thus strategies against criminal behaviour should begin at central government level, where a broad range of enabling and encouraging gestures might be made. Local government should reflect this social concern. Communities should then be educated in the importance of social concern for crime reduction. The police might be expected to offer leadership, advice and information. The independence of police in their constitutional and legal functions should of course remain unimpaired.

Chapter 21

Crime: prevention or enforcement?

There are a number of different approaches to the control of crime. The two most obvious are prevention and enforcement. It is because the preventive is so difficult and full of uncertainties that it dismays all but the most determined. Far simpler, on the other hand, is the approach through enforcement, since all that this entails is to await the commission of crime, pursue its detection and punish the offender. Admittedly the process of investigation is not easy in many cases; but the concept of enforcement is easier to grasp than that of prevention.

Another problem with the preventive approach is that it opens up the entire field of the body politic in the search for causes. Social, behavioural and political scientists and criminologists have all explored the vast and complex field of causation in pursuit of the answers to the problems of increases in crime in Western society over the last forty years or so. Geneticists and other medical scientists are entering the field with serious ideas. Their answers have been many and varied and often contradictory. Much has been made out of it but in the end the most distinguished criminologists have had to admit that there is no easy answer to the causes of crimes. If causes are founded with certainty, the preventive approach will come into its own, providing that the price is not too high.

The enforcement approach meanwhile carries few of these complexities. Provided that the law exists and the crime is identified, all that need follow is the pursuit and collection of proof. Discharging the burden beyond reasonable doubt raises difficulties, of course, particularly in the face of the many exclusionary rules of evidence and the right of silence enjoyed by the accused. Nevertheless the idea that the causes of criminality can be ignored and the blame laid at the door of the individual removes considerable moral burdens. In other words it is often said that it does not matter what is done to people in their growing and impressionable early years, for when they grow up they as individuals carry the responsibility for their crimes, and the rest of society should not feel guilty about it. There are a number of theories that strengthen this belief. In the first place, it is well known that out of similar circumstances some will "go straight" whereas some become delinquent. Secondly that, given the same opportunities, some will abuse them for criminal purposes, others will use them legitimately. Some offenders reject the chances they are given to reform, betraying the system which tried to help them. All of these instances can be verified, are easy to understand and are capable of reinforcing the view that only a "tough" line with offenders will solve the problem. The extension of this valid argument leads on to the demand for increased police powers and a reduction in the rights of accused persons in the criminal trial. It follows from this plausible line of argument that the attack on crime should be concentrated at this point and it makes an acceptable appeal to public opinion.

Meanwhile, the prevention school flounders in search of such concrete arguments as will also appeal to the general public. These are hard to come by, although they do exist.

That there is a degree of polarisation of view cannot be denied, and it is fuelled by the popular press using labels such as "do-gooders" (the preventers) and "hard-liners" (the enforcers). This is unfortunate and obscures more than it reveals. The position is further hardened by the political preferences of right and left, though there are many exceptions and contradictions to the general rule.

To induce a greater degree of rationality into the debate it is necessary to have regard for the strengths and weaknesses of both elements.

The enforcement approach relies for much of its success on the successful investigation of crime, followed by conviction and sentence. It follows therefore that any crime which does not come to notice, remains undetected or becomes the subject of an acquittal, may be regarded as a defeat for this approach.

It is generally agreed by those who have assessed or examined the phenomenon of crime unreported to the police that only some 10 or 15 per cent of the bulk of crime comes to notice. Sir Leon Radzinowicz estimated the figure to be 15 per cent and recent research by Sparks, Genn and Dodd in their book, *Surveying Victims*, suggests 10 per cent.

If this is near the mark, reliance on enforcement is considerably undermined. For example, in 1977 in England and Wales, some $2\frac{1}{2}$ million indictable crimes were reported to the police. If this figure represents one-tenth of all crimes, it follows that some 25 million crimes were committed. Further erosion of the effectiveness of potential enforcement is observed when it is realised that the police clear-up rate over the same period was 41 per cent of all reported crime, that is less than 5 per cent of all estimated crime. Even allowing for the deterrent effect of enforcement on would-be criminals, these figures seriously undermine the philosophy that pins its faith on enforcement as the *sine qua non* of crime control. Furthermore, the cost of dealing with only a small proportion of offenders is high when it is realised that the entire system of courts, penal, reformative and rehabilitative agencies is brought to bear on them.

Although a low proportion of all crime is reported it has to be remembered that a high proportion of serious crime comes to police notice and the police are able to concentrate resources on its investigation. Allowances must also be made for the fact that frequently one offender commits more than one crime; so that although the number of crimes committed represents a higher number of victims, the number of offenders responsible will be lower. Therefore while the enforcement approach is sound, indispensable and essential for society's survival, it is also true that too heavy a reliance on it, to the neglect of prevention, leaves society less well served than it otherwise may be.

Measurement of crime control in terms of prevention is even less exact than in those of enforcement. Save under very strictly controlled research, the prospects of reliable assessment are small. This is one reason why prevention has not had the attention it deserves— people are conditioned to look for justification in raw statistical proof. Prevention, on the other hand, can have significant impact on both collective and individual attitudes. The pursuit of preventive policies will help to create a more co-operative community through a heightening of its own potential for crime control. Similarly, individuals who are helped to avoid criminal behaviour will add to the pool of goodwill upon which enforcement policies rely for their better effect. Preventive policies are of course much cheaper than enforcement policies. The high and escalating cost of criminal justice is not reflected in preventive policies, since existing resources like education, the media and those of other agencies such as social services, welfare and probation can be made more effective by better co-ordination. It is also possible for the more obvious preventive policies, such as tactical deployment of police, the use of Special Constabulary and the organisation of the community against crime to reduce fear of crime and social tensions which make for disorder. The greater the success of preventive policies in organising communities against crime the greater is the contribution made to the quality of life and the more police can concentrate on enforcement goals. It goes almost without saying that physical security of property is of inestimable value in keeping crime levels against property down.

It seems therefore that polarisation of the enforcement and preventive schools of thought represent trends which are inimical to the balanced control of crime. A successful strategy will greatly depend on the successful fusion of the two.

Chapter 22

Terrorist crime

All Western societies suffer from increased terrorist crime, notably that associated with politics. The reflexes of a liberal society render it vulnerable to damage from political terrorism, but a liberal society and a superior democratic police will inevitably defeat political terrorism *in time*.

The police in the United Kingdom have largely been concerned, historically at least, with only spasmodic outbreaks of terrorism associated with the problems of Ireland and the British connection. But the United Kingdom, like all liberal Western states, is now open to the growth of international terrorism.

The vulnerability of liberal states is magnified by their liberalism, including freedom of movement. The ease now by which people can move from country to country by air, by sea or by land has rendered police counter-measures particularly difficult. Since this type of crime is motivated by the desire to terrify, the advent of television and the availability of uncensored news media generally have added to the seductions of terrorism and its effect. As has been said earlier, the terrorist concept of "the propaganda of the deed" exploits television. Thus a medium, made for pleasure and information, is turned on the public by those who use it to unsettle, to influence and to terrorise. On the other hand, portrayal of terrorism or its brutality, by causing public revulsion, can and does aid the police and others in helping to combat terrorism.

The ability of the police to combat the free-floating nature of terrorist violence faces a considerable challenge. Unlike crimes of violence normally encountered by the police where the victim and offender are usually related in some way or other, the terrorist's victim is usually chosen at random. It is of considerable significance therefore that the success of the police in England and Wales against recent terrorism has been pronounced. In his autobiography, *In the Office of Constable*, Sir Robert Mark was able to record that:

By the end of 1976 there had been 263 (terrorist) incidents in England and Wales involving 302 (explosive) devices. In London alone there had been 182 explosive devices and 11 shootings. Fifty-eight people had been killed and many more injured, but 148 persons had been arrested, 49 of them in London (99 in the provinces) where 68 per cent of all terrorist incidents had been cleared up. And throughout all this we had not killed or wounded a single terrorist![1]

The same high clear-up rate against terrorist incidents throughout the provinces had indicated that a liberal society where the police traditionally are part of the society, and the mass of the people themselves regard it as their duty to co-operate with the police, can develop a high rate of success against terrorism. Where, however, the police and public are alienated such success is unlikely. The police therefore have a vested interest in constantly improving their proper relationships with the public against such challenges as that presented by terrorism.

When threatened by terrorist campaigns it may be necessary for society to provide the police with powers of arrest and detention which they would not provide under more peaceful circumstances. The Prevention of Terrorism Act 1973, which gives the police powers of arrest and detention for dealing with terrorism, should rightly be repealed at the first opportunity. On the other hand, without such powers for police, society would be rendered more vulnerable. One is bound therefore to agree with Richard Clutterbuck in his book *Living with Terrorism* when he says: "The marriage between an uncorrupt police force and an alert and co-operative public is the healthiest guard against terrorism."[2]

The arming of the police and co-operation between the police and military are both matters which are likely to require consideration when terrorism is discussed, but these matters are referred to elsewhere.

NOTES

1. Sir Robert Mark, *In the Office of Constable* (Collins 1978), Chap. 14.
2. Richard Clutterbuck, *Living with Terrorism* (Faber & Faber 1975), Chap. 14.

Towards New Models

PART FOUR

Towards New Model

Chapter 23

Trends in policing

In setting out to consider new model police arrangements for the future, it is necessary to establish that the police are subject to the same forces of change as are other institutions of government. There is nothing immutable about a police system and it must give way or adapt to change.

Although it is said that history never quite repeats itself in the same way, it is possible to learn from it. Other police systems have existed, have become replaced by change and have had to be reformed or recreated. By a glance over the shoulder in time, it is hoped to show that in the evolution of the nation changes in political, social, and economic forces have fashioned new policing devices and systems. In this way it is hoped to foreshadow probable or possible trends and to identify contemporary pressures for change, which are significant in this connection.

GREEKS AND ROMANS

It is to the Greeks of course that we owe the term "police", stemming as it does from the Greek word *polis* (still pronounced in this way by some people in Scotland). It had a much wider meaning in the Greek city states, including as it did all the institutes of government. The *polis* was that part of civil administration for maintaining health, safety, and good order.

But if the Greeks provided the word, it was the conquerors, the Romans, who, as in so many things, provided the great bureaucracy of police administration. Carried forward on the tide of imperial Rome and its power to all parts of the Empire, the *politia* became the strong arm of municipal authority wherever the Eagle rested. In his book *Police State*, Brian Chapman records that: "... although Roman law accepted distinctive functions for different State institutions, the police powers were regarded as lying at the very heart of State authority".[1]

It is important therefore to remember two things in this connection: firstly that Roman police and legal systems were very advanced and very effective even by modern standards; and secondly that police power was centralised and at the heart of the central authority. The idea that, although ultimate police power resides at the very centre, the instrument of police can reside locally and be answerable to its locality was neither Greek nor Roman, but was to flower in Saxon England.

WESSEX WAYS

It was in the tribal villages of Wessex, in what is now England, that the early seeds of the present systems of policing based on common law might be said to have been sown. It is possible, even likely, that such tribal policing concepts were brought over by the Saxon settlers from Northern Europe and have Germanic origins; nevertheless it was in the settlements of Southern England that the great alternative to Roman systems was to take its first root. No doubt due to the difficulties of travel, the remoteness of the king and the vulnerability of the settlements to armed marauding bands, necessity required that all able-bodied males should accept responsibility for armed protection of their localities.

"From very early times, certainly from the reign of King Alfred, the primary responsibility for maintaining the King's Peace fell upon each locality under a well understood principle of social obligation, or collective security."[2] The point to be remembered here is that, although the police system itself has been modified out of all recognition by the passage of time, the principle of every man's responsibility for law and order has remained throughout in the common law.

The tythingman of the Saxon police system was the nearest equivalent to the modern community constable of the present. His responsibility lay in supervising the police protection of groups of some ten families, linked up with other tythings or tens to form the next level of administration (the hundred) and then higher still to a collection of hundreds to form the shire, whose senior police official, the shire reeve, is still a law enforcement official in many common-law countries. From a collection of shires came the kingdom with the king himself at the head of the policing system. It was through this simple police organisation and method that a semblance of law and order was maintained in a primitive tribal society under the laws promulgated by the kings in their Dooms; for example, the Dooms of Alfred (971–90). Setting aside wars between kingdoms and invaders, the policing of Anglo-Saxon England was both recognisable and reasonable in its constitution. But it could not last.

1066 AND ALL THAT

The first change was to come following the Norman Conquest in 1066 and the subsequent administration of law and order, which, under the Norman administration, was refined, strengthened and applied with greater precision. Under what has been described as the most significant and important police institution of that time, the Frankpledge, the Normans exacted a pledge for good behaviour from their subjects. This was preventive policing in a primitive form. All Saxons were bound over, to use the appropriate term. The police system was tougher, as one would expect it to be when an invading alien force is in the process of subjugating the conquered.

But with the passage of time, as conqueror and conquered moved slowly to an integrated and new nation, the rigid system with its strong central control relaxed a little to give more discretion to local courts and officials. "And somewhere about this time of general relaxation the Norman title of 'Constable' acquired a local significance it has held ever since."[3] The new administration had stamped its mark indelibly on the English police system of the time and had coined words which exist to the present day. The next set of pressures, however, were not long in coming.

The pattern of social change towards the end of the thirteenth century required that police control should be stiffened. The method devised was that the Crown, under the famous police provisions of the Assize of Clarendon appointed the conservators of the peace. These lay officers, known as knights, were deputed to administer the oath for good behaviour of all men over fifteen years of age and they largely replaced the many petty officials of local courts of the hundreds and of the counties.

PROSPERITY AND POLICE

It was no doubt due to the growing prosperity of the towns and cities in thirteenth-century England that the growing mercantile activity and the shifting population gave rise to a growth in crime, particularly crime connected with theft. "Whereas every day, robbery, homicide and arson are committed more frequently than used to be the case . . ." runs the wording of the Statute of Winchester of 1285. That strong king of law and order, Edward I, firmly reminded his subjects of their collective responsibility for undetected crime, for the payment of damages if they were negligent, and of their individual duties. "Moreover, it is commanded that every man shall have in his house arms for keeping the peace according to the ancient Assize." Such commands accord well with the concept of community policing in primitive style. They certainly accord well with the policing traditions of the American West in its early days of settlement!

The Statue of Winchester, however, was to introduce a new mode of policing more in keeping with the time. The cities were to supplement the old idea of amateur policing by the appointment of watchmen to "watch and ward". Furthermore, the closing of city gates between sunset and sunrise and the control of entry of strangers, the offence of harbouring offenders, all adumbrate the concept of prevention of crime of which the following passage of the Statute is a prime example:

> Furthermore, it is commanded that highways from one trading town to another shall be enlarged wherever there are woods, hedges or ditches; so that there shall be neither ditches, underlush nor bushes for two hundred feet on the one side and two hundred feet on the other, where men can hide near the road with evil intent.

The policing system of England was changing and taking on a new and interesting pattern as crime, associated inevitably with the birth of prosperity, posed its perennial problems.

JUSTICES

In less than 100 years after the passing of the Statute of Winchester, the social upheavals of post-war violence and disorder in the reign of Edward III (1327–77) required further developments of the policing arrangements. In between campaigning on the Continent, the various lords and their armies returning to England, flushed with loot and conditioned to violence, posed considerable problems for law and order. It seems that there was considerable and persistent anarchy. Not for the last time was England outgrowing its police institutions.

After numerous attempts to strengthen the power of the local gentry with only partial success, the key statute, the Justice of the Peace Act 1361, finally established the office of Justice of the Peace. Its enactments included:

> that in every County of England shall be assigned for the keeping of the Peace, one Lord and with him three or four of the most worthy of the County, with some learned in law, and they shall have power to restrain the offenders, rioters, and all other barators, and to pursue, arrest, take and chastise them according to their trespass or offence, etc., etc.

In this way there began a police system built around the Justice of the Peace and his enforcement officer, the constable, which served England and Wales as a police system for nearly 500 years.

The period of English history which followed saw considerable violence, with war, crime and disorder. This placed the police system under enormous strain, and at times overwhelmed it. The great civil Wars of the Roses were followed by the Tudor period with its strong rule and policing policies which reached their pinnacle under Henry VIII and his ace policeman, Thomas Cromwell.[4] The policing of Tudor England was given greater effect by a widespread network of spies and informers and the system of Justice of the Peace was brought up to a high level of effectiveness.

In essence, however, the main burden of law and order in England was placed to a large extent on the shoulders of the system in the form of Justices of the Peace. It was to endure from the fourteenth century to the early nineteenth century, although it had begun to break down under the accumulative strains of the Industrial Revolution in the eighteenth century. A police system which had been designed for a largely rural population with only a few major cities of note and with London as a special case, could hardly be expected to cope with a country where the most massive social changes so far witnessed were taking place.

REVOLUTIONS

By the middle of the eighteenth century the system was becoming inadequate, though what to do about it was the cause of much argument, theorising and experimentation. Spasmodic legislative efforts to curb the growth of crime, without having a strong police enforcement system, were many and varied. Towards the end of the eighteenth century, the great impact of the French Revolution only served to add to the fears and anxieties of the aristocracy and landed gentry, and accordingly ruled out the creation of a strong bureaucratic police system of spies and of armed force. Crime was preferred to police, which was an indication of the deep-rooted antipathy towards police reform.

The period of the Industrial Revolution witnessed growing crime, disorder and licentiousness on a scale that was to astound foreign visitors and to induce comment concerning the lack of a proper police force. In spite of it all, Parliament turned its face against police reform. Great pioneers of the age, such as Henry Fielding and his blind brother John, successfully proved that their experiment of Bow Street patrols was a model which prevented crime without threatening freedom. Their model was based on the historic relationship of Justice of the Peace and constable, but the constabulary part of it was to be more effective and better organised. Great names such as Patrick Colquhoun, Jeremy Bentham and Edwin Chadwick were connected with the subject of police reform; though the political will remained elusive. It was to the Home Secretary in 1829, Sir Robert Peel, that the final hopes for police reform were turned.[5]

WELLINGTON AND PEEL

Parliament was at last ready to compromise. Crime and disorder threatened and a police force was essential if the Army were not to be sucked into a role which ill suited their organisation and training. The Duke of Wellington supported Peel and eventually a new model police was devised. Once again it was based on the ancient system of Justices of the Peace and constables. The early Commissioners were Justices of the Peace and their constables inherited the traditional common-law position of constables throughout the age. The constables' constitutional position of independence under the Crown passed into the new Police Act of 1829. The establishment of the new police was in keeping with the native genius for adapting old institutions to new problems. Once again great social and political upheaval had produced a major change in policing systems which spread throughout the remainder of the country during the first half of the nineteenth century.

VICTORIAN AND SUBSEQUENT STABILITY

The great period of social stability marked by the Victorian era, the impetus of which carried on well into the twentieth century, seems remarkable when viewed in retrospect from the late 1970s. The police system was undoubtedly successful and fitted well into the culture of Victorian moral rectitude and the emergence of one nation at the Imperial fountain-head. The gradual attainment of universal male suffrage, the impact of two World Wars requiring national unification and the setting aside of other conflicts, together with an improved system of police, brought about a state of law and order in Britain which was remarkably stable compared with the historical past.

Beginning with the reform movement for political emancipation and the ensuing freedoms for the mass of the people from abject poverty, ignorance and other socially disabling conditions, this not only led to greater demands for more political and social freedom but, together with the rise of mass affluence, also created conditions for policing which in the 1960s and 1970s appear to have indicated the onset of new pressures for police change. Following upon the Royal Commission on the police of 1962, which reviewed the constitutional framework and the role of the police in the changing society, the number of police forces was drastically reduced. Following local government reorganisation in 1974 further reductions in the number of police forces brought the number down to forty-three.

Thus it is that great social, economic and political change has in the past required the police systems to be adapted to new conditions. The simple Anglo-Saxon tribal system had to give way in the cities to the watchmen of the thirteenth century, and the system of local informal responsibility for law and order had itself to give way to the Justices of the Peace of the fourteenth century.

The Industrial Revolution required a new police system which emerged with Robert Peel's reforms in 1829. Prior to these reforms, speaking in the House of Commons, Peel was moved to comment that:

> The time has come, when from the increase in its population, the enlargement of its resources, and the multiplying development of its energies, we may fairly pronounce that the country has outgrown her police institutions and that the cheapest and safest course will be found to be the introduction of a new mode of protection.[6]

This passage is of considerable interest, since it indicates the growing size, prosperity and dynamism of early nineteenth-century Britain. Today none of these forces creates pressure for change. Contemporary pressures are different, but include moral relativism, multiracial characteristics, a shrinking economy, technology, mass freedom and the speed of change.

As further changes have been brought about as a result of twentieth-century reforms, the question now remains as to whether the country has once again outgrown its police institutions.

NOTES

1. Brian Chapman, *Police State* (Macmillan 1971), Chap. 1.
2. T. A. Critchley, *A History of Police in England and Wales* (Constable 1978), Chap. 1.
3. Ibid., Chap. 1.
4. B. W. Beckingsale, *Thomas Cromwell Tudor Minister* (Macmillan 1978).
5. See Radzinowicz, *A History of the English Criminal Law* (Stevens & Sons 1968) generally on this period.
6. Parliamentary Debates 1828.

Chapter 24

Pressures of change

A society in which the consensus accepts authoritarianism presents police with fewer doubts and uncertainties than one which has cast off the yoke of authoritarianism and is revelling in its new-found individualism. It might be said that, at least traditionally, the police are the servants of authoritarianism, and are therefore bemused by the concept of policing a highly individualistic and plural society.

AN AUTHORITARIAN SYSTEM

Peel's police were an authoritarian solution to the problems of disorder in an authoritarian society. Drawn largely from the lower orders of late Georgian and early Victorian England, they were introduced with great reluctance on the part of Parliament and the privileged in society as a last resort to the growing disorderly behaviour of the urban poor. Control of the mob and the criminal classes of those days was placed in the hands of a police system, which was a product of its time.

Much has happened to change the nature of society since those days, and this poses new and considerable challenges to the police system. It is therefore necessary to anticipate changes in police which might be foreshadowed by recent and profound change.

In a passive, submissive society where consensus prevails, policing is a comparatively simple concept; but when a society begins to mount its challenge to authoritarianism, policing becomes more burdensome, particularly at the point where the challenge is rising but authoritarianism has not begun to recede. It is a turning point; since, if those vested interests in power refuse to give way, police will play the major part in maintaining a stagnant society. It is also likely that the static condition of privilege and deprivation will ultimately erupt in violence. The police will be amongst the victims of that eruption. Police, therefore, should be used only to contain excessive violence, that is violence which exceeds tolerance levels, so that arrangements can be made for the peaceful and constitutional redistribution of rights. The use of the police in Britain may be said to have conformed to a reasonable pattern in this connection.

148

The Reform Bill protests and Chartist riots of the nineteenth century were contained by the police system; and some may argue that in doing so it retarded the introduction of political freedom for the masses. This is a matter for the political historian to comment on, but it is pertinent in connection with this narrative to examine, albeit superficially, the impact on society and on the police of political liberation through universal suffrage.

The question "What happened to authoritarianism?" is raised; and the reason for this question is that something has happened to society which amongst other things produces more crime and disorder than there has been perhaps at any other time during the last hundred years or so. Much of this ground has already been covered but the search for solutions brings us back to this central issue.

PAYING THE PRICE

It is far too facile to say that crime has grown in proportion with the increases in the degree of individual freedom and affluence. It would be easy to stand by such an assertion, and merely to say that we must acknowledge that there is a price to pay for such changes and crime is part of that price. After all, it is self-evident that the glorious freedom of travel provided by motor transport in Great Britain alone exacts a price of some 7,000 deaths and 81,000 serious injuries a year. It is too uncomfortable to dwell on the thought that simple reductions in driving speeds alone would significantly reduce these figures. Society is prepared to accept these risks as a price for getting there more quickly and more often.

Why should society not accept crime with equal equanimity? Is there not a lot of hypocrisy about, or is it just that the public are not well informed or do not want to be well informed any more than they want to accept that driving speeds kill? What has happened to that world at the turn of the century of "domestic peace and neighbourly trust" described recently in the B.B.C. Reith Lectures by Professor A. H. Halsey?[1] Something has happened to make his descriptions appear to be quaint period pieces, and if we are to seek a way to understand the growth of crime we must begin by answering, or trying to answer, some of these questions.

Of all the checks on criminality in Western society, authoritarianism in all its forms seems to have had the greatest success. Even today the only developed societies in the free world to show a containment of crime, or its reduction, are those where authoritarianism to a greater or lesser degree still exists as part of the culture. Japan, Israel and Switzerland all manifest these tendencies, and all have so

F 149

far contained the growth of crime; though in Japan there has even been a reduction in the more serious crimes.

In his paper "Crime Trends in Modern Democracies since 1945"[2], Professor Gurr suggests that current trends of reported crime indicate that "a rising common crime rate has become a pervasive phenomenon in Western societies" and "a rapid and sustained increase in property crime in particular has become virtually universal". "Switzerland with stable property crime rates is the single European exception"; and he notes that Japan has not only reduced property crime as a whole but serious property crime most of all. The remainder of the developed countries all show increases in crime of considerable proportions, alongside a diminishing cultural authoritarianism. What happened to Western authoritarianism?

In Great Britain, it seems that the liberation from authoritarian control, from convention, dogma, ignorance and superstition, springs particularly from political emancipation over the last sixty years, as one would expect.

POLICING CHANGE

Released from the bondage of ignorance by mass access to higher education and through the information explosion associated with the news media, and particularly the window on the world provided by television, it is only to be expected that our society will continue to press for greater emancipation.

Keynes expressed his own views that: "When the accumulation of wealth is no longer of high social importance there will be great changes in the code of morals." He thought that "we shall once more value ends above means and prefer the good to the useful".[3]

New pressures for change are likely to come from the liberation from materialist values, but in seeking new and higher moral values greater freedom will be demanded, which might add to further police disorientation.

Halsey believes, as many do, that the keys to further moral progress include "full equality of the basic material conditions of social life" by what he calls "fraternal distribution". Progress in this field will not be without some civil trauma, but if it comes about there will be further demands for the liberation of the spirit. As women achieve full equality they will turn their thoughts, together with liberated men, to the condition of the young, then to animals and then to nature.

The pressures for change in social behaviour will require police action in supporting change rather than in preventing it. Therefore police will need to understand the forces of benign change in order to help society to attain its higher aspirations. For police this poses difficulties, since they are culturally and professionally concerned with the *status quo*. The idea of policing change will need to be understood, taught and acted upon.

The idea that there is one morality, a consensus view, belongs to yesterday's society. The forces of law and order are no match for the change of pace which has confronted them during the past twenty-five years. Not only is today's society the plural society of individual choice, but it is now and almost overnight multiracial as well. Policing such a society calls for experience and know-how which until very recently has not been available. Even now adjustments at the police/public interface are having to be made. It is a contradiction to expect a policing style and concepts of law and order fashioned on homogeneity and consensus to adapt easily and without friction in a heterogeneous non-consensual society. Conflicts inevitably arise and more crimes are recorded.

But the police are often only the scapegoats for the inability of society to make adjustments to ease these social tensions, in the same way that the immigrant may be made the scapegoat for what indigenous groups do not like about their own society. Immigrants have been singled out for this treatment throughout history, the greatest and most shameful example in European history being the treatment of the Jews.

If the changes from an authoritarian to a libertarian society have largely been achieved, it has not been without cost; and crime and disorder have been part of that cost. If the libertarian society is now to transform itself into a society of new moral dimensions, it will not be done without cost either. The police, however, may be able to help to reduce the cost if they can change fast enough in style to develop the arts and skills of policing change.

NOTES

1. A. H. Halsey, *Change in British Society* (Oxford University Press 1978), Chap. 3.
2. Professor Gurr, "Crime Trends in Modern Democracies Since 1945", *The Cranfield Papers* (Peel Press 1978), Supplementary Papers, 1.
3. J. M. Keynes, *Essays in Persuasion* (Macmillan 1931), Chap. 5, section 2.

Chapter 25

A quest for new models

PRELIMINARY CONSIDERATIONS

The chemistry of Western society today is volatile. It seems to be constantly in danger of disintegration, as wave after wave of social, political and economic change surges on. Those steering the ship of State have difficulty in keeping it on their selected course. The passengers and crew long for some kind of calm and stability to recover their sense of purpose and the values of social man.

THE POLITICIANS

Politicians such as Lord Hailsham, Jo Grimond and the late Anthony Crosland testify to this attitude.

In seeking what he calls "limited government" Lord Hailsham writes: "I believe this country requires a period of stability." Regretting constant ineffectual innovation he believes that "we have now to recognise that neither law nor political institutions, neither morals nor social habits can be respected if they are to be in a constant state of flux."[1] It is not so much a question of "stop the world I want to get off", but "stop the world we are dizzy from its turbulence and need respite to recover". This is the voice of one whose entire adult life has been spent in or around the centre of law and politics. It commands a respectful hearing.

Addressing his mind to the social problems of the modern welfare state, Jo Grimond deplores the suffocating tendencies of modern bureaucracy and its habit of worsening problems. He does not ask the machine to stop, but rather to go into reverse. Instead of the welfare state in a centralised form, he seeks a return to individual communities with voluntary effort being stimulated towards a common good. In appealing for this new version or style of social organisation he writes:

> I would like to see every individual developed to his or her fullest potential and not merely up to a minimum standard of well-being. I would like to see every community attempting to produce something pre-eminently good which they can feel proud of and which can attract other people.[2]

He asserts a strong belief in the creation of small communities, which will require a change in present attitudes to achieve, and believes:

It may seem difficult to accomplish, but it is certainly no more difficult than continuing with the present (bureaucratic centralist) system. And it holds out far greater hopes for the future.

C. A. R. Crosland writing in the 1967 edition of *The Future of Socialism*[3] believed that:

As our traditional objectives are gradually fulfilled, and society becomes more social-democratic with the passing of the old injustices, we shall need to turn our attention increasingly to other, and in the long run more important, spheres—of personal freedom, happiness, and cultural endeavour; the cultivation of leisure, beauty, grace, gaiety, excitement, and all of the proper pursuits, whether elevated, vulgar, or eccentric, which contribute to the varied fabric of a full private and family life.

There are of course implications for the police in policing the kind of society envisaged here, but clearly what emerges is the accent on the individual and family benefits. Some fifteen years after these words were written, it might be suggested that a free society, to preserve its freedom, needs to move the emphasis from family to community if the quality of life is not to be retarded through community-induced delinquency and crime. The extended family may be the clue to progress.

AN ECONOMIST

The idea that smaller communities might help to bring more social stability and prospect for survival of our democratic values was given great currency by the economist the late E. F. Schumacher. Imploring belief in "small is beautiful", in his book of that name, he suggests that:

The hope that the pursuit of goodness and virtue can be postponed until we have attained universal prosperity and that by the single minded pursuit of wealth without bothering our heads about spiritual and moral questions, we could establish peace on earth, is an unrealistic, unscientific and irrational hope.[4]

It might be regarded as equally irrational for a society to expect crime, alienation and political violence to be controlled and reduced where materialism and acquisitiveness are regarded as the givers of status, or where they represent the major ethic. Some would argue that tougher laws, more police with more powers, would maintain stability. This is a false hope and a dangerous one. Where society is flawed, as in Italy, Northern Ireland and in the black ghettos in the U.S.A., the external forces of law and order can only buy time for the flaws to be repaired. But however that may be, and it will be taken up again, Schumacher's observation that, if the economic structure of society requires the average amount of capital investment per work place to exceed the annual earnings of "an able and ambitious industrial worker" (if costs are higher than earnings), there are likely to be serious social repercussions. This may lead to "undue concentration of wealth and power among the privileged few; an increasing problem of 'drop-outs' who cannot be integrated into society and constitute an ever-growing threat; structural unemployment; maldistribution of the population due to excessive urbanisation; and general frustration and alienation, with soaring crime rates and so on."

Therefore we can observe politicians, one a former Lord Chancellor, and an economist, all expressing their thoughts about modern Western society, each in his own way suggesting that social organisation and its fulcrum should move towards smaller communities. Police will not allow it to escape their notice that alienation, disorder and crime are much more the creatures of excessive urban anonymity than of smaller, more homogeneous, social groups. In *A Blueprint for Survival*[5] ecologists record, for example, that violent crime appears to be four times greater *per capita* in cities of 250,000 than in towns of 10,000. The sociological concept of *Anomie*, used to describe people who, though part of suburban society, do not share its advantages and consequently feel rootless, disorientated and alienated, is a human condition loaded with potential damage to the social order.

SOCIOLOGISTS

Let us turn now to the opinions and comments of sociologists so far as they relate to prospects for the survival of public order as we in Western societies might wish it. It is intended to quote two, both of them distinguished B.B.C. Reith lecturers. Ralf Dahrendorf records:

> The justice of man's social institutions is threatened too by the uncontrolled power of organisations and firms and bureaucracies, by shifting equality and impotent participation. And the solutions offered by some for these problems make matters worse: the authoritarianism of a small élite which is supposed to assure survival along with law and order, the egalitarianism of a tyrannic majority for which justice has come to mean that no man must have or do anything which is different. The price for these mistakes is liberty, and it is too high, because liberty alone gives survival and justice their meaning.[6]

It seems that Dahrendorf regards the law and order solution as being, if not bankrupt, at least unhelpful if it is seen as the salvation for man's social institutions, precisely because it demands liberty as the price, and that price is too high.

Police should note this view as an important statement, not as a simple dismissal of the need for some order maintenance (such a need is axiomatic) but as a warning that they should not reinforce communal belief that laws, police and courts are an acceptable substitute for the use and development of individual liberty in the pursuit of a better society. Again "better" in Dahrendorf's terms does not depend on expansion but rather improvement of habits, attitudes and expectations, in the public mind, which police cannot cultivate to any great degree; but they can avoid impeding their growth by not offering security as a substitute for freedom. Dahrendorf's analysis of and prescription for forms of alleviation and perhaps a cure for some of society's current dilemmas is full of hope, and challenges the imagination of police amongst others to reconsider the contribution which each can make to the "new liberty". Although he does not explicitly champion small as beautiful, nevertheless implicit in much of his argument is the need to nurture resources by curbing and controlling growth of bureaucracies and wasteful ambitious political and industrial prospects. His arguments point towards communities being conceived in smaller and more neighbourly form.

The second sociologist, A. H. Halsey, in charting change in British social order. He sees the pathway for improvement in our sick social many of the informal social controls of the past which gave cohesion and consensus. The rapid development of liberty into permissiveness and the increased equality of opportunities are commented on, though with many reservations; for example, he sees social justice in economic terms as crucial to peaceful progress. These gains stand out against the loss of fraternity, which is so much the cement of healthy social orders. He sees the pathway for improvement in our sick social conditions:

> Britain is to take its own traditions of citizenship and democracy seriously in all their richness and inspiration. They offer the basis for a new fraternity without which both liberty and equality are impoverished. They offer also the political and social means of progress towards a newly integrated society.[7]

The stress on a newly-integrated society is of importance to police who are themselves bewildered by the turn of events in the plural multiracial society. Policing a disintegrated or disintegrating society has a tendency to drive police into their own culture more deeply,

155

since they find it increasingly difficult to integrate with those whom they police. A move towards a better-integrated society is in the police interest and calls for police to assess the prospects of their own contribution. Halsey reminds us of the distinction between the political organisation of citizenship, which is democracy, and the social organisation of citizenship, which is community.

Citizenship itself is political fraternity. Now one of the purposes of the police is to reinforce the community in its organised state as well as protecting and serving the individuals within it. Whilst avoiding political involvement itself it is concerned with upholding democracy. Police in society where democracy is weak or broken take on unpleasant characteristics and can no longer be called superior; for it is the strength of democracy that reflects itself in superior police.

Since the mind of the reader will shortly be asked to address itself to the question of what role the police may have to play in the future and how they in turn can affect that role, it is important to bear in mind Halsey's caveat that:

> the greatest danger is precisely the offer of simple solutions to our complicated plight. Simple solutions can only lead to political tyranny, whether from the right or left. Either would destroy that fundamental element of our social life and tradition in which we can take pride—our long developed and tenaciously held civil liberty.

And so the second sociologist like the first concludes by stressing that the life-blood of even a battered and bemused social order is liberty. Police as defenders of liberty have no difficulty in relating to such ideas.

THE FUTUROLOGIST

A futurologist poses the question "Can one live in a society that is out of control? That is the question posed for us by the concept of future shock."[8] The writer is Alvin Toffler, coiner of the phrase "future shock". Although writing some ten years ago when the U.S.A. itself was reeling from various shocks including Vietnam, much of his thinking still bears consideration. He is concerned not only with the unleashing of science and technology, but also that other social processes have "run free", including urbanisation, ethnic conflict, migration, population, crime and other examples. He is concerned that we shall be unable to keep pace with change. But it may already be that the slowing down of Western economic growth is causing countries of the West to register a falling of the pace of change, coupled with a reaction to the profligacy and excesses of limitless economic wealth, a reaction which could contain the seeds of backlash.

Toffler also registers the terrible vulnerability of Western society, particularly the cities, to disruption by the few (the handful of computer operators, for example, who might bring whole systems to a halt). The interdependence of modern giant concerns renders security more tenuous than ever. People feel vulnerable as they are. He therefore believes that people should be asked "What kind of world do you want ten, twenty, thirty years from now?" This is what he calls a "continuing plebiscite on the future". If he were to ask his question he may, of course, and probably would, get the answer which our politicians, economists and sociologists prescribe, namely a greater feeling of common identity and purpose, more spirit of community and fraternity, and concern for improvement without the expansion which induces "future shock".

THE HISTORIAN

Before closing this list of commentators, the historian might be allowed the last word. Hugh Trevor Roper, speaking at the London School of Economics in 1968, said: "To understand our own country, we need to see it in its wider context of space among other countries. Equally, to understand our own age, we need to see it in its wider context of time, among other ages." It seems therefore that he would have approved of our approach to considering contemporary and future policing against those "trends in policing" which we have discussed.

But his distinguished fellow historian, the late Arnold Toynbee, writing in the *Observer*[9] in 1974 following the economic setback after the Yom Kippur War, believed that we had no option along with other developed countries but to face up to seige economic conditions. He prophesied that we should have to get used to the idea of economic setback and develop a new way of life because of it, and that, as there would be a scramble for a share out of goods and supplies, life would have to be severely regimented. Police would have a large role to play in Toynbee's world, for society would have to accept the need for its new way of life "to be imposed by ruthless authoritarian government".

Now, ruthless authoritarian governments have to employ ruthless authoritarian police and this is not in the British tradition. Police will have to think of ways of coming to terms with Toynbee's world without having to resort to the role he forecasts. In Britain we can think of many ways of co-operative policing under seige conditions, our most recent example being the two World Wars. Shortage and rationing prevailed and survival depended on social discipline. Perhaps we could do that again if put to it.

DISCUSSION

The purpose behind considerations of political, economic, social, futuristic and historical views of the condition and prospects of our society has been justified on the grounds that although police in all societies with democratic characteristics are creatures of the law, in superior democratic systems they are much more than this. They have an enlarged moral purpose which leads them into areas of social affairs for preventing the growth of crime and disorder, of creating a feeling of safety by reducing fear and tension, and of manifesting care and compassion as a higher calling and as a social example; in short they have a contribution to make to liberty, equality and fraternity. Messrs. Hailsham, Grimond, Schumacher, Dahrendorf, Halsey, Toffler and Toynbee have helped us off on our pilgrim's progress to "new models" of policing. Other companions may join us, but essentially we shall have to be our own guide, philosopher and friend in much of what remains to be said.

POLICING DEFINED

So far sufficient has been said to allow for an assessment of what is meant by policing and who is responsible for it. If we speak of preventing things happening by policing (that is preventive policing), do we mean to use the word policing in the wide sense of civil administration or do we mean policing by a special force set up for that purpose? It is important, even crucial, to get this right.

There is a sense in which the concept of police can be used to mean a whole range of government departments; indeed almost the entire resources of the Home Department (including prisons, probation and, together with the Lord Chancellor's department, criminal justice), plus parts of the Department of Health and Social Security (including Social Services) and the Department of Environment (including transportation, pollution, trading standards) have policing characteristics in the widest sense of the term. If to this battery of government resources one adds the idea that the common law explicitly commits the entire population to some policing responsibilities, that is the duty to uphold the law, to serve on juries and so on, all added to the police forces and kindred local government bodies, one is beginning to think in terms of policing by the body politic. Now if the idea that policing is an action entered into by the combined resources of all these parts, it means something essentially different in both philosophical and practical terms from policing by a civil force set aside for that purpose. If the narrower view of policing is taken that it is something done by police forces, this may encourage the idea amongst the public that policing is nothing to do with them, and among police that it has little or nothing to do with anybody else. This in turn will affect attitudes towards responsibilities which may be inimical to good civil government and may actually lead to a waste of resources.

Drawing the wider concept of policing through the body politic is likely to lead to improved co-operation with its several parts; drawing the narrower one may, on the other hand, reinforce existing discussions and create gulfs.

The implications of this philosophical discussion for the police are profound. To approach the policing of a community with a co-ordinated group of various services on a wide front would require a good deal of energy and enterprise. Common goals would need to be clarified, for example the prevention of juvenile crime, and all parts of the policy directed towards its achievement. The concept would have to be carried over into the field of police training and into that of associated bodies. Police leadership would need to grasp the idea and policies be fashioned to accommodate it. For society as a whole, beset with and bemused by crime as it is, the feeling that all the resources of combined departments working together to prevent crime, to protect people and communities, to detect and deal with offenders, would be likely to enhance the feeling of security and be a greater contribution to the common good.

To persist with the narrower meaning of the term makes things simpler and reduces conflict or potential conflict. Police training would be simplified, objectives clarified, policies narrow and certain, and police objectives more readily understood and achieved. The tendency for police to define their own role ever more narrowly as their professionalism increases might conceivably lead to concentration of resources on reactive styles and eventually to purely "criminal" policing with no concept of service, prevention and crisis management. The police may drift further from the public and the public become less willing to "serve" the police. The options towards the new model policing are at this stage open to these competing philosophies. It is intended to opt for the wider meaning of policing through the several parts of the body politic, for in this way scarce and valuable resources will be better used, the control of crime made potentially more effective, the common good facilitated and the contribution to human happiness increased thereby. It accords with the search for a new spirit of fraternity in action.

NOTES

1. Lord Hailsham, *The Dilema of Democracy* (Collins 1978), Chap. 35.
2. Jo Grimond, *The Common Welfare* (Maurice Temple Smith 1978), Chap. 13.
3. C. A. R. Crosland, *The Future of Socialism* (Jonathan Cape 1967), Chap. 20.
4. E. F. Schumacher, *Small is Beautiful* (Abacus Books 1976), Chap. 2.
5. *The Ecologist, A Blueprint for Survival* (Penguin 1972), Appendix B.
6. Ralf Dahrendorf, B.B.C. Reith Lectures (Routledge & Kegan Paul 1975), Chap. 3.
7. A. H. Halsey, *Change in British Society* (Oxford University Press 1978), Chap. 8.
8. Alvin Toffler, *Future Shock* (Pan 1973), Chap. 20.
9. Arnold Toynbee, the *Observer* 1974.

Chapter 26

Who defines the police role?

The role of police in a given community can be defined by the law, by senior police, by junior police or by the community itself. Since it is not possible to define precisely what the police role will be at any time, there are bound to be conflicts concerning what it should be.

It is because of the complexity of policing that a good deal has to be left to the common sense and discretion of the man on the spot. This again will differ according to whether the man on the spot becomes the men on the spot or the senior officer on the spot, or whether what is being done is under public scrutiny and so on. There are so many variables in the nature of the police task and in the nature of the police response that only generalities can be formulated.

The law requires that it be enforced by the police, and the High Court will consider compelling the police to enforce it if they are pusillanimous in the matter.[1] On the other hand the High Court recognises that it would not be realistic or in the public interest to expect the police not to use their discretion.[2] The two cases involving Sir Raymond Blackburn and Metropolitan Police Commissioner are useful to the police in that they reveal the High Court's attitude to the role of the police in law enforcement. On the one hand the court wants to see the police taking their enforcement duties seriously and it wants to check any tendency on the part of chief officers to prevent their constables from enforcing Parliament's will. On the other hand, it would make nonsense of the law and criminal process if the police were expected to enforce every infringement, or if they were expected not to use their discretion in the proper use of police resources.

After the law has had its say about the police role, the importance of the chief police officer's policies is of paramount importance. Having the statutory duty to direct and control his force[3] he is responsible for the orders and policies which result from that duty. His policies stem from a basic philosophy of policing to avoid being capricious or inconsistent. The basic philosophy may from time to time stress the preventive role of the police or the law-enforcement role. He may have to follow the direction being dictated by events, or influence events to accommodate policies. It is possible therefore to

161

find different values being placed on the police role from time to time, and from place to place.

Promotions and appointments will reflect the values of the chief officer and his closest colleagues, and will in turn influence the role of junior officers. There are other ways in which the chief officer will influence role definition and these will include organisation, disposition and training of officers and public relations programmes. By allocating officers to specific tasks, for example liaison with schools, the intention to reduce juvenile delinquency and create trust for his force amongst young people will be indicated.

By allocating extra resources to the enforcement role, policing values will be indicated, always allowing for the need to respond to external stimuli which leave little room for manoeuvre, for example threatened large-scale public disorder.

It may, on the other hand, be the intention to move a force in the direction in which the policed want it to go and if this is done the police will move towards having their role defined by the public. This is not only a sophisticated notion if done intentionally but it is one which police find difficult to accommodate. In the first place it is difficult if the interaction between the police and the policed is of a poor quality or if it is largely based on conflict. A further reason for police not feeling comfortable in having their role defined by the policed is that the definition may vary from neighbourhood to neighbourhood. It is thus easier for the police to accommodate role definitions in areas which are traditionally law-abiding. This is not to say that the accommodation of role definition cannot be achieved or to deny that it occasionally is achieved, but as a generality the assertion will hold good.

This does not mean that this notion is wrong, on the contrary, it would be capable of producing democratic policing of the highest quality. If it is accepted that the police role could be defined by the policed (the major influence together with that of the law), then more informal crime control can develop out of the partnership. This trend has important implications for police since they would have to develop services in keeping with public wishes and even deployment of forces would be influenced by what the public wanted. This is exemplified where, through public clamour, officers have been returned to beats and foot patrols where the public have become disenchanted with motorised and impersonal policing.

An influence of the greatest importance in this connection is that of constables themselves. Where constables work alone on their own beats they will tend to acknowledge some defining of their role from the neighbourhood being policed. This form of policing is fulfilling for the officer and satisfying for the community and takes policing to a high level. It presents a considerable challenge to the officers concerned since they may find themselves under conflicting pressures. The policies of the force may require one thing and the neighbourhood culture may desire another. This kind of policing is greatly facilitated where the chief's policies acknowledge that conflict is likely, but permit wide discretion to the officers on the ground. In these circumstances police officers should be specially selected for this role, since it demands considerable abilities including self-reliance, confidence, good judgment and so on.

Where officers police town centres, conflicts of this kind will diminish. The commercial interests may induce pressures for tolerance in law enforcement and some may be called for, but care has to be taken here since the police may attract censure from other vested interests and allegations of partiality. Nor is it likely that town-centre policing will develop relations with the public of anything approaching the quality of that in neighbourhoods. It is here that the police role is more likely to be influenced by the officers themselves.

Groups of officers such as task forces take on characteristics different from unitary or small patrols. These are often implicitly defined in the nature of their task. Their use may produce the results intended, for example reduction of hooliganism, dispersal of crowds, counteraction of robbery, which individual officers could hardly achieve, but the dilemmas facing the police in this role almost inevitably preclude role definition by universal public consent.

Specialists in the detection of crime, in traffic policing, and many smaller departments will of course tend to have their role more clearly defined by the task itself. It is axiomatic that the object of the Criminal Investigation Department is detecting crime, but its trial and sentence is the concern of courts and penal establishments. Traffic policing has options to educate or enforce, for example,

Thus it is that there are many pressures and forces at work on the defining of the police role. At least four have been mentioned; the law, the chief and senior officers, the constables and the policed themselves.

One of the dangers inherent in creating ever larger, for example national police forces, with constantly developing professionalism, is that the most important element of all in defining the role of the police may be underestimated or overlooked. That element is the policed themselves. Thus the police role is subject to competing pressures for definition.

NOTES

1. *R. v. Commissioner of Police of the Metropolis Ex parte Blackburn* 1968 2 Q.B. 118.
2. *R. v. Commissioner of Police of the Metropolis Ex parte Blackburn* (No. 3) 1973 Q.B. 241.
3. Police Act 1964.

Chapter 27

Ten declarations

It is now proposed to make a number of declarations and to test them with argument so that if they stand up to rational examination they can be carried forward to be used as material for building a New Model Police System. It is assumed that the reader will accept that where the argument deals in matters outside the writer's expert knowledge and experience, reliance has been placed on the explicit references to authorities earlier in the text or on the implicit authority of their works.

DECLARATION A

POLICING A COMMUNITY IN A LIBERATED PERMISSIVE SOCIETY CANNOT RELY SOLELY ON FORCE AND THE CRIMINAL PROCESS

In an authoritarian society which is stratified, static and homogeneous, a criminal code can be devised to represent the moral consensus. The enforcement of that code can be seen as the application of the will of society. Generally speaking, this might be said to have been the position in Britain until 1918. Since then, and accelerated by the Second World War, the gap between our criminal code and popular morality has widened. The law, as we have seen, has retreated considerably from control of private morality. It can now be said that the moral relativity of modern society is an accepted fact which weakens and finally destroys the controlling vestiges of yesterday's criminal sanctions.

If the law is changed in this way social control against excesses, at least in this area of private morality and moral choice, must lie in individual conscience.

Most individuals have sufficient strength of moral conscience with which to handle and control their liberty; but many have not. Thus those who have not will go beyond even the considerable areas of moral freedom available into the areas still controlled by the criminal law. The majority are not going to give up their freedom of choice in order that the minority who commit excesses can be better controlled, therefore the criminal process is called into action.

More people will need to be dealt with by the criminal process as

165

more and more freedom is demanded and gained, since the greater the freedom the more people there will be who cannot cope with it, without coming up against the framework of the criminal law.

For although the law retreats, it takes up new and firm positions. The challenge of a free society therefore is not to give freedom to those who can handle it and to use the criminal sanction for those who cannot, but to strive to teach them how to handle it better. To demand more and more freedom knowing with certainty that many more will fall by the wayside is immoral, unless those who can handle it have concern for those who cannot.

The assertion that policing a community in a liberated permissive society cannot rely solely on force and the criminal process is therefore true, since it relies also on the need to educate the less capable to handle the disorientating nature of the permissive society.

DECLARATION B

ATTENTION TO "THE COMMON GOOD" WILL BRING ABOUT IMPROVEMENT IN ATTAINING POLICING OBJECTIVES. NOR IS THE CONCEPT OF THE COMMON GOOD IN CONFLICT WITH THE NATURE OF THE PLURAL SOCIETY

There are a hundred different ways of saying that men in authority should use it in the general interest and for the common good; that the interest of the people should be the rule of their decisions and the public good the end of their actions.[1]

Police, being persons of authority, are no exceptions to this exhortation, since the aim of the police is not to enforce the law for its own sake but in the interests of the common good. But the interests of the individual cannot always be sacrificed for the common good because the common good by its nature requires that individual rights be upheld and individual duties performed.

Police may also be expected to protect the common good against the actions of a few more powerful, or of many more numerous, than those seeking the common good. The law will prescribe the occasions when it can be used thus. An example might be where the common good requires that every man has the right to enter his place of employment though others, in pursuit not of the common good but of personal advantage, may try to deter him. This may reach the point where police have to act to uphold the individual's right, for it is in the common good that it should be upheld.

There are many who have subjective ideas of what is involved in the common good, but there are a number of "goods" which are "common" to all; and the public tranquillity borne out of mutual respect is one of them, it might be agreed. But where "mutual respect" is neither mutual nor respectful the law may be required to supplement it in the public interest. This concept of public tranquillity, or the Queen's Peace, is therefore a common good.

It may be said that it is in the common good for freedom of speech and assembly to be allowed, and this may be agreed as far as it goes. But when freedom of speech or assembly is used for protest, it may offend other sections of the community, a feature which is not in the common good since it may result in violence. Thus freedom of political extremists to have their views and to express them is in the common interest as an exercise of a right; but when exercise of such rights causes violence it is in the interest of the bulk of the community to prevent them.

Man is essentially a social animal and cannot exist in isolation. Therefore some notion of the common good is an imperative both of survival and of civilisation. The police exist to preserve both. In a plural and mobile society, however, communities keep breaking down and changing but sometimes re-forming. This is inimical to the common good, as social obligations are weakened and sometimes destroyed by a society in flux. The police can provide an element of stability in such societies provided that their intentions are recognisable. They can act as conductors or messengers of the common good and by giving or helping to give some form to a community they are contributing to its common good.

Thus it is argued that an understanding of the concept of common good by police, articulated and activated in a community, can assist police to achieve progress against crime and disorder. Furthermore, since the common good permits and defends individual rights, the plural society is not in conflict with the concept of common good.

DECLARATION C

AFTER ATTAINMENT OF BASIC NECESSITIES PEOPLE HAVE TWO
YEARNINGS WHICH GO TOWARDS THE SUM OF HUMAN HAPPINESS AND
THE QUALITY OF LIFE, NAMELY FREEDOM AND SECURITY. THEY REACH
PERFECTION WHERE PEOPLE FEEL COMPLETELY FREE AND TOTALLY
SECURE, BUT THIS SITUATION IS NOT ATTAINABLE

Police can be used to guarantee security but at the price of the loss of freedom. Police controls, police supervision, sanctions and regulations can all help to provide security; but carried to excess they deny freedom. On the other hand, the Utopian dream of a policeless society without the need for the security which police provide is not, in human experience, viable. The power vacuum created by absence of police would readily be filled by those attracted by it.

A superior democratic police, however, is concerned with the preservation of freedom gained by societies, enshrined in their laws and hallowed by their customs. It is also concerned with the development of freedom to come. This latter statement is true in the sense that police stand against unlawful seizure of power and for a condition of public order in which rational debate can take place, so that the minds of free men can be influenced. Without superior police existence, the processes of orderly evolution would be retarded or denied.

It would be wrong, however, to see these processes as an exact science capable of being regulated with precision. The processes of human affairs require that police can give gently against pressures, though without giving way to excesses. The laws which are fashioned by legislative process on the other hand are generally precise. There is, therefore, much room for misunderstanding and difference of opinion about the whole matter of enforcement. Law in theory and law in its police application are often of different dimensions. The balancing of security and freedom therefore rests on two levels: the level of the law's making and the level of the law's enforcement.

If police do stand as guarantors for orderly evolution, there are problems over the concept of "orderly", since some social pressure resulting in disorder is often the energy of evolution. The policing of such social movement, if not an exact science, is very much an inexact art. Free interplay of social forces within the broadest discretion, short of unacceptable social damage, may therefore not be against the whole public interest. For police to act too harshly at the slightest sign of social and political restlessness which manifests itself in action may be inimical to the public good. The police are not at their best when used in the suppression of social movement; but are undoubtedly well cast in a democracy to prevent change through violence. It is a matter for governments to assess the implications of such violence and either to continue to resist change or to recognise the underlying causes of it and to adjust. An example of this social phenomenon would be the suffragette movement of the second decade of the twentieth century.

Questions of balancing security and freedom become most acute as societies become more complex and permissive and as the ability to amass and control information develops. It is remarkable how easily most people will give up their freedoms in the hope of acquiring security.

This is particularly noticeable when they are afraid. In time of war people will submit to mobilisation, service in armed forces, direction of labour, food control, identity cards and so on. They will submit to being searched before boarding an aircraft if threats of bombs exist and will accept orders from complete strangers in times of crisis. Some people have no tradition of freedom, historically speaking, and seem generally content with safety. This is an accusation levelled at his countrymen by Alexander Solzhenitsyn.

The condition of proper social freedom requires that the holder recognises his duty towards the freedom of others, and in this way he begins to limit his own freedom; thus there is no such thing, at least in social terms, as complete freedom.

Security, on the other hand, may be provided by forces external to the individual; in which case he carries no duties or responsibilities in that connection. But where there is no guarantee of security from an authority such as the State, the individual will turn to protecting his own security either by himself or with others. This is the vigilante syndrome and can lead to further conflict and sacrifice.

The police, therefore, have to regard amongst their primary aims the protection of freedom and the creation of security. This is not because freedom and security are good in themselves but because together they offer the best chance of human happiness and high standards in the quality of life. But since some security must be sacrificed for freedom and some freedom sacrificed for security it is not possible for total freedom and complete security to exist side by side.

DECLARATION D

THE RESOURCES AVAILABLE IN SOCIETY FOR CREATING CONDITIONS OF
PUBLIC PEACE ARE IMMENSE. SOCIAL ORGANISATION OF SUCH
RESOURCES IS OF A NATURE TO ENCOURAGE THEIR DISSIPATION
THROUGH LACK OF MUTUAL CONCERN AND CO-ORDINATED ACTION.
WITH BETTER COHESION, IMPROVEMENTS IN POLICING COULD BE
BROUGHT ABOUT

The effort to justify the above declaration must be approached on three different levels. The first level is where action is taken which may reduce the possibility of juvenile delinquency. The second involves the use of resources to prevent crime through security measures. The third level concerns measures taken to deal with offenders.

The resources available to prevent delinquency are many, and they vary considerably. The most important are the resources of the home. Where the family background is stable, children are healthy and parents competent, the optimum chances of avoiding delinquency exist. This can be called situation A.

As these factors diminish in quantity or quality, so the chances of avoiding delinquency are lowered. Thus broken marriages, maladjusted children, incompetent parents and degrading living circumstances produce the optimum chances of delinquency. This can be called situation B.

Once the circle of delinquency in families begins, criminal habits pass from father or mother to son and daughter and from big brother or sister to young siblings. If this is true, and experience and research[2] suggest that it is, then efforts might be induced to change situations such as B into those such as A. In cultures where the extended family exists children are less vulnerable to condition B, since the "family" provide this support.

In complicated modern urban societies where only the "nuclear" family tends to exist there is no such support for the broken family, hence social disorder and delinquency arise. Because of this cultural omission the State has to step in by providing parental care, support and guidance, but it is a poor substitute. The result often is delinquency and the criminal sanction. The criminal justice system is a poor substitute for good family care, and, although deterring the deterrable, it tends to have little effect on those who have become confirmed in their delinquent habits.

The only other possible source of help for such broken or delinquent families is the neighbourhood or community, but since this is the age of the nuclear family little is done about mobilising it. Therefore society will have to accept that some, probably much, delinquency is inevitable in the existing social arrangements; though to organise the community may help its reduction.

The second great resource in controlling delinquency is the school. Ideally the school and the family should be compatible, as to condition the young to one standard of behaviour at home and another at school creates conflict and confusion in the child. In extreme cases this can result in the child being regarded as a school rebel with all the unfortunate consequences for the child. The parent/teacher associations are therefore potentially sound relationships. Unhappily, however, the very parents it is desired to help seldom belong to such movements. Such parents are, generally, not known to the teachers except by repute, but they are often known to the police since they head delinquent families. Thus the teacher and the police have an issue in common—the delinquent family.

Often other officials become involved, including social workers. Teachers are generally able to identify early signs of potential delinquency but do not have the means to do anything about it themselves. Thus the teacher resource element is inhibited in action. It is for this reason that police, social worker and teacher should team up to prevent the potential delinquent from becoming one. Too often concerted action, if it takes place at all, takes place after the delinquent is confirmed and hardened. Resources have thereby missed their opportunities and in that sense have been dissipated.

Outside school the pressures on the young towards delinquency can be considerable. Where the family fails the child, the neighbourhood gangs or groups will take over. Some of such groupings will result in mischief which is quite in keeping with youthful exuberance. Petty damage and theft may follow. At this point the chance of a caution by the police may be the end of the official delinquent phase of the child. But in all such cases the chances of a hardening of the condition is possible. At this stage the combined action of parent, police, social worker, probation officer and education welfare officer will have considerably greater chances of success if working together and in consultation, than any of them will have separately. This is the way to use resources for maximum effect.

There are many other agencies whose resources can be directed towards a conscious effort in the prevention of delinquency.

DECLARATION E

SOLUTIONS TO THE CRIME PROBLEM HAVE BEEN SOUGHT IN INCREASING RESOURCES. IN THE FUTURE, RESOURCES OF BOTH MONEY AND MANPOWER WILL FAIL TO MEET THE DEMANDS OF THIS APPROACH AND MAY ALREADY HAVE REACHED THEIR OPTIMUM. THE FUTURE WILL DEMAND A BALANCE OF RESOURCES AND NEW IDEAS

Since some crime is inevitable and the bulk of crime is of a petty nature (though it cannot be overlooked) it is not possible to eliminate it entirely, and not worth bankrupting society in this pursuit through methods known not be be cost-effective. The great cost of attempting to control crime through public spending is centred on the police, the courts and the penal, reformative and rehabilitative agencies, and on the growth of legal aid. It is possible to envisage an increase in police effectiveness in discovering and processing crime to such an extent that the courts and related agencies would have to expand to such a degree that they would swallow funds at a prodigious rate. The money for these purposes would have to be drained away from other deserving but less alarming social problems, including care of the sick, the aged and the incompetent.

The vicious circle of expanding police, requiring expanding legal aid, requiring expanding penal services, requiring expanding aftercare is not inevitable. The circle can be broken, though not easily. To break it will require action under the following heads.

1. A more rational and less emotional debate about crime.
2. A system of public education about crime, its nature and impact.
3. From 2 to the explosion of the myths about crime, perpetuated

by, amongst others, the media, the police and the legal profession.

4. A modification of the preoccupation with offenders to added concern for potential offenders.

5. Combined operations against crimogenic social conditions.

6. Increase of police activity in preventive measures.

1. A more rational and less emotional debate about crime should begin by acknowledging that the bulk of crime does not threaten the personal safety and security of people. Britain still has one of the lowest murder rates in developed countries; and the chances of being killed by a stranger are very remote and much less than those of being killed by a relative, a friend or an acquaintance.

A good deal of crime is related to the materialism and acquisitiveness of modern society and such crime is an indicator of relative affluence. House burglaries are unacceptably high, but a large number (estimated at some 45 per cent) are committed by children and young persons, and occupants are seldom harmed.

It should also be noted that organised serious crime is being strenuously and successfully countered by modern policing methods.

Putting crime in perspective and keeping it there should be an important police responsibility. Crime is news and there will always be a tendency to get it out of proportion, as its news treatment depends not on the police but on the preference of newspaper editors and writers.

Where crime is exaggerated and made to appear as a constant and impending threat to people, it is capable of inducing hysteria or anxiety, which will result in demands for harsher penalties and more spending on law and order. In both cases demands might be lessened if a rational debate and thoughtful portrayal of the phenomenon of crime were set about.

2. A system of public education about crime and of society's counter-crime measures and potential, begins of course with dissemination of facts. Police therefore have a responsibliity to release facts to give proportion, but it is in the explanation of the facts that the difficult challenge lies. The media of course represent the most potent and wide-ranging way of disseminating information. Just as the subject of personal and public hygiene is taught and is part of everybody's education, so should crime and criminality become part of educational curricula. Adult and junior evening and day schools, together with a young persons schools programme, offer important opportunities. Modern policing calls for a considerable effort in public education about crime. The media comprise as yet an almost untapped source in this connection.

A public well informed is less likely to feel threatened. Ignorance and fear of the unknown often cause greater anxiety than proper knowledge, but more knowledgeable people are also likely to play a greater role in combating crime. One of the problems is that simple solutions are peddled to the public who naïvely grasp at them only to be disappointed when they do not work.

Equally unsettling is the excessive politically-biased remedy offering control, resulting in exaggeration of causes and remedies. The belief that only the police can understand crime leads to public apathy. Lack of a rational educational dialogue about disease, for example, is known to induce anxiety.

Those who have suffered from cancer and other frightening diseases and who together with the medical profession have explained their fight against them and the nature of disease to the public have helped to allay some public anxiety.

The same may be said about crime. Knowledge can dispel fear. Ignorance may be bliss only when ignorance is total. Education therefore in the nature, causes and characteristics of crime is likely to produce a more knowledgeable and secure public and one able to play its own part in reducing crimogenic conditions as well as in the administration of criminal justice. The police can only benefit and enhance their work with an enlightened public around them. Additionally, an enlightened public will facilitate the search for alternatives to criminal justice for the prevention of crime through the concept of deterrence.

The advent of local radio, for example, offers massive scope for police and public to deter crime through the prospect of their combined resources. Serious crime which generates public anxiety can be made the subject of ten thousand pairs of eyes through one broadcast appeal. In local conditions residents have a vested interest in participating and will do so if properly informed and appealed to. The latent policing ability of the community can be activated to offset the alternative—higher taxes and rates for more police, more courts and so on.

Should shortage of public money restrict growth of police and other parts of criminal justice, and should public ignorance or apathy be condoned, the result must surely be uncontrolled crime. It is essential to progress by shifting the emphasis from resources to ideas.

3. There are a number of myths concerning crime which it is not in the public interest to perpetuate. It should be understood at the outset that most of the bulk of crime is for a variety of reasons never reported to the police. That the police are only able to detect a small proportion of crime reported to them if, at the time of reporting, a suspect or the actual offender is not nominated by the victim. Thus, although

the chance of detection is from the offender's point of view a crucial deterrent, the chances of detection are in most cases remote.

There are many people with a vested interest in perpetuating the myth that society is made up of the criminals and the non-criminals, and that if the police and criminal courts and penal institutions are only given sufficient resources the time will come when all the criminals will be caught and sentenced and all will be well. It goes even further in some cases with the assertion that improvements in the criminal law itself will make it possible to "win the war on crime". Much of this is simplistic though often well-meaning.

We have already quoted the statistics but they bear repetition. The facts are that, in 1977, 2,463,025 indictable crimes were recorded by the police in England and Wales. This is estimated to represent 10–15 per cent of all such crimes committed.[3] If this is accepted, and it is realistic to accept its general purport, then some 25,000,000 crimes were committed in 1977. In 428,735 cases offenders were found guilty. It seems possible therefore that some 4,500,000 offenders were not caught or convicted. Therefore the entire range of the criminal process and penal, reformative and rehabilitative measures were concentrated on some 10 per cent of offenders. This is not to say that it is not an important 10 per cent, for it is an important symbolic act for society to indicate its abhorrence of serious crime and its disapproval of crime generally.

It is, however, misleading to suggest that crime can be properly controlled in this way. So long as people are prepared to pretend or indulge in make-believe, so be it, but if society is serious in its attitude to crime and criminality it will have to begin by acknowledging the facts; then steps can be taken to make other efforts towards the control of crime.

Since crimes, in the main, therefore, are not reported to the police, the only other course open is that of prevention. The first step towards a purposeful and meaningful preventive policy is the acknowledgment of the limitations of treating crime *ex post facto*.

4. It seems therefore that progress is not to be made through abandonment of offender-orientated measures but to modify a preoccupation with such measures in favour of added concern for potential offenders. This is not always a popular approach with those who stress the concept of individual responsibility for criminal habits. At its most crude this may mean: "I don't care what sort of background this person comes from or what excuse they give for committing crime, but they should be punished for it."

Most people, however, hold a balanced view and are prepared to accept some mitigation for circumstances; others may go to the other extreme and blame society for everything. It is an area of human conduct where people tend to hold firm opinions (though these are often based on misinformation or misunderstanding). It is all the more enlightening therefore to note the comments of West and Farrington in their recent publication *The Delinquent Way of Life* where they report on an incredibly painstaking and thorough survey of some 400 young males in inner London over a period of ten years. They concluded that: "Help received voluntarily via health and welfare agencies would be more acceptable and might prove more effective than a direct attack upon delinquent habits by agents of the criminal courts."

Now this is not a popular thing to say, but it smacks of experience and is the result of extremely good research. They accept that ordinary penal measures are necessary as a last resort, though criminal justice can hardly be expected to succeed where educational and welfare agencies have failed. They further conclude that:

> Ordinary penal measures may persuade into conformity those who are capable of conventional social adjustment, but they are unlikely to improve individuals whose deviant attitudes and way of life have been ingrained from an early age and are continually reinforced by their social situation.[4]

The importance of a fresh approach to crime control lies in having it work effectively in the seed beds of crime wherever possible. For the police this means analysing crime in neighbourhoods in order to damp it down, together with all other agencies and resources, including the local residents. A great deal can be attempted in the form of proactive policing by both police and community. Policing is not just a question of reacting to the bad but includes activating the good in society, and in so doing reducing the number of offenders.

5. The police, however, cannot afford the manpower, nor do they possess all the skills and understanding required to produce a meaningful proactive crime prevention scheme.

The first requisite is to develop mutual confidence among the various statutory agencies working in the affected areas. Social workers, teachers, probation officers, youth workers, housing managers and planning officials can all in their own way contribute towards diminishing the crimogenic characteristics of a neighbourhood or reducing the criminality perpetuated in some families. These agencies together with parents and voluntary organisations represent the first echelon of measures to prevent crime, with the police providing the back-up of the authority of the law itself. Together much can be accomplished.

6. The final measure which is suggested as going towards preventing crime by preventive policing is the increase of police resources on neighbourhood duties. With responsibility for an area, the community constable is able to acquire a knowledge and understanding of the area and its inhabitants. He is able to provide the leadership necessary to stimulate and activate others. Unlike the roving mobile units he has a commitment to a group of people to whom he is a known individual, and a personality, distinct from the anonymous crews of prowling cars.

It is on his presence and position of trust that the edifice of community policing is to be built. It is a good investment of police manpower. Nevertheless it is not an easy task and calls for officers of considerable ability.

DECLARATION F

SOCIETY IS DISINTEGRATING AND THIS CONDITION INCREASES THE PROSPECT OF A BREAKDOWN IN SOCIAL DISCIPLINE. BUT AS SOCIETY DISINTEGRATES FROM ONE FORM OF SOCIAL ORGANISATION IT CAN REINTEGRATE INTO ANOTHER. A HEALTHY REINTEGRATION IS IN THE INTERESTS OF SOCIAL POLICING

As the Industrial Revolution gained pace in the eighteenth century, the disintegration of rural Britain began. Declining and poverty-stricken villages were deserted, as workers flocked to the industrial towns to take advantage of the growing boom and the prospects of increased material standards. The scale and speed of growth of urban centres, and London in particular, produced social problems, some of which, in relation to crime, have similarities to those of today. According to Asa Briggs:

> During the eighteenth century the population of East Anglia had declined while that of Tyneside, Yorkshire and Lancashire had increased. Surrey and Middlesex grew with the growth of London while the population of the West country, the South and East Midlands had remained relatively static.[5]

In London by 1800 the "population had risen to nearly 900,000 (from 674,000 in 1700)".[6] Insecurity and crime were worrying problems. There was no adequate police force, and the increase in wealth in a society grounded in inequality widened the range of criminal opportunity. Organised crime plagued the rural areas, including the destruction of woods for timber, the stealing of sheep and growing crops. "To put a check to these enormities, an association has been formed in the neighbourhood of Bideford, and this will most probably be soon followed by others in the country."[7] The urban crime however posed a far greater problem: "London is really dangerous at this time; the pick-pockets formerly content with mere filching, make no scruple to knock down with bludgeons in Fleet Street and the Strand."[8]

Thus the disintegration of society in the late eighteenth and early nineteenth century produced severe policing problems. Later, as the cities prospered and urban life entered into its halcyon phase (1870–1950), the crime problem was brought under control and London and the provincial cities and towns generally enjoyed both prosperity and security. Now that society is disintegrating again with the fall in economic prosperity, the high cost of urban living and working, awareness of pollution, travel problems, strikes and an unco-operative work-force and crime to top it off, the big Metropolitan areas appear to have passed the peak of their socially-organised sophistication. Aided by the motorcar and cheaper and better living environment the move back at least to semi-rural life has begun. The city centres decay and many incompetent people find themselves stranded in poverty, though surrounded by the remaining affluence. Crime thrives again.

The vulnerability and unfriendly nature of city life calls for fresh social organisation and a reintegration. All the indicators are that reintegration should begin in the creation of smaller communities. Just as rural village life begins to prosper and provide security, friendship and community, so should that pattern of the rural village be introduced and strengthened within the city. Reintegration may conceivably come through "the village in the city". The recreation of community is an urgent and feasible prospect.

DECLARATION G

THE DECAYING INNER CITY AREAS ARE BREEDING GROUNDS OF CRIME AND DISAFFECTION. TO LEAVE THE PROBLEM TO THE VAGARIES OF LAW ENFORCEMENT WOULD BE UNWISE, AND THE ADMIRABLE SOCIAL CONSTRUCTION TAKING PLACE SHOULD BE MAINTAINED AND INCREASED WITH POLICE BEING AN INTEGRATED PART OF THIS MOVEMENT

There are sufficient examples of how neglected social problems which have been allowed to fester to a dangerous state, but which have been covered over and policed by force, can break out into public disorder. In such cases the police are trapped into the dilemma. On the one hand they perceive the problem but not having the solution they gradually allow themselves to become a solution of expediency, though sooner or later social repair and reconstruction has to begin. From a police point of view the sooner the better. However, it is not enough for police to deplore these situations, they have to contribute towards the debate for a just solution. It should be remembered, for example, that the catalyst for the present phase of violence in Northern Ireland included the Civil Rights movement sparked off by social inequalities.

The Cameron Report[9] included amongst its conclusions for the immediate and precipitating causes of the disorders which broke out in October 1968 the following general observations.

(1) A rising sense of continuing injustice and grievance among large sections of the Catholic population in Northern Ireland, in particular in Londonderry and Dungannon, in respect of (i) inadequacy of housing provision by certain local authorities (ii) unfair methods of allocation of houses built and let by such authorities, in particular, refusals and omissions to adopt a "points" system in determining priorities and making allocations (iii) misuse in certain cases of discretionary powers of allocation of houses in order to perpetuate Unionist control of the local authority (paragraphs 128–131 and 139).

(2) Complaints, now well documented in fact, of discrimination in the making of local government appointments, at all levels but especially in senior posts, to the prejudice of non-Unionists and especially Catholic members of the community, in some Unionist controlled authorities (paragraphs 128 and 138).

(3) Complaints, again well documented, in some cases of deliberate manipulation of local government electoral boundaries and in others a refusal to apply for their necessary extension, in order to achieve and maintain Unionist control of local authorities and so to deny to Catholics influence in local government proportionate to their numbers (paragraphs 133–137).

(4) A growing and powerful sense of resentment and frustration among the Catholic population at failure to achieve either acceptance on the part of the Government of any need to investigate these complaints or to provide and enforce a remedy for them (paragraphs 126–147).

(5) Resentment, particularly among Catholics, as to the existence of the Ulster Special Constabulary (the "B" Specials) as a partisan and paramilitary force recruited exclusively from Protestants (paragraph 145).

(6) Widespread resentment among Catholics in particular at the continuance in force of regulations made under the Special Powers Act, and of the continued presence in the statute book of the Act itself (paragraph 144).

(7) Fears and apprehensions among Protestants of a threat to Unionist domination and control of Government by increase of Catholic population and powers, inflamed in particular by the activities of the Ulster Constitution Defence Committee and the Ulster Protestant Volunteers, provoked strong hostile reaction to civil rights claims as asserted by the Civil Rights Association and later by the People's Democracy which was readily translated into physical violence against Civil Rights demonstrators (paragraphs 148–150 and 216–226).

In the United States the police and residents of the largely black ghetto areas have been described as "warring minorities". Hans Toch in *Police and Law Enforcement* describes the situation as:

> an internal cold war. Militant ghetto residents are pitted against militant members of metropolitan police forces. Each group watches the other with apprehension, and each plots countermeasures against expected aggression. On both sides are those who proclaim that they will experience Armageddon in their day, in the shape of a premeditated massacre by the opposing force.[10]

The title of Toch's article, which describes both blacks and police as minorities, reveals the irony of it all. Both are trapped within the boundaries of the social/cultural problem, and being threatened each by the other produces the chemistry for eruption sooner or later if nothing is done to defuse the situation.

It is, of course, in the interests of the police who find themselves in these situations that prospects for a better and more understanding relationship with the area residents should be developed. They should not only be respected for their upholding of the law but they should be respected for their concern for social justice and be associated with ameliorative programmes. Seen on committees and belonging to other social bodies they can improve relations between themselves and other area workers, and they can be valued for their contribution to the common good. In this way tension between police and the policed can be reduced and a better spirit introduced into the affected areas.

DECLARATION H

SELF-REGULATION AT INDIVIDUAL LEVEL AND AT GROUP LEVEL EXISTS; ITS EXTENSION IS BOTH POSSIBLE AND DESIRABLE. POLICE HAVE A VESTED INTEREST IN STRENGTHENING GROUPS FOR REJECTION OR CONTAINMENT OF CRIMINAL BEHAVIOUR

Where social organisation is based on smaller groups with common values, police problems diminish, at least within the group. They may of course become targets, or prey, for external hostile groups as, for example, where an affluent group lives cheek by jowl with a poverty-stricken group, when the latter may be expected to prey on the former. But even within the poverty-stricken group there is room for strengthening self-regulation. However, as De Jouvenel so clearly expresses:

> The wider and more developed a society is, the less can the climate of trustfulness be the fruit of the spirit of community; the widening of the circle and the growing diversity of personalities tend to destroy that spirit. For that reason the climate of trustfulness comes more and more to rest on the guarantees provided by the Law.[11]

We are almost back where we started with this statement, which describes the dilemma of the plural society tenuously being held together by police law enforcement or its threat. This role for the police is a new one and has the potential for increasing their isolation, since, sooner or later, all individuals or groups in a permissive society are likely either to find the police irksome or a nuisance and an impediment to their civic freedom.

However, it has been noted that feelings of insecurity will cause people to group together to dispel such feelings. Since crime threatens, the call to community concern for the prevention of criminality has a chance of a favourable reaction so long as vestiges of common interest can be raised. The neighbour who guards his friend's house during the latter's absence on holiday is a good example since it promises the quid pro quo. The escorting of neighbour's children to and from school to protect them from offences or going missing from home is another. There are innumerable examples of informal social organisation which testify to the need and desire for group self-regulation, and the police should help to identify such needs and encourage and participate in the necessary group action.

Such group action can become antisocial and counter-productive if carried too far. Intergroup rivalries in industrial disputes and vigilante groups which usurp the police function and create potential or actual crimes of violence, are cases in point. Examples include the use of strong-arm men or "heavies" to police places of entertainment, intimidatory neighbourhood picketing to coerce unwilling fellow workers, and, at the extreme, private armies such as the "Black Panthers" in the black ghetto areas of cities in the U.S.A. or sectarian "private armies" in Northern Ireland.

Thus it seems that self-regulation as a social phenomenon exists and can be benign, but carried too far there are dangers; police should be aware of their responsibility for enabling self-regulation, whilst at the same time controlling it where it manifests malign characteristics.

DECLARATION I

MUCH CRIME IS TOLERATED WHICH COULD AND SHOULD BE
PREVENTED, SINCE IT IS IMMORAL AND COSTLY TO IGNORE IT

In an affluent materialist society where consumer goods abound and cash and securities in transit are at a high level, the opportunities for acquisitive crime abound. Where accounts, credit cards and financial systems are commonplace, the added opportunities for "white-collar" crime such as embezzlement add to the growing bulk of property crime. Crimes against property amounted to 80.9 per cent of all crime reported in 1977. D. P. Walsh[12] records that in 1977 £500,000,000 worth of goods was stolen by shoplifting in England and Wales, an alarming proportion of which was committed by children, young people or ordinary adults who would never stoop to any other type of crime.

The appropriate subtitle of his book is "Controlling a Major Crime", because that is what it amounts to in social and economic terms. In the first place, the cost of preventing it, increasing it or making it up in one way or another is passed on to the customer. Shoplifting has, like other acquisitive crime, increased with opportunity and the advent of the walk-round store and supermarket. Shoplifting, theft of and from motor vehicles continue to keep pace with the growth of opportunities, whilst thefts from automatic machines or meters decline as the machines are withdrawn or redesigned.

This is what one would expect. Crime trends are largely dictated by opportunity. Therefore every effort should be made to reduce opportunity. Built-in thief-proof devices in cars and better security in stores would dramatically affect petty crime. The tendency to pass the costs of crime on to the consumer or on to the insurance companies, who again pass it on to the consumer, merely induces indifference to crime. Paradoxically, reluctance of manufacturers to increase purchase price inhibits provision of elementary aids to security. This in turn is immoral, since offenders who fall are drawn into criminality through excessive temptation and blatant opportunity. Though most people are able to resist the temptations of acquisitive crime there are those who fail.

This is not to condone their actions and certainly not to overlook the other group of offenders who are organised or purposeful in their criminal activities. It is to assert that much crime could and should be prevented if greater concern were to be shown by those who afford the opportunity blatantly.

The control of white-collar crime, that is crime by professional and executive workers, presents considerable problems not only of discovery but of reportage. If embezzlement or falsification of accounts are discovered, but not disclosed to prosecuting authorities, the crime is compounded. It is odd that people are more ready to seek the punishment of the petty juvenile offender whilst feeling less hostile towards much white-collar crime. Whatever forces activate public concern, it should never be forgotten that indifference to crime of these kinds produces a society which eventually fails to distinguish the rights and wrongs which sustain a healthy community.

DECLARATION J

ALTHOUGH THERE IS CONSIDERABLE SCOPE FOR IMPROVING THE
CONTRIBUTION OF COMMUNITIES AND THE BODY POLITIC IN POLICING
MEASURES, POLICE HAVE A PARAMOUNT DUTY TO ENGAGE IN
COUNTERING THE GROWTH OF ORGANISED CRIME, SINCE IT CONTAINS
THE SEEDS OF CORRUPTION, INTIMIDATION AND BLACKMAIL

The destruction of a society can begin with the unchecked growth of organised crime on the grand scale. Although law-abiding members of the public may assist the police in combating such crime by offering information, for example, the control of organised crime is essentially a matter for the cleverest investigatory skills and the highest standards of organisation.

Police, therefore, have to make value judgments and attempt to conform with the views of the general public in determining priorities and the allocation of resources. Therefore, although individual members of the public may have been the victims of ordinary thefts, they would not expect the police to devote the degree of attention to that offence as they would expect to be given even to a stranger who had suffered a grievous crime.

In policing there have to be priorities of action. Just as concern for violence in public demonstrations may require large numbers of police to be withdrawn from their normal day-to-day preventive function to control the crowds, so the combating of organised crime requires an adequate concentration of detective forces sometimes numbering hundreds in dealing with one crime. The police, therefore, recognise that there are two broad areas of policing to contend with: on the one hand, the ordinary, generally law-abiding but occasionally offending public, and on the other the few who have taken a conscious decision to operate beyond the law. The former are the concern of community policing, the latter are the natural quarry of the police supported by the community.

NOTES

1. Bertrand De Jouvenel, *Sovereignty* (Cambridge University Press 1957), Chap. 7.
2. West and Farrington, *The Delinquent Way of Life* (Heinemann 1977), Chap. 6.
3. (a) Sparks, Genn and Dodd in *Surveying Victims* (Wiley 1977) estimate some 10 per cent. (b) Radzinowicz and King in *The Growth of Crime* (Hamish Hamilton 1977) estimate some 15 per cent.
4. As in 2 above, Chap. 9.

5. Asa Briggs, *How They Lived* (Basil Blackwell 1969), Chap. 1.
6. Ibid., Chap. 3.
7. Ibid., Chap. 12.
8. Ibid., Chap. 12.
9. Disturbances in Northern Ireland, Cmnd. 532.
10. Hans Toch, *Police and Law Enforcement* (A.M.S. Press Inc. New York 1972), Chap. 3.
11. As in 1 above, Chap. 8.
12. D. P. Walsh, *Shoplifting* (Macmillan 1978).

Chapter 28

A reconstruction

The point has now been reached where it is possible to assess the prospects of constructing a police model for the future. In Chapter Twenty-five the commentaries of observers of the political, economic and social scene were noted, and in Chapter Twenty-seven the ten declarations on aspects of policing were tested and defined. It now remains to use all of these as materials upon which to erect a new model police fitted for a free, permissive and participatory society. There is, however, one doubt, one cloud on the horizon to be studied before we can start to build a brave new system on the lines desired, and that is what might be called the Toynbee scenario. It is essential to dispose of this at the outset.

The reader's attention has already been drawn to the late Arnold Toynbee's forecast, when writing in the *Observer* in April 1974, that developed countries would have to resort to siege economies in order to cope with their steadily deteriorating economic condition. The 1973 Yom Kippur war and the use of the oil weapon by the Arab countries had highlighted the vulnerability of Western economies. It is possible to envisage an economic as opposed to a conventional or nuclear war in which supply of food and goods would have to be controlled by the Government. There is nothing new in this since the rationing of food, fuel and consumer goods was efficiently and successfully administered by the British Government in the First and Second World Wars. With Ministers of Food, Fuel and other commodities, together with Ministers of Information and Home Affairs, having extra powers, this can easily be contemplated when society's existence is at stake.

Toynbee, however, went beyond envisaging a true social contract in these matters and forecast that public disorder and squabbling would be at such a pitch that the Government would require to be "ruthlessly authoritarian". Now if a government is to be ruthless and authoritarian it will need an arm of power capable of ruthless authoritarian enforcement, and that means the police. A police system designed to sustain this kind of government would need to take on appropriate characteristics. It would need to be under central control with a Minister of Police. It would need fairly arbitrary powers and it would need to develop a strong third force or mobile *gendarmerie* and a secret police. The arbitrary powers of arrest, search and seizure of people and property would be closely allied to the control of rationed goods, and here a department of trade police may have to be formed to enforce the myriad regulations associated with imports, exports and rationing. If this were not done, a thriving black market would burgeon as it does in totalitarian regimes of this kind.

The *gendarmerie* style third force on the lines of the French and continental systems generally would be required to maintain public order, since the tensions and disaffections which spring up under ruthless authoritarian governments would need to be put down. This force would need the sophisticated weaponry of crowd control and have recourse to arms and other paraphenalia. It would have to be a strong quasi-military force to avoid being overborne by numbers and would require extra powers and procedures for arrest, detention and conviction of offenders. There would be a clamour for universal fingerprinting and identity cards, with liability for arrest if they were not carried or if persons refused to comply. In view of the increase in numbers which might be arrested, concentration camps would be required and a system or string of Gulags may have to be set up, as in the U.S.S.R., for political as well as for criminal internees. Movement of suspected persons may require restrictions within the country and systems of reporting to public officials would be required.

A secret police organisation might be set up, with wide powers of access to private information and entry into private premises, and above all to police the police themselves, since a ruthless authoritarian government would wish to keep the police on their toes and out of sympathy with the populace.

This, then, is the kind of set-up to which an extrapolation of the Toynbee theme would lead. It may seem fanciful, when considered from the comparative freedom of the permissive society, but when people feel threatened by shortages of food, shelter, clothing and widespread disorder they would willingly sacrifice their freedom and grant powers such as these to a government to bring order out of chaos. The instinct for survival is greater than the instinct for freedom. Equally, it would be a bold man who would prophesy that economic problems for the developed nations would not become acute enough for contemplation of ruthless authoritarianism.

There is however an alternative scenario to the dark and dispiriting one of Toynbee. It is possible for a developed nation, with sufficient deep-rooted traditions of stability in its institutions and cultures, to cope with economic decline without resorting to the kind of police state just considered. A society capable *in extremis* of finding its soul and a sufficient well of decency in its culture and traditions with which to cope with its traumas is a possibility. There are, in Britain, prospects for a better solution.

Writing in his book *The British Experience* in which he reviews Britain's problems between 1945 and 1975, Peter Calvocoressi concludes:

> British democratic instincts and institutions remain intact. This does not means that the democratic processes cannot be improved or that they do not require vigilance. But they have persisted and functioned despite the pressures and perplexities of the most taxing age in British history, and this may well be the single most important feature of the British case. Without them Britain would be unrecognisable, which it is not.[1]

This summation helps to redress the balance and points away from the dark Orwellian world of thought police, newspeak and Big Brother, where the Ministry of Truth concerns itself with law and order and the Ministry of Plenty with economic affairs.

But if an attempt is to be made to further the construction of a police system to match a free, permissive and participatory society, we need to take advice again. Ralf Dahrendorf, who has enlightening counsel to offer, writes: "A period of expansion, economic and otherwise, is coming to a close; the problems with which we are faced can be solved only if we change the subject and concentrate on the improvement of our lives."[2]

This surely is a touchstone. "Improvement without expansion" concentrates on the quality of life and human relations in the broadest meaning of the term. It goes with a proper extension of liberty, and superior police are companions of liberty. In the light of such possibilities it would be a betrayal of all that the superior police stand for if we were to construct a Toynbeean model. It is proposed therefore to set aside further treatment of the concept of a ruthless authoritarian system and to set about constructing police for an enlightened society, the society of Dahrendorf's *The New Liberty*, in which "improvement instead of expansion, good husbandry instead of affluence, human activity instead of work, and of course one word which is quite old, liberty"[3] provide the guiding light.

THE VILLAGE

The social control of crime and misbehaviour in a village community is facilitated by the very nature of that community. It is usually homogeneous, has shared values, and achieves stability through the general will. That is not to say that a village cannot contain a wide variety of people of differing social status and still achieve stability,

186

or to deny that a village without social stratification has a good chance of producing a common will. Clearly there are examples of both. The traditional village of rural England and Wales exhibits the former and the many new worker villages clustered around industrial centres exhibit the latter. The key to social stability in villages does not seem to depend on social stratification or its absence.

It is in the opportunity to relate as one individual to another and to the identifiable and meaningful community, which helps to strengthen community order in a village and it brings benefits which are apparent to the residents. The security provided by the group and the opportunity for frequent interaction strengthens the feeling of belonging, which man as a social animal needs if he is to be at his best.

The first quality of village order is living in sympathetic proximity and having a system of shared values. The second is the feeling that one counts as an individual and is not just another ant in the seething anonymity of the city. It is acknowledged, however, that the city has many advantages, if not in its environmental qualities then in the proximity of facilities such as education, shops, entertainment and cultural amenities of one kind or another. The lack of public transport to and from the village is largely compensated for by the motorcar, a feature which keeps the village alive.

Police in villages, therefore, are seen by the residents and ultimately by themselves as part of the milieu and consequently of the system of values. The policing of a village is not therefore the application of remote rules by remotely-based and anonymous officials but by one of the villagers. This is a very important point to bear in mind. Maureen Cain in her book *Society and the Policeman's Role* is quite right when she says, when referring to village policing: "The members of the community defined for him what was trivial and what was important. What was real police work and what was not."[4]

Thus where modern police systems have withdrawn police from villages and substituted mobile patrols based on urban centres, the village communities have judged the change harshly, and police relations with the public have suffered greatly because of it. This deterioration, in turn, has affected trust in the police and the free flow of information. Equally, it has resulted in loss of police understanding of and sympathy for the policed. The nature of police work has changed and moved toward the dominant city style of anonymous officials policing anonymous people.

THE CITY

Save for those city enclaves which still retain a semblance of village life, the general condition of heterogeneity, centralised bureaucracy and, above all, social mobility, creates a milieu in which it is more difficult to share community values. It is likely in the course of daily life that interaction with strangers exceeds that with people of the neighbourhood. The outsiders, who pass through or invade the home territory, prevent it from developing village cohesion. Although it is said that in the more static pre-motor-vehicle city neighbourhoods were communities, these have largely been destroyed by the pace of change, the planners and housing policies and the alienating style of much modern urban development.

The nuclear family has arrived in the city, and with it a police system to match. City police seldom police the community in which they live. Like any other commuter they travel from their own suburban homes into the urban centres to work. The localities where the police work may seem to them to have different values and even appear like foreign countries or strange lands. For police and community to relate as in the village is impossible. Since the urban residents often do not have a community to which they may relate then neither do the police, but of course there are exceptions to these general comments.

If the police cannot relate, save as an occupying force, the potential for misunderstanding and lack of co-operation is considerable and this can turn to hostility.

The police only come into contact when law is to be enforced. Stability is not maintained by a social contract between police and the policed, but by what appears to be outside coercion. Furthermore, the gulf between the parties can lead to police apathy and even occasional corruption. On the other hand, police in the city may themselves feel threatened by an environment which is hostile. This fear increases the need for solidarity between the police themselves and their collective ability to ensure their survival against the "other side". If the police and policed have few shared values, or the opportunity for non-conflict interaction on an individual and continuing basis, cultural sympathy and understanding are elusive. There is less opportunity than in the village for the public to transmit their hopes and aspirations to the police, and for the police to ease their own apprehensions. The prospect of the public defining or expecting a diverse service role and transmitting what they regard as "trivial" or "important" is reduced. In an authoritarian society this is not so important since the police would be expected to be authoritarian but in a permissive, free society the expectations are different.

The police are, within reason, expected to be responsive not only to the abstract legal values, but to the infinite and delicate range of social values as well. Cain, in the work already referred to, found that "neither the community nor the senior officers predominantly defined the policeman's role", but that this was largely done pragmatically by the officers themselves. This should not surprise anyone familiar with police work since, if uncorrected, it is in the nature of the work to seek its own level under given circumstances.

OFFICIALS AND VOLUNTEERS

But it is not only the police who "police" society. The whole range of official and unofficial organisations and groups affect the presence or absence of crime and delinquency. In a village they are not faceless officials or volunteers, but again are known individuals who can relate to the residents. They can envisage the needs of the community and in relating to them they learn sympathy and understanding for the hopes, fears and wishes of those whom they have to organise socially or to serve so that they may organise themselves. Again, in the city, the commuting official may not develop empathy but can leave behind the "foreign land" and return to the different values of his suburban dormitory. Those who remain and live amongst the community are left to cope, and often do. Religious leaders and volunteer committees, youth workers and so on have better understanding of the social and crime problems so often related. The National Youth Bureau in its evidence to the Royal Commission on Criminal Procedure stresses this point when it records:

> ... the Bureau notes with deep regret the fact that very few members of the Commission appear to have a specialised interest, knowledge or responsibility in connection with young people. In particular, it is felt that the absence from the Commission of any member who works in continuous contact with young people, and who is in a position to understand the meaning of their viewpoints and their experiences, is a serious deficiency in its composition.[5]

The village police and other officials, conversely, are often socially involved with the residents. Either as youth leaders or committee members, or in some such roles, they both control and serve the community. This is not to say that there are not many shades of grey in between these black and white assertions, but it is the *tendency* to these situations that has to be borne in mind.

Perhaps sufficient has been said at least to raise the question of whether or not it is desirable and possible, in the interests of superior policing, to transplant or create village characteristics within the city.

THE VILLAGE IN THE CITY

It is in the urban sprawl, and particularly the inner core of many cities, that policing problems tend to present themselves in acute forms. The seeming anonymity of modern estates in the suburbs and high-rise tower blocks in city centres appears to militate against concepts of communal policing or co-ordinated social action in some of crime's breeding grounds. Policing here is generally regarded as a matter entirely for the police themselves; but this would be to neglect the considerable scope for community action to check crime and the ability to reduce it.

There are, of course, many faces of a city—from outer suburb to inner city, from business area to enclaves of entertainment and shopping facilities. The city by day and the city by night also offer different characteristics and problems. The traffic rush hour, requiring maximum traffic police attention, turns into deserted commercial centres, or busy night life, and so on. In this great age of vociferous protest, the city centre becomes the platform and the scene of procession and demonstration. The city is like a kaleidoscope in the way that it presents differing and moving patterns of human activity, including of course crime and disorder. Violence is often near the surface in some parts, though as far removed from others as it is in a country town.

Thomas L. Blair in his book, *The International Urban Crisis,* describes the Janus-like city countenance where:

> The great metropolitan centres of population and wealth contain, on average, the richest, healthiest, best educated, housed and serviced people in the world. Their administrative, professional and business élites pride themselves on being innovators in a quick reacting, wide-open cultural system, and use the metropolis as a vast staging-ground for the mobilisation of manpower and the expansion of productive capital. But each new state of metropolitan development reveals grave and fundamental structural defects at all levels of society and tremendous problems of alienation and social conflict that grow in virulence with quickening tempo of change.[6]

The picture of the city as described by Blair in this passage indicates where the seeds of conflict lie, and shows that the juxtaposition of goods, wealth and poverty in the city gives rise to the criminal entrepreneur.

The police have no part in the creation and development of the city and yet the germs of petty delinquency, serious crime and violent behaviour are all problems for police to control. This state of affairs places the police in a disadvantaged position, which is neither in their own interest, nor in the interest of the city administration. Since the police have an unrivalled view of crime, its causes and manifestations, it is highly important that city administration should have access to, and use for, police information of this kind. The police might be expected, in a sense, to develop a fairly dynamic and positive approach to influence city planning and reconstruction. This has taken place where new cities have been developed in recent times, notably with the Thames Valley Police at Milton Keynes.

The problems of the older cities are of course profound and cannot be treated lightly but attempts to find ways out of the existing tensions and hopelessness of run-down areas on the one hand and the fears and apprehensions of the more orderly areas on the other might be considered. One such strategy might be that of "the village in the city" (*see* Appendix 6).

The village it seems can be of help to the city in setting a model of social organisation. This kind of social strategy would obviously not be suitable for centres of commerce and entertainment, but would be well suited to the residential and suburban enclaves. In most city areas, there are tightly-knit communities in existence which would lend themselves to a resurgence of village organisation. There are others more loosely-knit which could be drawn together, and there are those where little or no social identity exists and where a good deal of effort would be needed to create any kind of unity.

Since most people who live in cities, whether well-to-do or not, are on occasions victims of fear and apprehension, if not of crime itself, and since all are potential victims, there is likely to be considerable interest in neighbourhood activity designed to reduce crime.

The city village might well begin to form an identity where local communications exist. Local newspapers, radio or even television such as in Greenwich, London, can soon stimulate mutual interest and concern. But the most potent jolt to "village" consciousness comes from a demographic survey of local crime and its public propagation. Where the police illustrate neighbourhood crimes and crime patterns on view-foil maps at public meetings, two reactions may be expected. Either the crime exceeds common opinion and agitation is increased, or if it falls short of common reputation there is feeling of relief, both of which the police might take up to stimulate action. Whichever it is, the village in the city has taken the first and important step of getting to know its own crime. This new awareness can then be used as a means to the creation of schemes and action for the prevention of crime through social co-operation. At this juncture, other agencies are likely to become interested.

The local school staff, social services, probation officers, magistrates, youth, housing and planning officers can become involved and further the movement towards social identity, as well as participating in joint schemes for the prevention of crime. The police may well have to play their vital early leadership role; but there is no reason why others should not do this, provided that the police are prepared to put their knowledge at the village community's disposal. A city able to develop and proliferate patterns of village activity would be likely to become a happier and safer place. It is, however, important that the *residents* should be active, for the statutory agencies are apt to stifle community initiative through professional (and sometimes misplaced) zeal.

In many cities, there still remain enclaves of former villages, and there are neighbourhoods of one kind or another with much in common in cultural terms. On the other hand there are tracts of anonymous estates and high-rise tower blocks where the paradox of isolation in a crowd characterises life. The sympathetic association which characterises community life rarely exists there. Communities in cities have either disintegrated spontaneously, or have been destroyed by new buildings and modern planning notions, whereas, in the past, many of these communities had a sufficient cohesion for people to relate to one another in mutual support. The Isle of Dogs in London's East End is a good example.

But with the brave new welfare state and nuclear life styles, the State itself has become the provider. Community care has nothing to do with the community. In cities there is often apathy towards community affairs, though there are exceptions. An echo from the inner city was reported in *The Times* in June 1978 when a Mr. Kelly of Spitalfields was interviewed and was reported as saying:

> In a way too much money is being spent in Spitalfields on useless things. We have social workers and others pulling this way and that. But we really need less money and more encouragement to do things ourselves. For one thing we would like to build parks and plant trees. Somehow someone has to have the imagination to give us some hope.

SURVEYING COMMUNITIES

To give inner city residents in deprived centres particularly "some hope" fits in well with the concept of the village in the city. The idea would be firstly to carry out numerous surveys to identify existing communities where community spirit is noticeable; secondly to identify quasi-communities where there are remnants of communities but where there is a need for stimulus (these areas will be remains of the old parishes where church, school, pubs and council offices used to denote community); thirdly to identify areas where ethnic minorities are concentrated and where new communities could be established; fourthly the polyglot areas where there are people but no sense, no hope, no remnant of community. These are usually the twilight areas around railway termini or the decayed areas awaiting demolition, and so on. It will be necessary for projected communities to be small enough in size for people to relate to them, perhaps as small as the beat of one community constable.

Having plotted possible, viable and non-communities, the next stage would be the production of graphic presentations of the results of a demographic survey of crimes and criminality within that community. The object of the survey is to produce pictorial evidence of the state of crime within the area and its relation to other aspects of social organisation. Help is needed here from agencies other than the police. Social services, probation, youth, housing and planning officers, can all find an interest for themselves in this exercise. The juxtaposition of crimes and amenities will reveal much and can act as the community's catalyst for action.

Calling a public meeting within a defined community to illustrate pictorially the neighbourhood's demography on crime and related matters is a salutary experience. It can electrify the community and can produce hostility too. Nevertheless, it is in keeping with the free permissive and participatory characteristics of modern society that inhabitants should be asked to face up to the condition of crime. Some areas will find relief in the paucity of crimes, others in the nature of it, others will demand action from a variety of agencies to reduce the prospects of juvenile crime and so on. The dialogue has begun, the community, the quasi-community or just the neighbourhood has taken a step towards creating the village in the city. Much energy, leadership and activity are required to keep this early and sometimes minimal interest alive. The press and the other media can help considerably. Schools can become involved by inviting police in to explain their purpose and aims.

Since the village in the city is for the purpose of preventing crime and delinquency problems, it will have no resources other than those provided by local government and by charities. It does not need resources much beyond those already available, but the most important resource is the residents. The residents will be asked to form a Community Policing Advisory Group with its own terms of reference. This is an important stage.

At this juncture, it may be helpful to summarise the necessary action.

1. Police initiate action to identify possible "villages".

2. Police set up a small group to analyse crimes and other social phenomena within the village.

The Group's terms of reference are as follows.

1. To examine selected areas with a view to identifying crime and relevant community problems.

2. To devise crime prevention initiatives and encourage interest in them.

3. To encourage and direct police resources towards the prevention of crime.

4. To activate public interest and participation in the creation of good citizenship and community awareness thereby helping to control crime.

Police will need to penetrate the community in all its aspects and develop personal relationships at beat level. Co-operation between police, social workers and probation officers should now begin. Community links with the police, probation and social services should now be fostered. Schools, particularly those with delinquency problems, should be asked to increase co-operation. Parent/teacher associations should be informed and involved.

In community policing (and that is the term to be used henceforth in describing this action in the village in the city) there can be no set pattern, no blueprint. Communities are organic and will develop in different ways. Flexibility and the need to experiment will be paramount. This exercise is based not on resources but on ideas. The community must be involved. To encourage self-help and increase the feeling of security through growth of care and the lowering of neighbourhood tensions, and to capitalise on existing social organisations to achieve these aims, is the concept. Police have to lead and thus they have to become socially-orientated and in sympathy with their embryonic villages. All are out to contain delinquency and reduce it through proactive community organisation.

If the community is to become committed in a sustained form, some shape must be given to its obligations. This begins with the Community Police Consultative Group. Press, education, transport, highways, health, social security, employment, magistrates, licensed victuallers, councillors of all parties, churches, trade unions, chamber of trade etc. are all eligible to serve on the Group's main body. This has no power resources of its own, nor does it need any. Its role is persuasive only and to encourage co-operative effort in community affairs. In order to get things done the Group requires a small steering committee with the following terms of reference.

1. To provide a forum for considering ways in which to reduce crime by social as well as by legal action and for sharing ideas and initiatives.

2. To identify community needs and to formulate possible action through a combined agency approach and to report where necessary to parent bodies.

3. To make best use of joint resources.

4. To stimulate, review, support and monitor local community initiatives.

194

5. To determine joint agency training programmes.

This small steering group might comprise police, probation, social services, health, community volunteers, planning, housing, youth and leisure.

Through these devices the community will begin to see its own form and be strengthened by its image. Co-operation between the many social agencies will be advanced and the community will benefit. Sharing of knowledge, expertise and resources, and discussion before policy-making, are all benefits to be gained. Experience will show how crime and delinquency can be affected and reduced or minimised by joint action of this kind. The community policing plan should be buttressed by a good Victims' Support Scheme, since in this way not only are victims helped but the community is drawn further into the self-help role. Victims' support schemes require only that police co-operate by identifying victims and notifying their needs to a volunteer body who provide support of the human kind.

Having embarked on this form of social action to reduce crime, fear, tension and apathy or defeatism, the potential for its growth and purpose is only limited by the scope of imagination. If social organisation is community, then the reduction of crime through better social organisation is community action at its best. The village in the city may even increase fraternity. At all events, community policing is a viable concept.

LEGAL LONG STOPS

If the village in the city is designed to disperse crimogenic social conditions the police will still have to face up to crime and its many challenges. In this sense the police are the legal long stops. With the accent on preventive policing, the future role of the police in a free, permissive society is seen as primarily one of caring, informing, persuading and generally enforcing their way towards a semblance of "orderly disorder". The police are not to see the law as an end in itself but as a means to an end. But, when all has been said about the prevention of crime, there has to be an enforcement of laws in keeping with the times. Crimes in the future are likely to concentrate on new forms of antisocial behaviour as well as the traditional crimes concerned with violence and theft. Now that private morality is hardly any business of the criminal law, offences concerning pollution of the environment and undue damage to nature's balance will become of greater concern and indicate the continuing shift in society's values.

NOTES

1. Peter Calvocoressi, *The British Experience 1945–1975* (The Bodley Head 1978), Part 4, D.
2. Ralf Dahrendorf, *The New Liberty* (Routledge & Kegan Paul 1975), Chap. 2.
3. Ibid., Chap. 6.
4. Maureen E. Cain, *Society and the Policeman's Role* (Routledge & Kegan Paul 1973), Chap. 2.
5. *Young People and the Police* (The National Youth Bureau 1979), Chap. 1.
6. T. L. Blair, *The International Urban Crisis* (Hart-Davis 1974).

Chapter 29

A new model police

It should be understood at the outset that any model of police designed to fit a free, permissive and participatory society cannot, and should not, be limited to the police alone. By this is meant that the reduction of levels of criminality requires not only legal action and enforcement, but proactive elements as well.

TO DIMINISH CRIME

Police leadership however will count for much and a police force will have to be designed to be able to activate the latent energies and powerful good in identifiable communities, which, in going towards the diminution of levels of crime, will proportionately diminish the need of the police to activate the system of criminal justice. Since it has been argued that criminal justice alone cannot and will not be able to deal with all but a small proportion of offenders, since most offenders are never discovered, a superior police system will need to acknowledge the ethical and utilitarian advantages of proactive measures in the prevention of crime. Policing a future society is very much a matter for society itself.

Thus, instead of freedom bringing an absence or diminution of responsibility to the individual, it requires precisely the opposite. The more freedom that people claim, and rightly claim, the more they should be prepared to accept the concomitant responsibilities. Therefore, policing freedom requires an activation of the sense of civic responsibility in individuals in order to achieve a diminution of police activity to enforce the criminal law. Not only of course is this ethically superior but it is economic sense to develop self-policing rather than rely too heavily on expensive reactive and post-crime measures.

BEGINNING WITH PRINCIPLES

The first step in pursuit of a new model police is to address oneself to the problem of objectives.

The primary objects of an efficient police were first laid down by

Sir Robert Peel on the foundation of the Metropolitan Police in 1829. Peel said: "It should be understood at the outset that the principal object to be attained is the prevention of crime." At that stage of course there was no question of a criminal investigation department, nor of a traffic department. The police were there solely to prevent crime by foot patrols in dense urban areas. The modified objects as expressed in the *Metropolitan Police Instruction Book* are as follows.

Primary Object of Police—The primary object of an efficient police is the prevention of crime; the next that of detection and punishment of offenders if crime is committed. To these ends all the efforts of police must be directed. The protection of life and property, the preservation of public tranquillity, and the absence of crime, will alone prove whether those efforts have been successful, and whether the objects for which the police were appointed have been attained.

Although the prevention of crime remains the primary police responsibility, it will be readily seen that objectives laid down for more rudimentary and primitive police systems leave much to be desired as we approach the twenty-first century. The Royal Commission on the Police, in their report in 1962, addressed their minds to the purposes of the police, and thought that basically their task is the maintenance of the Queen's Peace—that is the preservation of law and order. But this generalisation does not take us very far, since it fails to point in particular directions. Acknowledging that:

the policeman works in a changing society, there is nothing constant about the range and variety of police duties, just as there is nothing constant about the pattern of crime, the behaviour of criminals, the state of public order, or at deeper levels the hidden trends in society that dispose men to crime, to civil and industrial unrest or to political demonstration. The emphasis on particular duties varies from one generation to another.

The main functions of the police were summarised as follows.

1. The police have a duty to maintain law and order to protect persons and property.

2. They have a duty to prevent crime.

3. They are responsible for the detection of criminals and, in the course of interrogating suspected persons, they have a part to play in the early stages of judicial process, acting under judicial restraint.

4. The police in England and Wales (but not in Scotland) have the responsibility of deciding whether or not to prosecute persons suspected of criminal offences. (The Director of Public Prosecutions decides in certain cases.)

5. In England and Wales (but not in Scotland) the police themselves conduct many prosecutions for the less serious offences.

6. The police have the duty of controlling road traffic and advising local authorities on traffic questions.

7. The police carry out certain duties on behalf of government departments—for example, they conduct enquiries into applications made by persons who wish to be granted British nationality.

8. They have by long tradition a duty to befriend anyone who needs their help, and they may at any time be called upon to cope with minor or major emergencies.

To express the objectives of the police system in such a particular way as the Royal Commission did tends to encourage ossification or, to put it another way, does not encourage evolution of police contributions to the change around them. Police objectives need to be expressed in principles which allow for growth, both of the police themselves in their own professional contribution and of public awareness; since it has already been stated that a future police system, at least in a democratic society, can only be meaningful in the context of joint police community activity. The first thing, therefore, that needs to be done is the restating of objectives.

RESTATING OBJECTIVES

The objectives of a police system for the future in a free, permissive and participatory society should be as follows.

1. To contribute towards liberty, equality and fraternity in human affairs.

2. To help reconcile freedom with security and to uphold the rule of law.

3. To facilitate the achievement of human dignity through upholding and protecting human rights and the pursuit of happiness.

4. To provide leadership and participate in dispelling crimogenic social conditions through co-operative social action.

5. To contribute towards the creation or reinforcement of trust in communities.

6. To strengthen the security and the feeling of security of persons and property.

7. To investigate, detect and activate the prosecution of offences within the rule of law.

8. To facilitate free passage and movement on highways and roads, streets and avenues, of public passage.

9. To curb public disorder.

10. To deal with major and minor crises and to help and advise those in distress, where necessary activating other agencies.

LIBERTY, EQUALITY AND FRATERNITY

The police contribution towards concepts of liberty are of paramount importance, since without proper police of a superior kind, liberty for many would not exist. By the meaning of liberty of course one means freedom to exercise one's rights without let or hindrance, provided that the rights of other people are not invaded.

Police in inferior systems represent one of the main threats against liberty. So far as equality is concerned the police have a paramount ethical and legal duty to ensure that enforcement or non-enforcement of the law is carried out impartially and equally without regard for social standing, race, creed, religion, colour or class. Police in superior systems will understand this and act accordingly, but inferior police will be partial and show favouritism towards those of influence, either political or social or even economic, and will neglect the less able and less influential and certainly the people at the bottom of the pile. Fraternity in human affairs can be helped considerably by the police in the way that they deport themselves and propagate concepts of self-policing through their educational involvement and through their public actions and pronouncements.

FREEDOM AND SECURITY RECONCILED

To help reconcile freedom with security has been the great challenge to government throughout recorded history. It was argued earlier that the desire for freedom and security are the two great human hopes since they go towards the purpose of life, happiness and those police systems capable of bringing about a balance within the rule of law will be the more triumphant. The rule of law itself should be seen to be in one sense a fragile thing. The legislature should be aware that pressing legal issues too far against the public will result in the rule of law being damaged through popular resistance towards law and the police.

This was exemplified during the discontent in trade union circles following the Industrial Relations Act of 1971 when mass disobedience to the picketing restrictions brought about a national crisis. The police, however, have a duty to uphold the law as long as is humanly possible; but they also have a duty to advise governments of the limitations of the rule of law in practical affairs. This is not to fail to recognise that the concept of the rule of law is the *sine qua non* of democratic societies.

PURSUIT OF HAPPINESS

As people reach out for more freedom and justice the concern for human rights, human dignity and the pursuit of happiness will grow. These are amongst the highest goals of mankind and the superior police system will be capable of understanding these great human instincts and of assisting their attainment. Above all, the police have a moral responsibility to avoid degrading people and taking away their dignity. In helping people in the pursuit of happiness, police should not lose sight of the fact that restraints on some persons are essential if the mass of people are to achieve a greater happiness.

POLICE LEADERSHIP

Since communities will be involved in the reduction of the levels of delinquency the police will be required to provide leadership and to participate in helping communities to dispel social conditions giving rise to crime. One cannot sufficiently emphasise that the seedbeds of crime have to be tackled through preventive measures, and this is one of the main requirements of a modern police system. The bringing together in communal and fraternal activity of the latent social energies and resources, to reduce crime, is likely to provide a new police with their greatest challenge.

REDUCING FEAR AND TENSION

One of the paramount aims of a modern police system is the reduction of fear and of tension in communities and neighbourhoods. People who are afraid of being victimised by crime are indeed victims of crime. Sometimes inferior police systems generate fear in people, as a means of control or as a means of acquiring greater resources, but this is immoral and stands to be condemned. In providing security for persons and property a superior police system, if faced with defining priorities will put persons before property and will put poor and inadequate persons before the property of the more well-to-do. This is not because the police should take up particular positions, but because the moral/ethical principles of their work demand that the security of persons is put before that of property. This is not to say that the security of property is not of great importance, and police should strain all their resources to reconcile these difficult choices.

PRINCIPLES OF INVESTIGATION

During the investigation of crime superior police will act within the law and the rules laid down for their guidance. It is offensive to the notion of superior police that illegal practices should be justified by the results. The end can never justify the means if they are offensive to civilised instincts or are illegal. Superior police must seek new definitions of laws and the extra powers necessary for discharging their duties efficiently. If the legislature refuse to grant such powers then the police have to make it abundantly clear that their efficiency will be reduced. These decisions are outside the scope of the police who have to perform their duties under the conditions existing and not under the conditions they would like to exist.

In detecting crime all the scientific aids available should, and no doubt will, be put to use by the police. There are, however, devices which in the superior systems are unacceptable. The polygraph or lie-detector is an example of this. The use of such things as truth drugs and hypnosis, disorientation, abuse, torture and deprivation are offensive to the civilised notions and unacceptable within the practices of a superior police system. In seeking to activate the system of criminal justice through prosecution the police, in all but the most minor cases, will seek independent legal opinion or refer to the appropriate prosecution authority.

FREEDOM TO PASS

It is essential that the police should continue to discharge the task of facilitating free passage and movement on the highways, roads and streets and other avenues. It is often argued that such duties could be delegated to a different organisation, such as a traffic corps, but this solution is considered to be an inferior one. It is inferior since crime and the motor vehicle, crime and the highways, crime and the use of streets are inseparable. Therefore to open up a gulf between criminal police and traffic police would not make for efficiency, even if it made for expediency and convenience.

FREEDOM TO PROTEST

The subject of public order in a free, permissive, and participatory society requires that great allowance should be made for freedom of speech, of expression and of protest generally. The police should not be used to put down freedom of expression or protest but merely to facilitate it within the law. There are times, however, when in order to preserve order the police will have to educate the public through the media and other organs of communication as to the desirability of the curbing of protest from time to time. It is essential that this should be understood in a plural and multiracial society since what might be inoffensive in a homogeneous society can be extremely offensive in a heterogeneous society.

202

It is not only a question of law: custom, religion, tradition and beliefs are so varied, and so sincerely and profoundly believed in, that to permit excessive freedom of protest would be inimical to the general interest and must be curbed. There is no doubt that in a future society the question of protest will remain popular, particularly in view of the existence of television. Thus to protest in an international capital in one country is to flash a message round the world within seconds. This availability is too attractive for activists not to use. The police, therefore, in a future society, should expect more use to be made of protest mechanisms.

THE LAST FRIEND

The police have built up over the years a reputation for accepting the responsibility for major and minor crises and in many cases providing the main resource. In a future society, where many people will work for shorter time and will need things to do, the concept of voluntary bodies will need to be developed further. Voluntary emergency services should be given every encouragement though they will need to be under official control to avoid misunderstanding and aggravation. It is under the principle or objective of offering help and advice to persons in distress or in need of advice that the police have great opportunities for development.

The advent and availability of mechanical recording on computers and better communications networks means that the police can store items of public information which they could make available to members of the public on request. But the police could also act as a link between other agencies and those requiring their services. Again, voluntary bodies such as guidance councils, consumer councils, advisory bureaux and so on, can all be linked into the same network, so that by dialling one number a member of the public could find access to every part of the system.

These, then, are the objectives of a superior futuristic police force operating in a free, permissive and participatory society. It now remains to look at the police themselves as an organisation.

NEW ORGANISATION

The organisation of police in the future will have to take account of a number of emerging truths. In the first place, policing in the future will be a combined operation between the police, other statutory agencies, voluntary bodies and the general public. Policing will have to take account of the fact that greater participation by those affected by the making of policies and their execution will be inevitable. The free-ranging democratic society, with myriads of small communities all wanting to be involved in the control of their own destinies, will require shortening of hierarchical chains of command. As concepts of criminal justice become overtaken by social change and attitude, excessive reliance on such systems for social control will have to give way to informal arrangements. Therefore, a police organisation of the future will not set its own goals alone or have them set totally by Parliament or government, but will have its goals set in part by those who are on the receiving end of police policies, or at least by a combination of local and official thinking.

PREVENTIVE POLICING DEPARTMENT

The police therefore will require a preventive policing department headed by an assistant chief constable. This department, as the title suggests, will be responsible for helping the community to police itself. The department will require a battery of initiatives with which to discharge its task. The discharge of the task will begin with the establishment of a network of community police officers with a wide-ranging brief for discretion and initiative. The role will go beyond that of the traditional "village bobby" but will embody the spirit of that tradition within it.

The community constable will be a high status officer. Around him will revolve the community's informal organisations, using their own ideas, imagination and energies for making their community more secure, less delinquency-prone and, a happier place in which to live. Co-operation with other workers in the area will be of the utmost importance for the sharing of knowledge, understanding and information. The department will need to supply an advisory service available to communities, in particular their action groups, in order that they can help themselves in the care of their youth, their incompetent families and in leisure pursuits. This will be in addition to the emergency service to be provided by the emergency department.

LEISURE POLICE

Since a large proportion of the future society will be in part-time employment only, there will need to be a branch of leisure police responsible for liaison in the management of leisure facilities. For example, in a future society on a crowded island, amenities such as the Lake District, Dartmoor or Snowdonia would be in danger of being overcrowded, and it may be necessary to ration access to such leisure pursuits, inevitably involving some policing function.

204

CHILD PROTECTION

Since the police are responsible for securing human rights the manifestation of police concern will inevitably require expansion of children's departments. The right to more freedom from cruelty and excessive authoritarianism (but not from proper discipline), will require the police to develop greater skills and understanding in this entire field. It will be necessary to be able to work with the medical, education and other professions in the pursuit of safeguards for children.

EDUCATIONAL SUPPORT

The input to education from the police will need to be stepped up, since in a popular democracy people will demand that the police explain themselves. The police will need to develop this ability in the schools and in public meetings and classrooms in institutes of further education and higher education. This will require a continuing and questioning dialogue and the police will need to develop the ability to stand up to these demands. It will not be acceptable to retire behind the traditional barricades of police mythology.

ENVIRONMENTAL CONCERN

Under the preventive department will come a police environmental branch or section, concerned with the prevention of pollution and destruction of the environment. In the main this will be concerned with co-ordinating activities and controlling volunteer groups to police the environment. This department can be expected to develop new ideas for the prevention of unacceptable human behaviour through influence rather than through coercion or repression.

PUBLIC ORDER

The public order police department will need to retain the ability to apply force as at the present time and to develop skills concerned with the management of public attitudes towards disorder. An upsurge of popular condemnation of violence should be striven for, to the point where undue violence becomes socially unacceptable and disabling in the sense that the privileges of citizenship should be withdrawn from those who use such excessive violence. Since more people will have more leisure and more time to consider these things, the public order police will require to hold public meetings to discuss the issues involved in policing protest, demonstration and hooliganism. In this way, they will be capable of generating popular democratic sentiments conducive to an easy control of public order, and one less charged with violence, counter-violence and the inevitable escalation towards further police use of technological means for disabling protesters.

Sometimes the demeanour of the police is determined, not by their own wishes in the matter, but in the type of public they have to police or by the nature of the laws which they have to enforce. Violent societies get violent police forces eventually, it is true, and if in addition the police role is to suppress resistance to legislation which is widely unpopular the high road to civil disorder is opened up. The rule of law has its breaking-point and it is not wise for the legislature to place it and its upholders under too great a strain. The debate on these issues is of prime importance to us all.

If the public are to help the police to avoid the escalating violence of public protest, some steps towards a programme of public education would provide a useful beginning. The following seven suggestions may help in this direction.

1. A campaign of public information concerning the democratic nature of our police and the danger which undue politically-inspired violence poses to the continuance of its passive role. The political education of our youth should stress this element.

2. Leaders of public opinion should speak out without equivocation and condemn the resort to violence for political or sectarian purposes.

3. Undue violence by the police should not be tolerated and the principle of minimum force should be adhered to.

4. Police manpower resources should be increased sufficiently to allow the proactive and preventive work among neighbourhoods to be strengthened and to flourish, particularly among the disaffected and underprivileged.

5. A halt should be called to the creation of bigger police forces and every effort made instead to involve local communities in police affairs. This would rule out the creation of regional forces.

6. Serious and gratuitous assaults on unarmed police in the execution of their public order duties should be the subject of condign punishment, to avoid any drift towards riot police which could, otherwise, become the only alternative.

7. The police should not be expected to provide force as a substitute for the solution of social problems and current tentative hints of the "politicisation" of the police and criminal justice should continue to be firmly put down.

FREEING THE C.I.D.

The detective police department will require to be liberated from its bureaucratic crippling burden of paperwork. If this is not done detectives will continue to spend more and more time writing about crime instead of detecting it by enquiry. This is an abuse of their skills and their proper function. The detective department therefore will require considerable back-up in the way of legal clerks and advisers, so that their time is spent in pursuit of proof, and balance is thereby restored to their function. The use of computer storage for criminal intelligence will continue to be a sensitive issue but the public will insist on watchdog bodies, not to seek knowledge of particular information but to be able to reach an understanding of the *kind* of information which the police are assembling for this purpose.

As technology becomes more powerful and people feel more threatened by it, the detective department will need to conduct its own public educational programmes explaining the nature of crime, the nature of detective work and the limitations placed upon the function by law, custom and civilised standards. Once the technical difficulties are overcome there will be further demand for interrogation procedures to be conducted with audio-visual records. When this comes about the whole technique of interrogation will need to be reassessed and account taken of the skills required to achieve the aims of interrogation whilst under scrutiny from camera and microphone. This will not deter the best detectives, since through their own skills and appeal to fairness, justice and the public good, they will commend themselves to the public and surprise them by the high quality of their work. This will not so much create problems for the police, as relieve them of some of the existing burdens of suspicion, hostility and lack of public co-operation. When this comes about, there will be a gradual drift from the present system of justice, particularly in minor cases, to more informal enquiries and disposals.

When suspect, accuser and witnesses can be brought together with lawyers on both sides before cameras and microphones, the possibilities for instant hearings, where appropriate, will have arrived. The press will be able to monitor such proceedings and report on them and the record of film and tape will be available for any appeals and administrative procedures. The taking of evidence by audio-visual teletransmission will become acceptable to save travelling, and such procedures will merely follow the familiar down-the-line interview on television as presently practised.

Micro-processing and storage will enable courts to have access to documentary evidence, statements and other written evidence without the need to produce bundles of paper. When technology begins to move into the field of criminal procedure there could be considerable benefits for the detective and perhaps for justice itself.

TECHNOLOGY AND TRAFFIC

Traffic policing will rely more and more on electronic control and co-ordinated visual facilities. The requirement to have radio in every car capable of receiving police information, which would be a rather more sophisticated version of the present B.B.C. traffic reports, would facilitate orderly and safe control of traffic. Transmission of information concerning detours, weather conditions, hold-ups and so on would be extended to every car under the construction of new regulations.

In this way most traffic policing could be done by remote control and even excessive speeding could be monitored by camera, tachograph and similar devices. The offender would then receive notification and the printout of his alleged speed. If in agreement, he could then pay his fine without contesting the issue. As traffic policing becomes more and more electronic and technological the present mobile traffic units would take on much more of a helping role and advisory programme. In a popular democracy it will not be acceptable to rely on the maxim that ignorance of the law is no excuse. The police will need to educate the motoring public and to appear as helpers and advisers through a whole process of public relations education and concern for road safety.

INFORMATION SYSTEMS

The emergency response police will need to be deployed much less on a random *ad hoc* basis and more on a predictive course stemming from operational information systems. The concept of prowling around in cars by instinct rather than by an information-based system is wasteful, and will not be in keeping with the need to make the maximum use of scarce resources. In communities, it should be possible to maintain a community/communications link with responsive police in that community. Community-policing consultative groups, through their nominated representatives, will be able to make their own contribution to establishing communications with the police for emergency assistance, and in this way bring the community into closer participation in police activities.

Police communications themselves will need to take advantage of satellite communication as soon as technology produces a version which is sufficiently cheap.

DEMOGRAPHY, HUMAN AFFAIRS AND PSYCHOLOGY

Other developments which will need to be considered will be Demographic Sections capable of measuring social change impinging upon crime and offences generally. They will measure such things as the transient nature of some communities, the elements of stability in communities, and acquire social information of this kind in order to advise the community concerned on how better to cope with its social and communal problems.

It will need to develop a Technology and Human Affairs Section in order that the impact of technology on police officers and individuals and upon their work can be monitored, explained and assisted. There is little doubt that the speed of change in technology will severely affect the ability of police officers to understand its nature and its use. The behavioural factors stemming from such change will be disorientating and could build up resistance towards its use.

Closely allied to this section will need to be a Psychology Section capable of making an input into training as well as operational affairs. The use of psychological advice at the scenes of terrorist incidents has already indicated the potential for the use of psychology dealing with criminal investigation and the control of incidents. The psychology of crowds, the psychology of petty thieves and those with psychopathic tendencies, if better understood by the police, would enable a higher degree of efficiency to result from their work.

FUTURES

Future police forces will need what might be called Futures Sections. This will be not so much forward planning as forward thinking. The need to think ahead and to produce ideas for the planners to test and experiment with will be important. Since resources will fail to expand, the need for ideas will become paramount. In this section, of a "think-tank" nature, would need to be a mixture of police and people from other disciplines, as well as interested members of the community, who would take part in discussions by invitation; this would include, where appropriate, the press, for dissemination of information about the police.

Since future police will very much depend on the participation of communities it will be essential for the police to develop a Force Information and Communication Section. This section will grow in importance and become central to the main administration of a force. Through its officers on the ground and at the centre it will be in close touch with what the public need and want to know. Its relationships with the media would need to be made closer and the media used appropriately and properly to achieve the police purpose. But it will need to go beyond that and be capable of supplying information to communities themselves and interpreting police activity of one kind or another. Such a section will need to be able to produce literature, audio and visual tapes, and to arrange conferences.

In this new kind of approach to the police function in a popular democracy there will need to be a constant questioning of goals and a constant reappraisal of public desires and needs.

NEW INTERNAL ARRANGEMENTS

While the police will be called upon to make considerable adjustments to their role, to their styles and to their thinking, the internal arrangements for police forces will obviously need to come under reappraisal.

DECISION-MAKING

In the first place participation in decision-making processes will need to be increased (*see* Appendix 7). The policy-making will need to include a growing input from all levels of the organisation, both severally and jointly. Thus police of various functions, rather than ranks, would need to be represented, together with the civil staff on a functional basis, and members of communities where appropriate. It will be of extreme importance to devise systems to fit people, rather than the other way round. Policy-makers will have to study people rather than systems and, having acquired their knowledge, then devise systems to fit people.

Although participation of this kind may appear, on the face of it, to be likely to slow down policy-making, issues will have to be narrowed considerably and based on continuing dialogue rather than on occasional meetings. Since the police hierarchy will allow greater delegation of authority to flow to community police, many officers in the middle ranks will need to be redeployed in staff as opposed to line functions. This will mean that officers of inspector and chief inspector rank would be task-orientated and given particular jobs to do, requiring a higher quality of understanding. For example, a chief inspector with ten communities in his area could be responsible for securing the flow of information about ideas between communities and developing inter-community understandings and, in general, having an information role rather than supervising sergeants and constables on a day-to-day basis. The constables and their leaders, the sergeants, will be capable of doing most of their work on their own initiative.

Within the internal arrangements there will need to be administrative task forces. Instead of total adherence to the present system of lengthy negotiations and protracted arguments with the Home Office for the formation of rigid police administration establishments, the creation of administrative task forces with fluidity of function would be more in keeping with the proper use of scarce resources. Instead of creating rigid departmental systems, this course would fit more closely to a quickly changing situation.

NEW EXTERNAL RELATIONS

So much has been said about the need for the police of the future to become part of communities and for communities themselves to become part of the police that there is little to be added on the question of external relations. It remains to stress, however, that the social contract between the police and the policed will require considerably greater awareness on the part of the police, that they have to tell the public much more than they do at present and that, in its turn, the public will have to be trained or educated to see the policing of their community as very much a part of their responsibility as well. This will require continuing dialogues through meetings, exercises and joint participation in schemes of a social or morally constructive nature. The relations between the police and the public in a popular democracy are quite different from those in a hierarchical or authoritarian democracy. The demarcations between sections of communities and between professional officers are obviously much less clear in the former case than in the latter, and this will demand considerable adjustment of police attitudes. (*See* Appendix 8 for a Community Telephone Scheme.)

NEW POLICE OFFICERS

Police officers of a future police force, charged with the task of discharging the objectives of a police system in a free, permissive and participatory society as set out earlier in the text, will need to be people with considerable ability, adaptability and sensitivity.

If they are to police what Ralf Dahrendorf has described as a new type of liberty, in which he sees a society of people turning away from remote concepts of progress in the material sense and entering into fresh life-styles, hopes, attitudes and expectations, they will need to be much more socially aware than the present kind of legally-orientated officer. In a society where those things we have come to take for granted become more difficult to obtain, there would need to be a great need for leadership of a non-political, non-sectarian kind, and this would undoubtedly involve the police.

NEW TRAINING

If the police are to play an expanding role at least in quality, the training of officers as it stands today will need to be questioned at most levels. There is of course one vital pre-condition to any raising of levels of learning and understanding in police and that is in the recruitment of young men and women with the necessary academic achievement and learning potential.

In a ruthless authoritarian regime the police task of being merely repressive would appeal to different types of person than those we are accustomed to recruiting today. Being more like an occupying army than a democratic type British police force, the officers in an authoritarian regime would require training that follows military lines; police would be separated from the community, and deliberately so. That kind of police style would probably require officer élites and non-commissioned officers and men, as in the army.

The high standard of learning potential required by the future, and indeed the present superior democratic police, is almost completely of a different nature. Since, in the future, forces are unlikely to expand at any great pace, the accent will have to be on quality rather than quantity. Tasks not requiring the high quality of constables' ability will need to be delegated to auxiliaries. The present probationer training system would have to be scrapped almost entirely and redesigned to fit the needs of future police. In spite of recent improvement the present system would be incapable of developing the intellectual potential and practical ability needed by the community leader constable. Basic training would need to concentrate on a deeper study of society, on people and on human behaviour generally. The changing nature of the plural society, the demand for greater liberty, the need for greater security, the concern for human dignity and human rights, would all need to be highlighted in the basic training of a future constable. The legally-orientated training of today would take its proper place as only one of the many tools at the disposal of the community leader constable. The concept of teaching a number of situations and providing the constable with a drill-like response bears the marks of the nineteenth-century approach by the instruction book. Human behaviour being so unpredictable and infinite in its diversity calls for, and will call for, a qualitative kind of training to fit the constable, in the exercise of his manifold discretion, to provide high quality judgment and accurate service in the most complicated situations.

If constables are to avoid being perplexed by an inability to understand the apparent irrationality of behaviour stemming from modern social conditions, which causes, consequently, a drop in morale, they must be trained to cope with change, since the only permanence will be change itself. By A.D. 2000 this syndrome will be intensified and basic police training will need to be revolutionised to enable officers to cope. The police cannot rely on bigger and better battalions of shock troops, but will need all the intellectual power they can muster to cope with the challenges through improvement without expansion and by frequent proactive police measures (and not by permanent reaction).

Above all they will have to consider the impermanence of things, which is a difficult thing for police to do since they stand for stability and the protection of the *status quo*. The considerable increase in assaults on police may possibly arise from despair of change and an inability to understand and to cope with the tensions produced by modern society. The constable in uniform is often a scapegoat for a frustrated society, but by taking the debate *to* society the constable will strengthen his own security, since the public will be around him and not against him.

SENIOR OFFICERS

If the demands of the training of constables of the future will require radical reform, the needs of senior officers will call for the same urgent consideration. In an authoritarian world where hierarchies and bureaucracies are to be strengthened and no doubt lengthened, there is comfort for senior officers in the seeming permanence of things and the ability of the hierarchy to absorb pressures without disturbing itself too much. In the popular democratic communities of tomorrow, the concept of the hierarchy itself is thrown into question. The cramping of many written orders and instructions will already have given way to individual initiative, made possible by the superior intelligence and training of constables. The manager or leader enters the world of permanent reorganisation, and if not prepared for it will suffer from constant disorientation.

This kind of thing is already happening and many are finding it difficult to comprehend. There is even discernible reaction in the middle ranks of the police service both to change and to new ideas which they find disturbing and unsettling. The leader in the future therefore must no longer regard the serving of a long apprenticeship and a comforting mastery of the issues as if they are a qualification, but rather as a disqualification, since he will require great flexibility of mind to adapt to constant change. As he will be responsible for creating improvement without increasing resources he will need to innovate, seek the way to inspire those labouring at the task around him. His main study will be of people not systems, since again if he understands people he will be able to create new systems to meet the needs and aspirations of the people whose condition he has taken the trouble to understand.

In a police force of the future the hierarchy itself would be under some question, although indispensable in a disciplined uniformed service. The impact of technology has already hit hierarchical command systems hard. The passing up and down of orders and information is now short circuited by command and control systems which place the police task in the hands of constables and the direction in the hands of sergeants, at least on a day-to-day, minute-by-minute, hour-by-hour basis. This condition postulates examination of the adequacy of the training of sergeants in the present, let alone in the future. If routine operational policing is done effectively by the two lowest ranks, the necessity for higher ideas of police training to be pushed lower down becomes overwhelming. As the vertical chain of command is increasingly bypassed or short-circuited the leader will need to be trained to cope with increased management participation as pressures for change mount.

The growing indifference to promotion at all levels in the service today could be an indication of the onset of a disenchantment with the hierarchical structures, and this will need careful management in the future.

SPECIALISTS

It is not only the general nature of police duty, or what might be called the essence of police duty, that will need to be changed to face the future, but the increasing army of specialists also will have to be kept up to date with change. Such specialists are very numerous and there is a growing need for adequate time and facilities for their training and education. Although the skills and art of detective work stem from basic human qualities of shrewdness, intuition, determination, industry and dedication, consummated by experience; nevertheless the growing need to cope with changes adumbrated in other comments in this chapter will need to be taken into account. The detective, whilst keeping his professional nose to the ground, will have to perform the difficult feat of keeping his scientifically-trained ears alert for change. Training in technology for all police officers (detectives as well as those in preventive work) will need to be stepped up and maintained.

CHALLENGE TO EDUCATORS OF POLICE

The speed of change, the large size of police forces and distances involved will place an increasing responsibility on leaders to com-municate in a variety of circumstances. The public in a popular democracy will need and want to know, and to have instant response to complicated queries which present-day services would be unable to supply. The leader will need training to produce public infor-mation in all forms, from cassette recordings on the state of crime and means of prevention to a recorded talk on the concept of policing a popular democracy. Above all he will need the complete ability and training to cope with the pressures from the news media and to learn to communicate or be left behind.

The job of the trainer will become more complex and will demand the best of talent. Apart from the qualitative challenge of basic training in people, society and change, as well as the law, there will be the increasing ability of technical aids to efficiency. If the con-stable's notebook were to disappear in favour of the audio and, in due course, the video tape-recorder, that would not be surprising.

Training for the future police, given that the mental ability of those entering the service is adequate, should be capable of producing officers of sufficient insight, imagination and judgment, to be able to cope with an infinite variety of human problems and social change without suffering demoralisation through disorientation. It should enable them to use a wide variety of machines to provide their evidential records, their memory bank and their insight into the future. So far as the leaders are concerned, they will need to under-stand the pace of change in human behaviour, including changes in morality, social aspirations and motivations, particularly the desire for freedom, and they will need to be able to adapt systems to cope with such social phenomena. The concept of permanent re-organisation will require understanding as well as the accommodation of group aspirations for participation in decision-making processes.

If new police officers are to realise their full potential in the improving but not expanding society of Dahrendorf, they will need to secure the bridgeheads of understanding, new speeds of change and novelty, and be willing and able to act accordingly without reliance on orders coming down long chains of hierarchical control. Planning future training programmes should become a very interest-ing exercise indeed.

A POLICE RESERVE

A democratic community by its very nature is always at risk from organised violence. If this comes from an external power it is the task of the armed forces to contain and overcome it. If the threat is internal it is the policeman's task. If in either case the threat becomes too great for the professional army or the professional police, then the community has to be mobilised wholly or in part, if it is to survive intact. In two World Wars, Great Britain first of all mobilised its regular forces, then its territorial forces and then its citizens' army.

Policing conditions of extreme difficulty might reflect the same pattern. In the first place the police themselves heighten their state of readiness and capability, secondly the police reserve or Special Constabulary is put on an emergency footing, and finally the citizenry themselves are brought into the scheme of things. A police system which cannot obtain a volunteer reserve and citizen backing is on the high road to defeat. It is on the road to defeat because the lack of volunteers and citizen support indicates that the law and its enforcer are out of line with public sentiment. To put it another way, it may be said that, if the laws and those who enforce them are tolerable, then it is likely they will get the public support required in an emergency.

The police of today are presented with a most difficult task in trying to assess the future implications of keeping the peace. Not the least of the difficulties facing them is the ability to distinguish the voice of reason from amongst the more strident voices of discord, sectarianism, vested interest and xenophobia. It may be that the real voice of reason is not to be found amongst the many that daily assail the ears of the community, but in the neighbourhoods where the rationality of people as individuals is preferred to the reason of people as crowds. Police know that crowds develop their own peculiar characteristics which are more than the sum total of their several parts.

The police have to weigh in balance the ugliness and obscenity of the worst face of society, against the kindliness and public spiritedness of its better face. Although the former may attract most attention, the latter when concentrated upon will far outshine it. Facing the brutalities and violence of the twisted mind and the excesses of the disaffected, requires that the police have to feel fortified in the knowledge that the vast majority of the people stand behind them. The concept of policing a community which disapproves of, or even detests, all that the police stand for is an alien one.

When the prospect of widespread public disorder or the shadow of terrorist activity falls across the face of the community, the police have to assess their potential strengths. Having measured the capability of the police themselves, it is necessary to consider the willpower latent in the community to stand up to excesses of evil and intimidation. Police, and armies for that matter, have often been undermined and defeated by the failure of civil willpower. It is believed that the civil willpower in Great Britain is extremely strong and is the ultimate bank against total disintegration. The first thing the police have to do, however, is to inform the community frankly, accurately and without emotion of the problems which may have to be faced when public disorder is foreshadowed. It is by constantly keeping the public informed that the police will have built up a strong public psychological resistance to the challenge of grave emergency. The first police reserve in a democracy is to be found in the civil willpower and psychological strength of the community at large. The police have next to consider the physical reserves.

The police are brought up to understand that the law and custom of the common law requires every able-bodied citizen to assist in maintaining law and order. Not only does the law give power to citizens to effect arrest and to lay charges, but it requires them to assist the police when called upon. The police will know, however, the dangers of uncontrolled and amateur or vigilante groups, therefore the tradition of public spiritedness has to be channelled into a constitutional organisation and requires proper control. Just as the humanitarian volunteer in first aid to the injured is encouraged but controlled within the framework of medical practice, so the volunteer for keeping the public peace should be controlled within the professional police practice. The volunteer should not be seen to be in competition with the professional but as his friendly supporter. As in the saving of life, the protection of life and the prevention of crime permit of no compromise with belief in the common good. In times of crisis the volunteer has always played his immense part, and always will be prepared to.

The police, therefore, have to decide on how to organise and administer a volunteer reserve. In common-law systems this has generally taken the place of a Special Constabulary (where it exists), but there are a number of important principles to be borne in mind if relationships between the professional and the volunteer reserve are to be good. In the first place the professional police are entitled to guarantees. The reserve should not be used to inhibit progress in professional status, or as a cheap form of maintaining inadequate police strength in normal times. The volunteer should be seen solely as an aid to the professional and not as an amateur substitute. He, the volunteer, is only trained in the elementary theory and practice against emergencies of crisis proportions. In a prolonged emergency, of course, the volunteer will gradually raise his capability and be able to take on more duties.

Furthermore, the modern professional constable is by definition a leader and is well able to guide and control his own group of community volunteers forming a branch of the Special Constabulary reserve. There should be no need for a hierarchical reserve, since the existing police hierarchy is adequate to maintain and control both professional and volunteer constables. This obviates the need for parallel organisations which in themselves are divisive and rightly or wrongly can be seen by some as threatening. The status of the police constable can only be heightened by his being appointed leader of his own reserve group. He will realise that the nucleus of a volunteer body should be as well trained and active as circumstances will allow, but he will also remember that in times of great stress volunteers of all kinds, ages and experiences may be forthcoming, and therefore a second wave of reserve strength should be borne in mind. Those responsible for looking ahead and planning for eventualities have a heavy responsibility to get these relationships right (*see* Appendix 9 for a model scheme).

Chapter 30

Conclusions

The police face many conflicts in their role; but they also face conflicts within themselves. In some ways they have been outpaced by change, in others they have not. Over the last twenty years the police have maintained pace with new technology. From pocket radio to silicon chip, the police have harnessed or are harnessing technology to their purpose. In some ways, their success in coping with technological change has concealed the greater uncertainties in their attitudes towards the new society. Police are more comfortable in an authoritarian world. As we approach the twenty-first century, the belief that the technology of that century can be grafted on to a nineteenth-century philosophy, if adhered to, will cause the police considerable anxiety and disorientation.

The first question that poses itself is whether the military style hierarchical bureaucracy can adjust sufficiently to cope with the speed of change. When systems are not sufficiently flexible to allow for rapid change, they will put the brake on the necessary and desirable evolution of the police. As the speed of change makes most things impermanent, the police hierarchy has to regard its own role at any particular point in time as temporary in itself. Switching the hierarchy from task to task, from system to system, and new modes of deployment will call for greater adaptability than the police have so far shown themselves capable of producing. It is no good talking about massive stability when stability itself is an old-fashioned concept. It is in administering change that the hierarchy itself will have to be capable of quick shifts, changing values and what might in more stable times be called unorthodoxy. The key will obviously lie in the ability to police the changes, which is almost a contradiction in terms.

As in most things, liberation from rigidity and undue unorthodoxy should begin in education. The basic education of the police is still far too rigid and legalistic. As young people enter the service and go out to face the complexity of their problems on the beats they are bemused and disorientated by the seeming inadequacy of their training to measure up to the diversity and complexity of their task. Nor are their immediate supervisory officers always able to help them

219

much, since they themselves have been trained and conditioned to stable orthodoxy. Police training will have to take much more into account than it does at present, and start at the bottom level; the shift from its heavy legal orientation is long overdue. As the Police Training Centres are staffed by sergeants and inspectors who themselves have been brought up in the traditional ways, they will not be capable of responding to this challenge without considerable input from people in other professions. It seems likely therefore that the staff of Police Training Centres will have to be more diverse than it is, and certainly should include instruction in the modern sciences such as sociology, psychology and political science. The police however will have to stay clinically clear of political bias.

Access to the higher positions in the service for people of ability able to cope with change should be facilitated. This will not come about easily. The tendency to look for the archetype is stultifying. As imagination becomes just as important as technological hardware there will be a great need for this quality in police officers aspiring to command. If hierarchies are to change their characteristics they will not only need new systems but new people within those systems.

The traditional pattern of police force organisation will have to be questioned. The Holy Trinity of operations, crime and traffic will have to be prepared to accommodate new elements. Technological and psychological groups and sections will be required if the police are to keep pace with change. Ideas sections and Future sections will need to be given time and opportunity to probe with imagination the finer adjustments required in a modern police system.

The future will not only demand technological, organisational and personnel shifts, but there will need to be found room for shifts in the philosophy of policing. The police have done extremely well in accepting new technology, new hardware and new systems, but what is much more difficult is to get people to accept philosophical shifts. The idea that the contribution to policing an advanced society is mainly a non-police contribution will have to be better understood. Society can no longer be policed solely by the police. In many ways, coming to terms with this new dimension of policing will release both police and public from the mythology of crime and police omniscience. Much of crime is the inevitable result of the way of life of modern Western society, and if crime is to be significantly reduced, the public must realise that it is not just a question of more police, more prisons, more courts and harder punishment, but demands a change, and in some cases a fundamental change, in our way of life. Only this kind of understanding will bring about significant change in the place of crime in society.

Just as governments will need to consider the implications of the unemployed masses (or to put it another way the leisured people), so will the police. The idea that half of the population (of working age) will be working whilst the other half will be at leisure is a matter which both administratively and psychologically we have not yet come to terms with, but time to do so is short. The idea of helping a leisured society to police itself poses many interesting ideas. No longer would it be possible for society to say, "we cannot afford to look after and help the underprivileged", since there will be a mass of talented and able people with nothing much more to do than that. In this kind of situation, the police will become leaders of volunteer groups, helping to damp down crimogenic conditions in neighbourhoods. As society passes from the post-industrial age into the egalitarian, fraternal and leisured age, with possibly a new set of moral values, the police should be prepared to make a major contribution to its success. The creation of the village in the city would provide a suitable model of social organisation before this could take place. As people continue to struggle to escape from the physical and psychological ghettos of their daily lives, the police will not only have a considerable part to play as consultants to housing, planning and environmental authorities, but they should also play a leading part in creating completely new social organisations and groups to reduce fears and tensions and inequalities which lead to crime.

It will be essential for the intelligentsia of society to have a considerably better understanding of policing perspectives. Society's preoccupation with the theory of controlling crime only through punishing or treating offenders is clearly outmoded. Of course there will always be offenders to be punished or treated, but they represent the failures of society and of individuals. If sufficient people of sufficient talent with the right kind of influence and authority were to take an interest in the reduction of levels of delinquency in our neighbourhoods, it would not be long before considerable progress was noticed. Not only would such a course be more ethically virtuous but it would also be more cost-effective, since the massive amounts of public money being spent in piecemeal fashion would be better used by its co-ordinated spending. There will be a growing need for greater thought to be put into the entire field of crime control, if the methods are to match the aspirations of the new society and the potential of Western civilisation to rise above its current malaise.

Whilst all this is going on, the police will have as usual to contend with a likely increase, or at least a spasmodic pattern of terrorism; though once the Irish problem is solved (one hopes) the United Kingdom should be less affected than mainland states. Similarly there will be a constant need to break up and disperse incipient movements towards organised crime. An open, free, trusting, caring society is quite vulnerable to the organised criminal who will always require considerable expert, professional attention from the police. The police should approach the coming changes in criminal procedure and criminal trials with confidence.

Technology should not be seen as a threat but as an aid. The audio-visual camera at police interrogations will release police from the suspicions, doubts and misunderstandings which reduce the quality of their evidence and their standing in the eyes of the courts and particularly of jurors. It is now obvious that the role of the police in criminal investigations is to receive constant challenge and the police, therefore, instead of reacting defensively, should possess an open and co-operative attitude. The police have everything to gain professionally from change in this field.

When facing the need for change, the police should always bear in mind that the modern system devised and introduced in 1829 was regarded by many as a likely road to disaster, a threat to human liberty and incapable of reconciliation with a Parliamentary democracy.

Postscript

The foregoing narrative is not intended to be a comprehensive text on police and police organisation. The great debating points of local versus national police, the police role in pre-trial procedures and the criminal trial itself have barely been touched. Such omissions are deliberate, since the purpose of what has been written has been to pose questions and suggest ideas of a more philosophical kind. There is no shortage of police literature on the former, but there is considerable scope for the latter. It is in that spirit that this work has been compiled.

Appendix 1

Judges' Rules

Judges' Rules and Administrative Directions to the Police

JUDGES' RULES

The Judges' Rules, made by Her Majesty's judges of the Queen's Bench Division, are concerned with the admissibility in evidence against a person of answers, oral or written, given by that person to questions asked by police officers and of statements made by that person. These rules, which supersede rules previously made by the judges, are contained in Home Office circular No. 89/1978, issued in June 1978.

These rules do not affect the principles:

(*a*) That citizens have a duty to help a police officer to discover and apprehend offenders;

(*b*) That police officers, otherwise than by arrest, cannot compel any person against his will to come or to remain in any police station;

(*c*) That every person at any stage of an investigation should be able to communicate and to consult privately with a solicitor. This is so even if he is in custody provided that in such a case no unreasonable delay or hindrance is caused to the processes of investigation or the administration of justice by his doing so;

(*d*) That when a police officer who is making enquiries of any person about an offence has enough evidence to prefer a charge against that person for the offence, he should without delay cause that person to be charged or informed that he may be prosecuted for the offence;

(*e*) That it is a fundamental condition of the admissibility in evidence against any person, equally of any oral answer given by that person to a question put by a police officer and of any statement made by that person, that it shall have been voluntary, in the sense that it has not been obtained from him by fear of prejudice or hope of advantage, exercised or held out by a person in authority, or by oppression.

223

The principle set out in paragraph (*e*) above is overriding and applicable in all cases. Within that principle the following rules are put forward as a guide to police officers conducting investigations. Nonconformity with these rules may render answers and statements liable to be excluded from evidence in subsequent criminal proceedings.

RULES

I. When a police officer is trying to discover whether, or by whom, an offence has been committed he is entitled to question any person, whether suspected or not, from whom he thinks that useful information may be obtained. This is so whether or not the person in question has been taken into custody so long as he has not been charged with the offence or informed that he may be prosecuted for it.

II. As soon as a police officer has evidence which would afford reasonable grounds for suspecting that a person has committed an offence, he shall caution that person or cause him to be cautioned before putting to him any questions, or further questions, relating to that offence.

The caution shall be in the following terms:

"You are not obliged to say anything unless you wish to do so but what you say may be put into writing and given in evidence."

When after being cautioned a person is being questioned, or elects to make a statement, a record shall be kept of the time and place at which any such questioning or statement began and ended and of the the persons present.

III.—(*a*) Where a person is charged with or informed that he may be prosecuted for an offence he shall be cautioned in the following terms:

"Do you wish to say anything? You are not obliged to say anything unless you wish to do so but whatever you say will be taken down in writing and may be given in evidence."

(*b*) It is only in exceptional cases that questions relating to the offence should be put to the accused person after he has been charged or informed that he may be prosecuted. Such questions may be put where they are necessary for the purpose of preventing or minimising harm or loss to some other person or to the public or for clearing up an ambiguity in a previous answer or statement.

Before any such questions are put the accused should be cautioned in these terms:

"I wish to put some questions to you about the offence with

224

which you have been charged (*or* about the offence for which you may be prosecuted). You are not obliged to answer any of these questions, but if you do the questions and answers will be taken down in writing and may be given in evidence."

Any questions put and answers given relating to the offence must be contemporaneously recorded in full and the record signed by that person or if he refuses by the interrogating officer.

(*c*) When such a person is being questioned, or elects to make a statement, a record shall be kept at the time and place at which any questioning or statement began and ended and of the persons present.

IV. All written statements made after caution shall be taken in the following manner:

(*a*) If a person says that he wants to make a statement he shall be told that it is intended to make a written record of what he says. He shall always be asked whether he wishes to write down himself what he wants to say; if he says that he cannot write or that he would like someone to write it for him, a police officer may offer to write the statement for him. If he accepts the offer the police officer shall, before starting, ask the person making the statement to sign, or make his mark to, the following:

> "I,....................., wish to make a statement, I want someone to write down what I say. I have been told that I need not say anything unless I wish to do so and that whatever I say may be given in evidence."

(*b*) Any person writing his own statement shall be allowed to do so without any prompting as distinct from indicating to him what matters are material.

(*c*) The person making the statement, if he is going to write it himself, shall be asked to write out and sign before writing what he wants to say, the following:

> "I make this statement of my own free will. I have been told that I need not say anything unless I wish to do so and that whatever I say may be given in evidence."

(*d*) Whenever a police officer writes the statement, he shall take down the exact words spoken by the person making the statement, without putting any questions other than such as may be needed to make the statement coherent, intelligible and relevant to the material matters: he shall not prompt him.

(*e*) When the writing of a statement by a police officer is finished the person making it shall be asked to read it and to make any corrections, alterations or additions he wishes. When he has finished reading it he shall be asked to write and sign or make his mark on the following Certificate at the end of the statement:

"I have read the above statement and I have been told that I can correct, alter or add anything I wish. This statement is true. I have made it of my own free will."

(f) If the person who has made a statement refuses to read it or to write the above mentioned Certificate at the end of it or to sign it, the senior police officer present shall record on the statement itself and in the presence of the person making it, what has happened. If the person making the statement cannot read, or refuses to read it, the officer who has taken it down shall read it over to him and ask him whether he would like to correct, alter or add anything and to put his signature or make his mark at the end. The police officer shall then certify on the statement itself what he has done.

V. If at any time after a person has been charged with, or has been informed that he may be prosecuted for an offence a police officer wishes to bring to the notice of that person any written statement made by another person who in respect of the same offence has also been charged or informed that he may be prosecuted, he shall hand to that person a true copy of such written statement, but nothing shall be said or done to invite any reply or comment. If that person says that he would like to make a statement in reply, or starts to say something, he shall at once be cautioned or further cautioned as prescribed by Rule III (a).

VI. Persons other than police officers charged with the duty of investigating offences or charging offenders shall, so far as may be practicable, comply with these Rules.

ADMINISTRATIVE DIRECTIONS ON INTERROGATION AND THE TAKING OF STATEMENTS

1. *Procedure generally*

   (a) When possible statements of persons under caution should be written on the forms provided for the purpose. Police officers' notebooks should be used for taking statements only when no forms are available.

   (b) When a person is being questioned or elects to make a statement, a record should be kept of the time or times at which during the questioning or making of a statement there were intervals or refreshment was taken. The nature of the refreshment should be noted. In no circumstances should alcoholic drink be given.

(c) In writing down a statement, the words used should not be translated into "official" vocabulary; this may give a misleading impression of the genuineness of the statement.

(d) Care should be taken to avoid any suggestion that the person's answers can only be used in evidence against him, as this may prevent an innocent person making a statement which might help clear him of the charge.

2. Record of interrogation

Rule II and Rule II (c) demand that a record should be kept of the following matters:

(a) when, after being cautioned in accordance with Rule II, the person is being questioned or elects to make a statement—of the time and place at which any such questioning began and ended and of the persons present;

(b) when, after being cautioned in accordance with Rule III (a) or (b) a person is being questioned or elects to make a statement —of the time and place at which any questioning and statement began and ended and of the persons present.

In addition to the records required by these Rules full records of the following matters should additionally be kept:—

(b) of the time when a charge was made and/or the person was arrested, and

(c) of the matters referred to in para. 1 (b) above.

If two or more police officers are present when the questions are being put or the statement made, the records made should be countersigned by the other officers present.

3. Comfort and refreshment

Reasonable arrangements should be made for the comfort and refreshment of persons being questioned. Whenever practicable both the person being questioned or making a statement and the officers asking the questions or taking the statement should be seated.

4. Interrogation of children and young persons

As far as practicable children and young persons under the age of 17 years (whether suspected of crime or not) should only be interviewed in the presence of a parent or guardian, or, in their absence, some person who is not a police officer and is of the same sex as the child. A child or young person should not be arrested, nor even interviewed, at school if such action can possibly be avoided. Where it is found essential to conduct the interview at school, this should be done only with the consent, and in the presence, of the head teacher, or his nominee.

4A. *Interrogation of mentally handicapped persons*

(a) If it appears to a police officer that a person (whether a witness or a suspect) whom he intends to interview has a mental handicap which raises a doubt as to whether the person can understand the questions put to him, or which makes the person likely to be especially open to suggestion, the officer should take particular care in putting questions and accepting the reliability of answers. As far as practicable, and where recognised as such by the police, a mentally handicapped adult (whether suspected of crime or not) should be interviewed only in the presence of a parent or other person in whose care, custody or control he is, or of some person who is not a police officer (for example a social worker).

(b) So far as mentally handicapped children and young persons are concerned, the conditions of interview and arrest by the police are governed by Administrative Direction 4 above.

(c) Any document arising from an interview with a mentally handicapped person of any age should be signed not only by the person who made the statement, but also by the parent or other person who was present during the interview. Since the reliability of any admission by a mentally handicapped person may even then be challenged, care will still be necessary to verify the facts admitted and to obtain corroboration where possible.

5. *Statements in languages other than English*

In the case of a person making a statement in a language other than English:

(a) The interpreter should take down the statement in the language in which it is made.

(b) An official English translation should be made in due course and be proved as an exhibit with the original statement.

(c) The person making the statement should sign that at (a).

Apart from the question of apparent unfairness, to obtain the signature of a suspect to an English translation of what he said in another language can have little or no value as evidence if the suspect disputes the accuracy of this record of his statement.

6. *Supply to accused persons of written statement of charges*

  (*a*) The following procedure should be adopted whenever a charge is preferred against a person arrested without warrant for any offence:

  As soon as a charge has been accepted by the appropriate police officer the accused person should be given a written notice containing a copy of the entry in the charge sheet or book giving particulars of the offence with which he is charged. So far as possible the particulars of the charge should be stated in simple language so that the accused person may understand it, but they should also show clearly the precise offence in law with which he is charged. Where the offence charged is a statutory one, it should be sufficient for the latter purpose to quote the section of the statute which created the offence.

  The written notice should include some statement on the lines of the caution given orally to the accused person in accordance with the Judges' Rules after a charge has been preferred. It is suggested that the form of notice should begin with the following words:

  "You are charged with the offence(s) shown below. You are not obliged to say anything unless you wish to do so, but whatever you say will be taken down in writing and may be given in evidence."

  (*b*) Once the accused person has appeared before the court it is not necessary to serve him with a written notice of any further charges which may be preferred. If, however, the police decide, before he has appeared before a court, to modify the charge or to prefer further charges it is desirable that the person concerned should be formally charged with the further offence and given a written copy of the charge as soon as it is possible to do so having regard to the particular circumstances of the case. If the accused person has then been released on bail, it may not always be practicable or reasonable to prefer the new charge at once, and in cases where he is due to surrender to his bail within forty-eight hours or in other cases of difficulty it will be sufficient for him to be formally charged with the further offence and served with a written notice of the charge after he has surrendered to his bail and before he appears before the court.

7. *Facilities for defence*

(*a*) A person in custody should be supplied on request with writing materials. Provided that no hindrance is reasonably likely to be caused to the processes of investigation or the administration of justice:

    (i) he should be allowed to speak on the telephone to his solicitor or to his friends;

    (ii) his letters should be sent by post or otherwise with the least possible delay;

    (iii) telegrams should be sent at once, at his own expense.

(*b*) Persons in custody should not only be informed orally of the rights and facilities available to them, but in addition notices describing them should be displayed at convenient and conspicuous places at police stations and the attention of persons in custody should be drawn to these notices.

Police Discipline Code
(Police Discipline Regulations 1977)

1. Discreditable conduct, which offence is committed where a member of a police force acts in a disorderly manner or any manner drejudicial to discipline or reasonably likely to bring discredit on the reputation of the force or of the police service.
2. Misconduct towards a member of a police force, which offence is committed where:
   (a) the conduct of a member of a police force towards another such member is oppressive or abusive; or
   (b) a member of a police force assaults another such member.
3. Disobedience to orders, which offence is committed where a member of a police force, without good and sufficient cause, disobeys or omits or neglects to carry out any lawful order, written or otherwise, or contravenes any provision of the Police Regulations containing restrictions on the private lives of members of police forces, or requiring him to notify the chief officer of police that he, or a relation included in his family, has a business interest, within the meaning of those Regulations.
4. Neglect of duty, which offence is committed where a member of a police force, without good and sufficient cause:
   (a) neglects or omits to attend to or carry out with due promptitude and diligence anything which it is his duty as a member of a police force to attend to or carry out; or
   (b) fails to work his beat in accordance with orders, or leaves the place of duty to which he has been ordered, or having left his place of duty for an authorised purpose fails to return thereto without undue delay; or
   (c) is absent without leave from, or is late for, any duty; or
   (d) fails properly to account for, or to make a prompt and true return of, any money or property received by him in the course of his duty.
5. Falsehood or prevarication, which offence is committed where a member of a police force:

(a) knowingly or through neglect making any false, misleading or inaccurate oral or written statement or entry in any record or document made, kept or required for police purposes; or

(b) either wilfully and without proper authority or through lack of due care destroys or mutilates any record or document made, kept or required for police purposes; or

(c) without good and sufficient cause alters or erases or adds to any entry in such a record or document; or

(d) has knowingly or through neglect made any false, misleading or inaccurate statement in connection with his appointment to the police force.

6. Improper disclosure of information, which offence is committed where a member of a police force:

(a) without proper authority communicates to any person, any information which he has in his possession as a member of a police force; or

(b) makes any anonymous communication to any police authority, or any member of a police force; or

(c) without proper authority, makes representations to the police authority or the council of any county comprised in the police area with regard to any matter concerning the force; or

(d) canvasses any member of that authority or of such a council with regard to any such matter.

For the purpose of this paragraph the Isles of Scilly shall be treated as if they were a county.

7. Corrupt or improper practice, which offence is committed where a member of a police force:

(a) in his capacity as a member of the force and without the consent of the chief officer of police or the police authority, directly or indirectly solicits or accepts any gratuity, present or subscription; or

(b) places himself under a pecuniary obligation to any person in such a manner as might affect his properly carrying out his duties as a member of the force; or

(c) improperly uses, or attempts so to use, his position as a member of the force for his private advantage; or

(d) in his capacity as a member of the force and without the consent of the chief officer of police, writes, signs or gives a testimonial of character or other recommendation with the object of obtaining employment for any person or of supporting an application for the grant of a licence of any kind.

8. Abuse of authority, which offence is committed where a member of a police force:

(a) without good and sufficient cause makes an arrest; or

(b) uses any unnecessary violence towards any prisoner or other person with whom he may be brought into contact in the execution of his duty; or

    (c) is uncivil to any member of the public.

9. Neglect of health, which offence is committed where a member of a police force, without good and sufficient cause, neglects to carry out any instructions of a medical officer appointed by the police authority or, while absent from duty on account of sickness, commits any act or adopts any conduct calculated to retard his return to duty.

10. Improper dress or untidiness, which offence is committed where without good and sufficient cause a member of a police force while on duty, or while off duty but wearing uniform in a public place, is improperly dressed or is untidy in his appearance.

11. Damage to police property, which offence is committed where a member of a police force:

    (a) wilfully or through lack of due care causes any waste, loss or damage to any police property; or

    (b) fails to report as soon as is reasonably practicable any loss or damage to any such property issued to or used by him, or entrusted to his care.

12. Drunkenness, which offence is committed where a member of a police force renders himself unfit through drink for duties which he is or will be required to perform or which he may reasonably foresee having to perform.

13. Drinking on duty or soliciting drink, which offence is committed where a member of a police force, while on duty:

    (a) without proper authority, drinks, or receives from any other person, any intoxicating liquor; or

    (b) demands, or endeavours to persuade any other person to give him, or to purchase or obtain for him, any intoxicating liquor.

14. Entering licensed premises, which offence is committed where a member of a police force:

    (a) while on duty; or

    (b) while off duty but wearing uniform;

without good and sufficient cause, enters any premises in respect of which a licence or permit has been granted in pursuance of the law relating to liquor licensing or betting and gaming or regulating places of entertainment.

15. Criminal conduct, which offence is committed where a member of a police force has been found guilty by a court of law of a criminal offence.

16. Being an accessory to a disciplinary offence, which offence is committed where a member of a police force connives at or is knowingly an accessory to any offence against discipline.

Appendix 3

Guidance to Police

AN INTRODUCTION TO PROBATIONARY CONSTABLES ON THE NATURE OF SERVICE IN THE DEVON AND CORNWALL CONSTABULARY

Now that you have embarked upon a police career, you will begin to understand that the demands which will be made of you offer both challenges and fulfilment. You will need to develop your knowledge, understanding, skill and ability coupled with virtues of integrity, honour and courage of both moral and physical nature. The following comments, therefore, are intended to help you to attain a basic understanding of some of the principles of policing as required in the Devon and Cornwall Constabulary.

At first you may find the principles difficult to relate to the everyday problems you face as a police officer; but I urge you to persevere, for they offer an opportunity to enrich the community you serve and greatly enhance your professional status in a constantly changing society.

As you read these notes I ask you to bear in mind the concept of the police officer, not merely as a law enforcer, but as a community leader, for I firmly believe that modern policing is not simply a matter of controlling the bad but includes activating the good.

THE CITIZEN CONSTABLE
The outstanding feature of the office of constable which distinguishes the English police system from others is the concept of the citizen constable. In effect it means that a constable is acting for and on behalf of the other citizens as individuals under the law and not as an agent or servant of government. It follows from their position in the constitution of this country that police officers are independent officers under the Crown. The effect of this dual provision is to place a heavy individual responsibility on police officers. They are personally responsible for their unlawful acts. That is the legal effect. The social effect is that a police officer is expected by the public to have high personal standards. Apart from the efficient discharge of duties, the public expects a police officer to be courteous, helpful, resource-

234

ful, friendly, compassionate and understanding. These high standards are difficult to attain and maintain under the many stresses and strains of police duty, but every effort should be made to achieve them.

TWO ROLES

Police duties can be divided into at least two distinct roles. On the one hand is the officer of the law keeping the peace through enforcement of the law or by prevention of offences. On the other hand is the social agent to whom the public turn for an infinite variety of purposes. It should be remembered that the police are expected to be able to help any person who needs their help, and in cases where the police themselves cannot provide it, they should be able to activate the concern of other appropriate agencies, bodies or individuals. An efficient police service meets this public expectation and the accent is on giving a service over a wide field of human activity.

ETHICS OF POLICING

Being concerned, as it is, with power and its application, it is very necessary that police action, for moral as well as legal justification, should be bound by ethical and legal principles. The constable's oath of office expects a "solemn and sincere" affirmation of service to the Crown. It further requires that "favour, affection, malice or ill-will" shall not motivate a police officer to carry out or refrain from carrying out his or her duties. Police officers must develop an objective and impartial approach to their work. In carrying out their duties "to the best of their skill and knowledge faithfully according to law" they are likely to avoid many of the pitfalls and unethical practices that go with partiality.

In practice, the oath demands that all persons must be treated with the same consideration, irrespective of race, creed, religion or social standing. Personal prejudices, preferences and animosities are to be set aside. It should be remembered that the police are not set up to serve the nice, competent and clean people only, but they are to serve all members of the community including the incompetent, the poor and the needy. Good police officers, therefore, accept the community they serve with all its faults, since they are an integral part of it.

In applying the law the police officer has to have regard for the legal ethical rules which restrict his or her powers. It is a contradiction in terms for a police officer to act illegally since he or she is appointed to uphold the law. There are particular problems in relation to the arrest, detention and questioning of people since the police are often under pressures to achieve results, but it cannot be emphasised too strongly that no police officer is expected to act illegally to produce results. Such restrictive procedures which the law imposes are not impediments placed capriciously in the path of the police but safe-guards of individual rights and liberties which the police exist to protect. Unethical and illegal conduct erodes the self-respect and reputation of police, both individually and collectively, and should be studiously avoided.

POLICE RESPONSES

It is possible to describe two types of police response to their work—the proactive and the reactive.

The proactive style is one of "getting ahead of the game". It may be preventing offences by helping the community together with other agencies to remove or reduce the causes of crime. It may lie in working in schools to educate the young in responsible ways or in halls, meeting places or institutes to inform the general public of their own duties and the need for co-operation with police. It certainly includes using the media for news, current affairs, educational and informational programmes. A good programme of proactive policing is the hallmark of a forward-looking police force.

The reactive style aspect of policing is the response to crime, public disorder or service calls of one kind or another. Through communications, mobility and flexibility, police both individually and collectively have to provide a swift and efficient service. It is in this aspect of their work that the police find their efficiency being measured by such things as detected crime rates, response times, deployment and concentration of resources. Team work is vital in this area.

It is important for a police force to strike the correct balance of styles. Too much reliance on reactive policing can only lead to estrangement between the police and the public they serve. Estrangement can lead to public indifference, to misunderstanding, to suspicion, to animosity, to dislike and even, in extreme cases, to hatred. The police, therefore, have to develop contact in a variety of ways to offset the alienation that technological as opposed to human policing can bring about. Modern technology for police use is a great boon, but it also contains the seeds of alienation of police and must be counteracted by extra determination to maintain and develop human contact of a non-conflict style.

The strongest and most pervasive control in a community is provided not by law but by custom and convention. Therefore everything that the police can do to help strengthen lawful customs and conventions should be done. This amounts to social discipline and is strongest in homogeneous communities. Since the primary object of the police is the prevention of crime, the police have to be proactive in communities in building up trust and co-operation. Trust between

236

a community and the police as individuals, or collectively, is gained more quickly through contact before conflict or crisis intervenes. This calls for maximum police/public interaction. To further this interaction and co-operation, the police have to manifest their care and concern for people and their institutions.

Parents, teachers, pupils, other social agencies (social services, probation service, etc.), workers, employers, as well as the multitude of voluntary, statutory and government organisations, are all legitimate targets for proaction in the prevention of crime and the maintenance of public tranquillity. This aspect of policing calls for skill and imagination and its success is difficult to measure statistically. Its success can be measured, however, by public feelings and reactions as communities begin to notice care and concern manifested by the police. The degree of support for and co-operation with the police is likely to be higher in those areas where the police have been proactive.

EFFICIENT AND WELL-CONDUCTED

The object of probation is to provide opportunities over a period of two years for an officer to prove that he or she is likely to become efficient and well conducted, and it is for the chief constable to ensure that the means for doing so are provided. The notes that have gone before are intended to help young officers to achieve a little perspective in a most complicated task in a complicated society. The need to continue the search for knowledge and understanding in the pursuit of excellence is paramount. Reading over a wide field not only about law but about society and its institutions is vital. Discussion and argument also help to refine one's thoughts. Supervisory officers are expected to teach, inform and lead probationary constables to better and higher levels of understanding.

Beyond probation stretches a wide field of careers, all of them fulfilling, rewarding and satisfying. Each person has different choices and expectations, of course, but the happiest are those who have mastered their particular tasks and have pride and enrichment in their professional attainments.

CONCLUSION

I would like to conclude these comments by reminding you that as a constable you wield substantial power to affect the freedom of the individual. At the same time you have considerable discretion available to you in carrying out your duties, especially when dealing with minor breaches of the law. You will be well advised to balance the use of both; do not hesitate to seek the guidance of your supervisory officers when you have doubts.

Remember that it is very easy to resort to the authoritarian approach, especially when challenged, and I ask you to try to avoid this pitfall.

Of course there will be many occasions when firmness and direct action are required and there will be other times when the outcome of a situation hinges upon your own responses and self-control. Calmness and politeness are at a premium, however firm you may be.

In the final analysis, your success in balancing the use of power and discretion will depend very much on your personal attitudes. Try to put yourself in the position of a member of the public and consider your own reaction in similar circumstances.

I wish you well.

John Alderson

A community police order

INTRODUCTION

1. Social change exerts pressures on police systems which are thereby required to adjust.
2. The impact of change on the police due to increasing democracy and the unacceptability of authoritarianism requires fundamental readjustment of the basis of policing. That basis shifts its emphasis from reactive towards proactive styles.
3. Following experiments in Exeter Division over the last three years, it has become apparent that the public generally and other social agencies in particular can make significant contributions to the prevention of crime provided that the police are able and willing to co-ordinate their participation.

COMMUNITY POLICING

4. Following discussions with representative bodies and divisional chief superintendents it has been decided that this Force will introduce the concept of community policing as from 1st May 1979 in all divisions.
5. Community policing describes a style of day-to-day policing in residential areas in which the public and other social agencies take part by helping to prevent crime, and particularly juvenile delinquency, through social as opposed to legal action.

ARRANGEMENTS

6. The crime patterns in communities will be analysed, recorded and produced in graphic visual form.
7. Using the information as a basis for discussions with other agencies, joint conferences should be arranged. Other agencies include teachers, social workers, probation officers, housing, planning, youth etc.
8. The information produced should be made the subject of local public discussion with a view to consideration of social activity to assist the reduction of crime. Local consultative groups should be formed where appropriate.

9. Community constables (formerly described as residents) will perform a leading role in bringing about community concern for, and interest in, local policing arrangements.

10. Divisional plans already drawn up will be implemented on or following the 1st May 1979 and progress will be monitored.

RESPONSIBILITY

11. Responsibility for implementation of the community policing plans will fall heavily on all ranks. Supervisory officers will require considerable skills to sustain progress and constables will require much support.

12. To achieve proper impetus for this scheme prior discussion groups and question and answer sessions will be arranged in sub-divisions.

C.P.S.U.

13. The Headquarters Crime Prevention Support Unit (extension 273) will be available for advice and assistance and should be consulted where appropriate.

THREE-TIER POLICING

14. Community policing will represent the first-tier policing strategy. It should result in a closer co-operation between police and public in the general control of crime and disorder. Second-tier policing, by incident cars, task forces and the like, is the essential back-up to community policing in dealing with emergencies of one kind or another. Third-tier policing in the detection of crime should receive a greater input of community help flowing from the improved first-tier community policing.

CO-OPERATION

15. In setting out to achieve a better police service, together with our friends in other professions and the public generally, I wish you well.

Modification of national character: the psychological role of the police in England

I wish to advance the hypothesis that one of the techniques by which the national character of a society may be modified or transformed over a given period is through the selection of personnel for institutions which are in continuous contact with the mass of the population in a somewhat super-ordinate position. If the personnel of the institution are chosen chiefly for their approximation to a certain type of character, rather than for specific intellectual or physical skills; if persons with this type of character have not hitherto been consistently given positions of authority; and if the authority of the institution is generally felt to be benevolent, protective, or succouring; then the character exemplified by the members of this institution will to a certain degree become part of the ego ideal of the mass of the population, who will tend to mould their own behaviour in conformity with this ideal, and will reward and punish the behaviour of their children in the light of this pattern which they have adopted. As generations pass, the attempt to approximate to this ideal will become less and less conscious, and increasingly part of the unconscious mechanisms which determine the content of the super-ego or of the ego ideal; with the consequence that a type of character which may have been relatively very uncommon in the society when the institution was first manned will subsequently become relatively common, and even perhaps typical of the society, or of those portions of it with which the members of the institution are in most continuous contact or from which their personnel is drawn.

The institution which I propose to examine in detail are the English police forces; but the evidence which is available to me suggests that strictly analogous functions were performed during the period of the great immigrations of the half century ending in 1914, when masses of immigrants' children were transformed into "100 per cent Americans"; and that a similar attempt is being made in the U.S.S.R. where the members of the Communist Party are consciously presented as models for the mass of the population.

I should like to suggest that, increasingly during the past century, the policeman has been for his peers not only an object of respect, but also a model of the ideal male character, self-controlled, possessing more strength than he ever has to call into use except in the gravest emergency, fair and

241

impartial, serving the abstractions of Peace and Justice rather than any personal allegiance or sectional advantage. This model, distributed throughout the population (in 1949 there were 59,000 police officers, averaging one police officer for every 720 inhabitants; the force authorised was 71,000, one for every 600 inhabitants) has, I suggest, had an appreciable influence on the character of most of the population during recent decades, so that the bulk of the population has, so to speak, incoporated the police man or woman as an ideal and become progressively more "self-policing"; and with this incorporation there has been an increasing amount of identification, so that today, in the words of one typical respondent:

I believe the police stand for all we English are, maybe at first appearance slow perhaps, but reliable stout and kindly, I have the greatest admiration for our police force and I am proud they are renowned abroad.

If this hypothesis be true, then what started as an expedient to control the very great criminality and violence of large sections of the English urban population has resulted in a profound modification of the character of this urban population. In a somewhat similar fashion, the need to provide a common language and literacy for the children of immigrants in the United States placed the American public school teacher in a position of prestige which was not shared by her colleagues in any European society and turned her into a model of ideal American conduct and so modified American character with an incorporated school teacher to parallel the incorporated policeman of the English. There is not yet comparable evidence to show whether the communist party member in the U.S.S.R. (or, for that matter, China) is producing analogous results in the mass of the population; this institution is much more recent than the two others hitherto discussed, but the personnel is distributed throughout the populations in much the same proportions and similar relationship as the policeman and the teacher. The major contrasts are that the policy is quite self-conscious on the part of the governments, and that the Communist Party members are publicly connected with the whole apparatus of state power, in a way that neither the police nor the school teachers, both under the control of local authorities, are; and this public connection with state power may interfere with the processes of identification by the powerless; for, it would seem, it is by means of the more-or-less complete and more-or-less conscious identification with the members of an admired and succouring institution that the characters of the mass of the population are gradually modified or transformed.

(Extract from Appendix One of Geoffrey Gorer's *Exploring English Character*, The Cresset Press 1955.)

The creation of a village in a city

Creating a village atmosphere in an anonymous urban setting calls for a considerable level of leadership, energy and enterprise. That it can be achieved there is no doubt. This Appendix provides one example of such a scheme in the City of Exeter.

DEVON AND CORNWALL CONSTABULARY

CRIME PREVENTION SUPPORT UNIT

HOW WELL DO YOU KNOW WHIPTON?

One thing you may not know is that recent research has disclosed disturbing trends in your neighbourhood

If you care about your community we think you will want to hear more about the problems which could affect your way of life and your children's future

So we're inviting you to a neighbourhood meeting to discuss the results of the Whipton research project with the Police, Youth and Community Workers and the Social Services

The meeting is at 8.00 p.m. on
MONDAY, 14th MARCH, 1977
At Whipton Barton Middle School

We're ready to help but we need the support of the community
. . . . your help and ideas

Don't let Whipton down

DEVON AND CORNWALL CONSTABULARY

CRIME PREVENTION SUPPORT UNIT

WHO SPEAKS FOR WHIPTON ?

Whipton needs a VOICE—loud enough to be heard in official circles—persuasive enough to influence decisions affecting your future

We know you care about your neighbourhood because more than 150 people attended a recent public meeting to discuss the problems of Whipton

Now we believe you deserve a stake in the future and so with the Youth and Community Service we're inviting you to attend a second meeting with the single purpose of forming a community association for Whipton

A Community Association will :—

- Speak for the neighbourhood with one strong voice
- Enable official bodies to deploy resources to your best advantage
- Provide a focal point for newcomers arriving in the area
- Help to bridge the gap between adults and young people
- Organise social and neighbourhood activities

The meeting will be held on :

Monday, 25th April
At Whipton Barton Middle School
Starting at 8 p.m.

This is your chance to help your community

YOU speak for Whipton

I

STEERING GROUP LETTER ADVERTISING PUBLIC MEETING (DECEMBER 1977)

PUBLIC MEETING

Dear Friend,

You are invited to a public meeting called to propose the formation of the Whipton Community Association. The meeting will be held on Wednesday 7th December 1977 in the Main Hall, Summerway Middle School at 7.45 p.m.

A G E N D A

1. Introduction and welcome (Chairman)

2. What is the purpose of a Community Association?

   (Talk by Ray Sharland N.F.C.A.)

3. Proposal for the formation of the Whipton

   Community Association (Secretary)

4. Agreement of proposed Constitution of the

   Association

5. The Fixing of subscriptions for memberships

   Break for refreshments

6. Collection of envelopes. Only persons returning envelopes and thus becoming founder members of the Association will be entitled to vote in the Elections.

7. Discussion of Survey results - Ray Sharland

8. Election of Officers

9. Election of 15 Members for the General Council

10. Thanks and future plans (Chairman)

--- 0 ---

Please come along and bring this agenda. Support

your neighbours to form the Whipton Community

Association.

--- 0 ---

"Can the residents of Whipton work together for

their common good, through a Community Association?"

Denis Pearce

Secretary

18 Whipton Village Road

FORTHCOMING EVENTS

Here is a chance to get rid of all your unwanted goods
and chattels. Mrs. V. Bird will he holding a JUMBLE SALE
in the Whipton Church Hall, Pinhoe Road on SATURDAY MARCH
11th at 2.00 p.m. There will be a Draw, White Elephant
Stall, Cake Stall and Refreshments. Admission 5p.
HELPERS are required to collect jumble and also to help
bake cakes on the day. Anyone willing to help should
contact Mrs. V. Bird at the above address. Jumble can
also be given to Council Members.

PARENTS! Here is a chance to help your children. As a
result of our survey, there is to be a public meeting to
discuss the possibility of providing youth activities, in
the THORNPARK RISE/BIRCHY BARTON HILL area. All interested
residents welcome, particularly those who offered help with
youth work. The meeting will be held at ST. LAWRENCE CHURCH,
FRIDAY MARCH 17th at 7.30 p.m.

The children of Whipton invite you to enjoy an evening of
their own music and entertainment at a CONCERT at Whipton
Barton Middle School MARCH 21st at 7.00 p.m. The Concert
will be followed by a film on Community Association Work.
Refreshments to be provided during the interval.. Prog-
grammes can be obtained from Council Members and from the
Whipton News Shop in Whipton Village Road. Admission 20p
Children 10p under 5's free of charge.

You can take all the family (even gran and grandad) to
our SPRING DISCO-DANCE. Music to suit all tastes. The
Disco is to be held at Whipton Church Hall, Pinhoe Road
on SATURDAY APRIL 8th from 7.30 - 10.30 p.m. Admission
40p C.A. Members 30p Children under 15 half price.
Don't miss your chance to get to know your neighbours.
Offers of help would be greatly appreciated.

A DATE FOR YOUR DIARY! This is an advance notice of the
EXETER FESTIVAL. We will participate in the Festival by
putting on a FESTIVAL FAIR on SATURDAY JUNE 3rd in
Whipton Barton Middle School Fields. All local organisations are invited to provide events and stalls and
should contact the Secretary. Full details of programme of events will be available to residents at a
later date.

Our Fund Raiser Mrs. V. Bird requires the following
items:

Cushions or Pillows to make new cushions, also
dolls to dress, any size articles suitable for
White Elephant Stall, tinned food, homemade jam
and pickles, or any bottled sauce etc., packet
food, any handmade articles or any wool to be
knitted up, and jumble.

Please contact Mrs. V. Bird if you have anything to give.

JOBS FOR EVERYONE. Helpers are required for Community
Association bumf distribution. This newsletter will be
issued at regular intervals. The C.A. is open to other
organisations in the area such as Brownies, Girl Guides,
Scouts etc. who are welcome to use this newsletter to
publicise their own events.

***

WANTED

A TYPEWRITER IS
DESPERATELY NEEDED
BY OUR SECRETARY.
NO REWARD!!!

ALSO WANTED

BUDDING JOURNALIST REQUIRED
AS OUR PUBLICITY OFFICER.
DON'T MISS THIS CHANCE TO
IMPROVE UPON THIS NEWSLETTER!
YOURS COULD BE THE NEXT ONE.

PLEASE JOIN NOW TO GET FUTURE COPIES OF NEWSLETTERS

M E M B E R S H I P   A P P L I C A T I O N   F O R M

NAME ....

ADDRESS ....

....

INDIVIDUAL   FAMILY   ASSOCIATE
MEMBER   30p ____   MEMBER 60p ____   MEMBER   30p ____

                    AFFILIATED
                    GROUP   £1.00 ____

DEVON AND CORNWALL CONSTABULARY

CRIME PREVENTION SUPPORT UNIT

HOW WELL DO YOU KNOW WHIPTON?

You may remember that we asked you this question
nearly twelve months ago.

You responded well and attended our meetings,
following which you formed the WHIPTON
COMMUNITY ASSOCIATION.

You will recall that everyone was concerned about
the increasing number of young people living in
the Thornpark Rise/Birchy Barton Hill Areas who
were coming to the notice of the community
through criminal activity.

Let us keep our young people out of the courts,
and into the community.

We invite you to attend a Neighbourhood Meeting
to be held on the subject of youth activities in
these areas.

THE MEETING IS AT 7.30p.m.

ON FRIDAY, 17TH MARCH 1978

AT ST. LAWRENCE CHURCH

We are ready to help, your Community Association
is ready to help .... we ask your
support to help your young people.

DON'T LET WHIPTON DOWN

This is a community Newsletter, published by the Whipton
Community Association, written and produced by local
people. If you would like to get something instigated
in Whipton, or have comments or queries on certain
topics, or aspects which concern the area, we would be
pleased to hear from you.

Would your local organisation be interested in affiliating
to the W.C.A. We offer to publish forthcoming fixtures and
events and any other information you wish. A record of
all organisations affiliated will be printed in the next
issue of WHIPTON WORLD.

DIARY An events diary, for use by local organisations
and individuals, is kept in the Post Office in
the Village. Just fill in the dates of your
events and we will publish it in forthcoming
issues of the Newsletter.

DIARY
DATES May 8 Concert by Dudley Savage at the Mint
Church, Fore Street, Exeter. All pro-
ceeds to the "New Ear Campaign".

May 13 Jumble Sale in the St Lawrence Church
Hall, Hill Barton Road, Exeter, at 2.00 p.m.

May 20 On the last day of the Devon County Show,
there will be a "Hot Dog" stall in the car
park on the Half Moon pub.

June 3   Whipton Community Fair in Whipton Barton
Middle School, at 2.30 p.m., to be opened
by the Mayor.

May   A Binge Evening

July   Beach Barbecue

July/Aug   Children's Play Scheme

Sept   Cheese and Wine Party

Autumn   Christmas Bazaar

The Organisers of the "New Ear Campaign" are delighted
with their progress so far; they have collected
£600 in nine weeks!! keep your newspapers for
the campaign and let the Police in Pinhoe Road
have them.

Is there a Princess in Whipton? We are looking for a
little princess and two attendants for a float in
the Exeter Carnival procession. There are prizes
of £10, £6 and £2 respectively, in Premium Bonds,
to be won, and the Princess will be crowned by
the Mayoress at the Community Fair on 3 June.

How to enter the Whipton Princess competition?
Just contact Mrs. C. Treagale, 10 Thorn Close, to
obtain your Sponsor Form and information on what
you must do. Age must be from 8 - 13 years.

Now is the time to start thinking up ideas for costumes
for the CHILDREN'S FANCY DRESS COMPETITION to be
held at the Community Fair on 3rd June. For entry
application and further details contact either
Mrs V. Cassidy, 51 Lloyds Crescent, or Mrs. C.
Hawkins, 67 Lloyds Crescent. Prizes will be
presented by the Mayoress.

FAIR This big local event will be opened by the Mayor
and Mayoress of Exeter at 2.00 p.m. on 3rd June.
There will be Judo demonstrations, Police and
Vintage Motor Cycle displays, Sports by the
handicapped, Music by the Boys' Brigade, a
Children's Fancy Dress competition, and side
stalls.

Space for side stalls can be obtained from the
W.C.A. We need articles for the "Good as New"
and "Bric-a-Brac" stalls, also items for "Fancy
Goods" and oddments of materials, wool etc.
Further details can be obtained from Mrs. V.
Bird, 15 Summer Close, or Mrs. B. Lopez, 24
Whipton Village Road.

Help of all sorts is required to make this
fair a success. If you can do something -
anything - or donate articles, just let Mrs.
Lopez know.

ANTI-LITTER CAMPAIGN - 29th May - 24 June

It has come to the notice of W.W. that areas other than Whipton usually win this Campaign and he is rather disgruntled about it. If everyone in Whipton were to try and keep an area tidy, he says, that would be a start. How about picking up the litter that's blown into your garden, or outside the shops, and put it into a bin (not the gutter!) so that when the judges start their rounds in May, they will be impressed by how clean and tidy Whipton is.

THEATRE OUTINGS   There must be many people in Whipton who would love to go to a show from time to time, but, for lack of transport or company, seldom get to see one. Would there be enough interest to form a "Theatre Outing Club", where tickets could be bought in block and transport possibly arranged? Anyone interested should contact the Secretary.

Calling all GARDEN EXPERTS   How about forming a Garden Club where ideas can be swapped, guidance given and possible a cheap source of gardening materials? Interested? - contact Mrs. L. Saunders, 39 Kennerley Avenue.

Have you heard of the "Good Neighbour Scheme"? The W.C.A. plan to instigate something similar in Whipton but need volunteers to help. Would you be willing to help? Then contact Mrs. S. Tonks, I Woolsery Grove, or Mrs. V. Bird, to find out more about it.

More helpers are required, this time to run the new Youth
Club which is being started at the St. Lawrence
Church Hall, Hill Barton Road, on Friday nights for
8 - 13 year olds. Parents who wish to find out more
about the proposed Youth Club should get in touch
with Mrs. Treagale.

Yet another chance to off-load your unwanted "goods and
chattels". This time for a Jumble Sale to be held
in the St. Lawrence Hall on Saturday 13th May at 2.00 p.m.
Admission 3p. Helpers are required to collect
jumble, to make cakes and to help on the day.
Anyone willing to help should contact Mrs. C.
Treagale. Jumble can also be given to any Council
member.

How about that day out you've been wishing for? Fancy
a MYSTERY TOUR? Mrs. V. Bird has organised such a
coach trip for Whipton's Senior Citizens on 14th June
at a cost of 40p. W.C.A. members 30p. If you would
like to go, contact Mrs. Bird, but hurry!

SUCCESSES   The Jumble Sale on 11 March made a profit
of £55!! Many thanks to all those who contributed
jumble and helped during the afternoon. The Concert
in Whipton Barton Middle School, given by local children
on 21st March, was a great source of lively entertainment,
and the Disco/Dance on the 8th April provided an
opportunity for a good get-together. Our thanks are due
to MR. WAKEHAM (Whipton Ironmongers), MR. RAKES (Lords)
and MR. ROBERTS (Butcher) for donations of prizes, and
to all the business premises for displaying notices.

WANTED   A typewriter is required by the W.C.A. - any offers ?

M E M B E R S H I P   A P P L I C A T I O N   F O R M

Name ....

Address ....

....

Individual Member	Family Member	Associate Member
30p ____	60p ____	30p ____

Affiliated
Group   £1.00 ____

Appendix 7

A code of management practice

POLICE MANAGEMENT

A DRAFT CODE OF PRACTICE TO SUPPLEMENT THAT DECREED BY
POLICE REGULATIONS

1. It is acknowledged at the outset that the public interest is paramount. It is also acknowledged that no one person or group of persons has prescriptive right to exclusive influence in the conduct of the management of a police force in England and Wales. The arrangements for management of police forces must reflect these principles.

2. All those involved with the management of a police force should respect the rights, dignities, duties and responsibilities set out in the constitutional and legal arrangements which, in its wisdom, Parliament has seen fit to devolve upon persons or groups of persons.

3. It should be acknowledged that, though of necessity minimum guarantees for democratic consultation and participation may need to be enshrined by law in regulations, it is in the spirit of the conduct of human affairs by all the parties concerned that the highest levels of achievement and excellence are likely to be gained.

4. Notwithstanding the principles set out in paragraph 1 above, it should be acknowledged that for the proper and impartial discharge of duties the following persons or groups of persons are, in the final analysis, responsible.

(a) *The Home Secretary* is responsible for ensuring that the parties responsible are discharging their function in a proper manner and for providing inspection co-ordination and advice etc. in accordance with the Police Act of 1964.

(b) *The police authority* is responsible for ensuring the maintenance of an adequate and efficient police force in accordance with the Police Act of 1964.

(c) *The chief constable* is responsible for the direction and control of the police force in accordance with the Police Act of 1964.

5. In the discharge of his responsibilities at 4(a) the Home Secretary has recourse to advisory and consultative bodies and the same principle should operate at force level.

257

6. It should be recognised that the officers and members of the Superintendents' Association and of the Police Federation have not only a right of access to the chief constable, but also an obligation to assist him to discharge those of his duties which impinge upon the welfare and efficiency of the members of their respective bodies and of the force as a whole.

7. In order to achieve the objective set out in paragraph 6 above, joint consultation, either severally or collectively, should be instituted when issues affecting interests of the bodies concerned are under examination. Furthermore, there will be many occasions when participation on standing committees, working parties and planning will be more effective if carried out jointly. It must always be recognised, however, that in the final analysis the person responsible for the outcome must have the over-all authority to take the necessary decisions: responsibility without authority is as untenable, as authority without responsibility is imprudent.

8. In discharging his duties a chief constable is ultimately solely responsible for the final result, but there may be times when, in order to have fuller consensus within the organisation police committees, or indeed any policy-making body (if it is even the chief constable himself), he should consult with the representative bodies before declaring the ultimate decision.

9. Finally, it should be remembered that the management and leadership of the disciplined organisation in times of democratic involvement in affairs face particular problems in achieving the collective aim, whilst allowing for diversity of opinion within its ranks. There are times when orders have to be given and obeyed if the organisation is to hold fast and achieve its purposes, but there are also times when consultation and participation in planning and policy-making can be reconciled with the other characteristics of disciplined control. Generally, much will depend on the spirit within the organisation and the leadership of a police force, representative groups and individual officers should strive by every means to produce an internal atmosphere in which all ranks can fulfil their potential and prosper, while at the same time accepting that sacrifices are necessary if a police force is to operate successfully within our democratic society.

Police Advisory Telephone Service (PAT)

The Police Advisory Telephone (PAT) is a unique system for providing the public with a single simple method of contacting the police at any time of the day or night. Using the Post Office "Freefone" facility, PAT links a caller with an experienced local police officer trained to provide assistance, advice and information. First introduced in Cornwall in May 1976, the Police Advisory Telephone is identified by the symbol below which appears in public telephone kiosks.

DEVON AND CORNWALL

POLICE

POLICE ADVISORY TELEPHONE

embargo embargo embargo embargo embargo embargo embargo embargo embargo

E M B A R G O : To avoid public confusion, this press release

is embargoed until 0001 hours Tuesday May 24

Memo to News Editors: The PAT service will be launched at a

Press Conference at Camborne Police

Station at 10.30 a.m. on Tuesday May 24

You are invited to send a reporter/

photographer to this news briefing.

Press facilities will include

demonstrations on the PAT service and

officers will be available for

interviewing.

A unique problem-solving service designed to forge new links
between police and the public comes into operation in the
South West today.

The Devon and Cornwall Constabulary is to introduce a round-
the-clock free phone-in system offering assistance, advice
and information.

Called PAT - Police Advisory Telephone - the service connects
a caller free of charge with an experienced police officer at
any time of the day or night.

And the PAT team is geared to deal with enquiries from requests
for routine information to crime alerts.

Supplementing the existing "999" emergency service, the new
phone link provides instant contact with the police. Launched
as an experiment in the West Cornwall Division of the Force,
PAT adapts technology to recapture the spirit of the village
bobby.

Simply by picking up the telephone, dialling 100 and asking
the operator for "Freefone 9292", a caller will be able to
discuss problems or seek advice and information from an
experienced local police officer. Callers will not be asked
to identify themselves unless they want to and personal follow-up
visits from local officers will be arranged whenever desirable.

"PAT puts the police as close as your nearest telephone,"
explained Mr. Brian Morgan, Assistant Chief Constable - Preventive
Policing, who has devised the system to give the public easy
access to police resources.

"At three o'clock in the morning, for instance, the police
may well be the only source of assistance or guidance for
someone with a problem. But except in emergency situations,
there is no single, simple method of contacting the police.
Now PAT will be available to provide help and advice simply
by picking up the phone," he said.

Using the Post Office "Freefone" facility, PAT will offer a
comprehensive services: routine information on such local subjects
as availability of duty doctors and chemists; advice on domestic
problems, answer queries on the law and aspects of police work
and provide a police response for more serious problems.

Whenever necessary, calls will be referred to other social
agencies where direct police involvement is not desired and
Mr. Morgan said: "In the case of personal problems we will offer
sympathetic and confidential advice. In fact, we hope to provide
a quick and easy means of obtaining help and information on any
of the scores of problems which beset the community."

Mr. Morgan, who is developing new initiatives in police systems,
went on: "PAT does not replace the "999" service, it augments
it. Here the onus is not placed on the caller to decide what
constitutes an emergency. Quite often people are frightened of
activating an urgent emergency system when they are confronted
by a problem, and until now there has been no single easy way
of getting in touch with the local police whatever.the time of
day or night.

"Our aim in developing the PAT service is to put fast friendly
contact with the police back into everyday life. We're not
replacing the village bobby with the system, he's still there,
but because of the pressures of modern society, quite often
people just don't know how to reach him any more. PAT solves
the dilemma."

Posters and stickers are being distributed throughout the
Camborne Division, announcing the new service, and the pilot
project will be carefully studied for future application in
other areas of the Force.

"PAT also gives people a chance to have a say in the deployment
of their local police resources," added Mr. Morgan. "We hope
that the service will develop into a two-way dialogue so that
we can identify community requirements and tailor our resources
accordingly."

Force Information Services Devon & Cornwall Police Headquarters

Middlemoor Exeter   Tel (0392) 52101 extn 251/228

PRESS RELEASE

POLICE ADVISORY TELEPHONE

PAT arrives in Plymouth today to forge closer links between
the people of the city and their local police.

The Devon and Cornwall Constabulary's Police Advisory
Telephone is being launched in the city to provide the public
with a unique non-emergency service under which they can seek
advice and information from an experienced police officer at
any time of the night or day.

Police also hope that the public will take full advantage of
this free confidential service to provide them with information
which could help in the war against crime.

Specially trained officers will be operating the 24 hour-a-day
PAT service at Plymouth's Divisional Police Headquarters,
Crownhill. If the police cannot help, they will be able to put
callers in touch with the appropriate agencies to deal with
their queries.

Devon and Cornwall pioneered a service of this type when PAT was
launched in West Cornwall last May. The success of this experiment
has now led to the extension of PAT to an urban situation.

Mr. John Alderson, the Chief Constable, said today: "We shall
be continuing with the Police Advisory Telephone at Camborne,
and we feel that they system will also have tremendous potential
in a city environment. In effect PAT will be providing the
people of Plymouth with their own up-dated village bobby."

People living in West Cornwall and within the City of Plymouth
can now take advantage of PAT by calling the operator from
either a public or private telephone and asking for Freefone
9292.

Mr. Alderson said: "In the event of an emergency people must
still dial 999. But under PAT, we hope that the public will
feel free to telephone the police if their suspicions are
aroused or if they wish to seek advice without the fear that
they will be activating full scale emergency procedures.
The service is completely confidential for the benefit of callers
who wish to remain anonymous."

Officers operating PAT at Camborne have handled hundreds of
calls, ranging from requests for details of duty chemists and
doctors to information from people whose suspicions have been
aroused by activities in their localities.

Another Freefone service to link the people of Plymouth with the police was also in operation during the recent month-long Neighbourhoods Against Burglary Campaign. The system played a major part as local communities joined with the police in an all-out offensive against the burglar.

Mr. Alderson said: "Policing techniques have changed dramatically in recent years to keep pace with the requirements of modern society. The need for greater mobility and extra demands on our resources has inevitably meant that the valuable personal contact between the policeman and his local community has diminished. From many quarters have come pleas for the return of the policeman on the street corner.

"With the introduction of PAT the Devon and Cornwall Constabulary is now providing people with the opportunity to make a swift personal approach to their 'local Bobby' simply by lifting the receiver."

EXTRACT FROM *THE TIMES* DATED 24th MAY 1977

Police scheme for telephoned advice service

by Clive Borrell

An experiment aimed at forging closer links between the police and the public is to be launched by Devon and Cornwall police at Camborne, Cornwall, today.

Described as a "unique problem-solving service," the police plan to operate an advisory telephone (PAT) system where members of the public can telephone at any time of the day or night and seek advice and discuss difficulties. Callers will not be pressed to identify themselves if they wish to remain anonymous. They will be able to reach PAT by dialling 100 and asking the Post Office telephone operator for Freephone 9292.

Mr. Brian Morgan, assistant chief constable, who devised the scheme, said: "Our aim in developing the PAT service is to put fast, friendly contact with the police back into everyday life. We are not replacing the village bobby with the system; he is still there, but because of the pressures of modern society, quite often people just do not know how to reach him any more. PAT solves the dilemma."

The service will supplement the existing 999 emergency service. If the experiment is a success in Camborne the police hope to extend the scheme to other areas of the two counties.

Round-clock advice

Many of the most successful inventions have been simple, so simple that one wonders why they had not been thought of before. The same applies to a scheme initiated this week by the Devon and Cornwall Constabulary at Camborne.

Called PAT — Police Advisory Telephone — a caller can phone at any time of night or day by asking an operator for Freephone 9292. Callers will not be asked to identify themselves unless they wish to do so.

The difference between the new service and the 999 service is that it is not for emergencies only.

Except in emergency situations, there is no single simple method of contacting the police. At 3 a.m., for instance, the police may be the only source of assistance or guidance for someone with a problem that does not merit a 999 call.

The new service also relieves the caller on the onus of deciding what constitutes an emergency. Quite often, people are reticent about activating an urgent emergency system when they are confronted by a problem, and until now there has been no single easy way of getting in touch with the police whatever the time of night or day.

Long Overdue

On call now at Camborne will be routine information on such local subjects as availability of duty doctors and chemists, advice on domestic problems and queries on the law.

No doubt, local bobbies are thin on the ground these days and not always around when needed. The new service will not replace them but will be an addition long overdue.

A snag is that Devon and Cornwall Constabulary has to finance the scheme, but if the service is successful, savings will be made in various ways, such as the disposal of recording machines.

It is to be hoped that the response at Camborne to this invaluable service will warrant its use in the whole South-West.

EXTRACT FROM THE *WESTERN EVENING HERALD*
DATED 1st MARCH 1978

Local bobby is back-on phone

The friendly local bobby is back on the Plymouth beat — but this time he's on the phone.

PAT, the Police Advisory Telephone, came into service today at Crownhill police station. Anyone in Plymouth can now pick up a phone, dial 100 and ask for Freephone 9292 to speak to a policeman.

Police hope people will use the service to ask for advice and information on all sorts of things.

"There are many people who are alone, afraid, housebound and sometimes bedridden, who never see a police officer.

"They are unable to stop and talk to the local policeman because they are unable to get to him" said Chief Constable Mr. John Alderson, who launched the service today.

"There are many people in our complex society who need help and advice and we are trying to help them. We want to make today's police as close to the public as they were with the old village bobby."

The scheme was not a substitute for the local policeman but a "reinforcement".

Pioneer

People had used a similar freephone service during the recent . Neighbourhoods Against Burglars (NAB) campaign with great effect and he hoped PAT would be as successful.

"During the NAB campaign house burglaries in the city were considerably reduced."

The service, which was pioneered in Camborne, is the only one of its type in the world in a large city. Already Manchester and the Metropolitan police forces have shown interest.

PAT is not an experiment. It is now a permanent part of the Plymouth police service.

"In the event of an emergency people must still dial 999. Under PAT we hope that the public will feel free to telephone the police if their suspicions are aroused or if they wish to seek advice without the fear that they will be activating full-scale emergency procedures." said Mr. Alderson.

This will help save police resources by keeping officers available for real emergencies. Eventually the scheme will be extended to other parts of Devon.

"This falls in with our general philosophy of community policing — the police having more help from the public. This has got to be the trend for the future."

Thanks

Assistant Chief Constable Mr. John Morgan, who devised the service, said: "We want it to be like the old village bobby. He was there 90 per cent of the time to give advice and 10 per cent of the time in a punitive role."

Within about an hour of the 24-hour service being launched, the PAT centre had received a variety of calls.

The officers answering the first few calls were WPC Joan Harvey, 22, and PC Bob Ham, 38.

There was one call complaining about a car blocking a driveway entrance, a message of thanks to the police for seeing that street lights were mended and a call from a 15-year-old boy who wanted to know how to join the police force.

At their fingertips the two officers have a range of information from details of duty chemists to emergency numbers.

Police hope that in time Freephone 9292 will become as well known as 999.

EXTRACT FROM THE *WESTERN EVENING HERALD*
DATED 2nd MARCH 1978

The calls pour in for Pat

Plymouth's Advisory Telephone service, PAT, launched by the police yesterday, is already looking like a great success. In the 24 hours since the service started calls have been pouring in.

Chief Constable Mr. John Alderson when he launched the service at Crownhill yesterday raised fears that many people in Plymouth would be reluctant to use a phone. Early signs seem to have proved him wrong.

Constable Des Steer, who was in charge of PAT, said he was fast falling behind with the paperwork because of the number of calls.

"I have been extremely busy. There have been so many calls I have not been able to follow some of them up yet," said Constable Steer. "I am getting the sort of calls which as a PC I was getting when I was on the beat."

The sort of calls coming in on the Freephone (9292) have ranged from people seeking advice to those who want to make complaints.

A man rang from Plympton to complain that he was being pestered by gipsies, a learner driver rang to ask whether they could legally drive on a dual carriageway or motorway.

There were also a number of tip-offs which police are now investigating. One drew attention to a strange man who has been calling on old ladies and trying to sell them things.

Another reported that a woman was running an agency which they thought was a little suspicious because no books were being kept.

Special Constabulary: a police reserve order

REORGANISATION OF SPECIAL CONSTABULARY

INTRODUCTION

1. The responsibility of any police force and any police authority includes the need to train and maintain an adequate police reserve against times of national crisis or calamity. In wartime, the role of the Special Constabulary is highlighted, of course, but there are civil emergencies such as the breakdown of law and order in parts of the country, or action taken by groups within society, which would require the deployment of considerable police support units drawn from the regular force. It is in times like these that the public whom we serve should not be left without some adequate protection of their own. To fail to provide for this is only to give rise to the creation of vigilantism or private armies and this is a threat in itself to law and order. It has been the tradition of Anglo-Saxon policing for over a thousand years that the citizens themselves are partly responsible for maintaining law and order. Common-law principles require this not only as a right but as a duty.

2. There is also a very important secondary spin-off from arrangements such as those described above. This results in a number of members of the public being well informed about the police and acting as a reliable link between the police force and the community which it serves. It is well known that any police force relies heavily on pro-police citizens for its effectiveness. Many of the public only learn about the police from half-truths, opinions and sometimes lies, which appear through the media, and this needs to be offset by well-informed sources amongst the public generally.

3. It is for the above reasons that it is necessary for the Devon and Cornwall Constabulary to look carefully at the present state of the police reserve in the two counties. The attached order sets out the plan as agreed following discussion with the Police Federation, the Superintendents' Association and the Senior Officers of the Force, together with the members of the Special Constabulary themselves.

It is based mainly on the recommendations of the Home Office Working Party which was subscribed to by representatives of all ranks in the service, and it should therefore commend itself to the police service.

4. I hope therefore that our plan will commend itself to you, and that you will be able to give support and encouragement to the Special Constabulary. I also urge you to encourage suitable men and women to join the Specials—they can help you.

FUNCTIONS AND DUTIES

1. The Special Constabulary provides a valuable service, in particular by supporting the Regular Police Force in times of natural crisis, local emergency or special occasions.

2. The number of hours' duty per week performed by Special Constables should not, as a general rule, exceed four. Classroom training will not, however, be included in this total.

3. Special Constables will not be employed so as to deprive Regular Officers of the opportunity of working voluntary overtime.

4. Special Constables will not be employed on duties arising directly from industrial disputes, but there is no objection to them being used to take over routine duties from Regular Officers so employed.

GRADE STRUCTURE

5. There is a need in the Special Constabulary for grades above Special Constables. These grades, however, will reflect administrative rather than operational duties. The grades will be:

   (a) Section Officer;
   (b) Sub-Divisional Officer;
   (c) Divisional Officer;
   (d) Force Officer.

UNIFORM

6. All members of the Special Constabulary will wear shoulder flashes which carry the description "Special Constabulary—Police Reserve". Badges of grade will be in silver braid around the epaulettes:

   (a) 1 bar—Section Officer;
   (b) 2 bars—Sub-Divisional Officer;
   (c) 3 bars—Divisional Officer;
   (d) 4 bars—Force Officer.
   Caps:
   (a) Section Officer—ordinary cap;
   (b) Sub-Divisional Officer—Inspector's style cap;
   (c) Divisional Officer—Inspector's style cap;

(d) Force Officer—Superintendent's style cap.
(For the time being plain cap bands will continue to be worn.)

AGE LIMITS

7. The minimum age for Special Constables will be 20 years, but it is essential that persons of this age must show above-average maturity. Retirement ages will be:

(a) Special Constables, Section and Sub-Divisional Officers—55 years;

(b) Divisional Officers—60 years;

(c) Force Officer—65 years.

Appropriate arrangements will be made to phase the retirement of those serving officers who have already reached these age limits.

8. An extension of service may be granted annually to Special Constables over 55 but under 60 years of age on the recommendation of Chief Superintendents, and only in special circumstances.

INELIGIBLE PERSONS

9. Holders of the following offices or occupations are not eligible for membership of the Special Constabulary:

(a) members of police authorities;

(b) magistrates;

(c) clerks to justices;

(d) clerks of courts;

(e) members of employers' police forces;

(f) holders of liquor licences, managers of licensed houses and their husbands or wives;

(g) licensees of betting and gaming establishments;

(h) promoters of lotteries;

(i) bailiffs;

(j) members of private security organisations (whether directors, partners or employees);

(k) private detectives and enquiry agents;

(l) traffic wardens;

(m) school crossing patrols.

(This list is not exhaustive.)

ESTABLISHMENT

10. The authorised establishment of the Devon and Cornwall Special Constabulary wlil not exceed in over-all total that of the Regular Force. The distribution will not necessarily be the same, however, as it is extremely unlikely that in the foreseeable future sufficient new members can be recruited to the Special Constabulary to bring it up to the same level as the Regular Force.

11. The number of Section Officers and Sub-Divisional Officers per division will depend largely on local circumstances. Ideally one officer of the Special Constabulary should be appointed per section and subdivision, but where large numbers of officers or geographical consideration dictate more officers of these grades may be appointed.

PAY AND ALLOWANCE

12. Special constables will not be paid but will in general be protected from actual financial loss. Loss-of-remuneration allowance will be paid, as at present, only when an officer is required to attend for duty and actually suffers a loss of earnings. The present relationship of this allowance to the basic pay of a regular constable is appropriate.

13. Boot allowance will be retained as a separate allowance and paid annually. The rate will be £10 per year subject to periodic review.

14. The Working Party recommended that allowances other than loss-of-remuneration, subsistence and boot allowances should not be payable except with the approval of the Secretary of State, it being considered that reimbursement of actual expenses is generally more satisfactory than an allowance. However, in this Force the travelling allowance already approved by the police authority will continue.

RECRUITMENT

15. Local campaigns are the most effective form of recruitment. Such campaigns will be co-ordinated by the Force Information Officer. Chief Superintendents will consider the best means of achieving new applications in their respective divisions.

16. Community Constables should be involved in enquiries about and initial interviews with Special Constable applicants.

17. Each applicant will also be interviewed at subdivisional level by an officer not below the rank of Inspector, and the Sub-Divisional Officer of the Special Constabulary should be consulted whenever possible.

TRAINING

18. The Force Training Officer will revise the *Special Constabulary Handbook* and appropriate training programmes. Annual training will be organised in divisions at the discretion of Chief Superintendents. On appointment as a Special Constable each member will receive individual advice and guidance on his role, and Resident Constables, in liaison with Divisional Training Sergeants, should be closely involved.

DISCIPLINE AND COMPLAINTS

19. The procedure for investigation of complaints against Special Constables will, as far as practicable, follow that for Regular Officers, although important statutory differences will necessarily remain.

Index

adaptability, 26, 219
Administrative Directions, 20, 23n
affluence and crime, 149, 153, 172, 177, 180
agencies, statutory, 39, 47, 69–70, 175, 192, 203
alienation, 112, 123, 138, 153, 154
Anglo-Saxon police system, 44–5, 142
Anomie, 112, 154
arbitrary powers, 184–5
armed police, 25, 43, 49–50, 59, 71–3, 138, 185
army, *see* military
Army/Youth teams, 132
Australia, 49
authoritarianism, 12–13, 55, 148–51, 157, 184–5, 212, 219
decline of, 122, 150, 151
authority
changes in attitude towards, 55
sources of, 12–13, 27

bail, 21–2
Bail Act (1976), 21–2
Baynes, J. C. M., 79, 81–2, 83n
Belson, Doctor William, 55, 56n, 66
"Black Panthers", 180
Blair, Thomas L., 190, 196n
Blueprint for Survival, 121, 126n, 154
Bow street patrols, 145
Briggs, Asa, 176, 183n
British police tradition, 3, 16, 50, 53–6, 71, 74, 157, 241–2
bureaucracy, control of, 155
bureaucratic state, 58
Butler, R. A., 12

Calvocoressi, Peter, 186, 196n
Cameron Report, 178, 183n
change, 150–1, 152, 156, 213, 215, 219
policing, 150–1
Chicago police riots (1968), 59
chief constable, responsibilities of, 257, 258
child protection, 91, 205
Children and Young Persons Act (1969), 90–1
China, 45
C.I.A., 59
C.I.D., 60, 69, 163, 207–8
corruption in, 33, 67
citizens' powers, 11, 84
city, policing the, 187–9, 190–2 (*see also* village in the city)
civic responsibility, 197
civil and criminal actions against the police, 22
Colwell, Maria, 91
common good, 46–7, 63, 166–7
common law, 50, 129, 142, 158, 217
common-law system, 2, 11, 15, 58, 62, 146
communal policing, 43–8, 93 (*see also* community policing)
communication(s), 40, 41, 42, 100–4, 203, 208, 209, 215
communism, 57
community, 39, 47–8, 153, 156, 177, 187, 192, 195, 199, 201, 204 (*see also* smaller communities)
and crime prevention, 132, 136, 170, 191–2, 201
constable, 68–9, 176, 204

271